Black Religion and
Black Radicalism

Black Religion and Black Radicalism

BY GAYRAUD S. WILMORE

C. Eric Lincoln Series on Black Religion
Garden City, New York
Doubleday & Company, Inc.

Library of Congress Catalog Card Number 75-180116
Copyright © 1972 by Gayraud S. Wilmore

Printed in the United States of America

FOREWORD

THIS SERIES of books is about the Black religious experience. It is addressed to Blackamericans because the rich heritage that is their history has not been made fully available to them in the usual ways in which a society informs its membership about the significant aspects of its development. Blackamericans want to know—indeed they *must* know—more about who they *were* and who they *are* if they are seriously concerned about whom they intend to become. The Black man's religion is a critical component of his American passage from slavery to a freedom, which is still to be perfected.

This series is addressed to white America, too. The Black experience—religious, social, economic, political—is writ large in the cultural development of the larger society. Understanding it is crucial to an informed perspective of what America is or can become. To a degree not always recognized, America is what it is because the Black minority is here, and has been here since long before this nation came into being.

The Blacks brought their religion with them. After a time they accepted the white man's religion, but they have not always expressed it in the white man's way. It became the Black man's purpose—perhaps it was his *destiny*—to shape, to fashion, to re-create the religion offered him by the Christian slavemaster, to remold it nearer to his own heart's desire, nearer to his own peculiar needs. The Black religious experience is something more than a black patina on a white happening. It is a unique response to an historical occurrence which can never be replicated for any people in America.

The Black man's pilgrimage in America was made less onerous because of his religion. His religion was the organizing principle around which his life was structured. His church was his school, his forum, his political arena, his social club, his art gallery, his conservatory of music. It was lyceum and gymnasium as well as *sanctum sanctorum*. His religion was his fellowship with man, his audience with God. It was the peculiar sustaining force which gave him the strength to endure when endurance gave no promise, and the courage to be creative in the face of his own dehumanization.

This is the Black religious experience. This is what this book and this series is about.

C. Eric Lincoln
Union Theological Seminary
New York City

ACKNOWLEDGMENTS

THIS BOOK was written in 1970 during a six-month sabbatical granted me by the Council on Church and Race of the United Presbyterian Church, U.S.A. I am much indebted to the Council and to my colleagues on the staff of COCAR, who bore the heat of the day in the unabating struggle for racial justice during my absence. It would be remiss of me not to mention also with appreciation Dr. Charles Willard of Princeton Theological Seminary, Librarian of the Robert E. Speer Library, who made that excellent collection available and provided every convenience for quiet and unmolested study. I wish also to thank Dr. Charles Spivey, now on the staff of the World Council of Churches in Geneva, Switzerland, Professor James H. Cone of Union Theological Seminary in New York City, Dr. Edward M. Huenemann of the United Presbyterian Division of Evangelism, and my good friend and editor Professor C. Eric Lincoln, also of Union Seminary, all of whom read the entire manuscript and made several helpful suggestions. They are, of course, in no way accountable for my errors either of fact or judgment.

Finally, I acknowledge with thanks my wife Lee and those of our children who were still at home for giving me the encouragement and the solitude to work to completion.

GAYRAUD S. WILMORE, JR.
Princeton, New Jersey

CONTENTS

INTRODUCTION

ALTHOUGH RELIGION has always been one of the most important aspects of the life of Black people in the United States, it has been woefully neglected as an area of serious study by Black and white scholars alike. This partly because Black professional theologians, church historians and sociologists of religion have been few and far between, but also because seldom have they been fortunate enough to acquire the sabbatical leisure and research grants which white scholars have customarily enjoyed. It is also true that white scholars, for their part, have rarely expressed great interest in Black religion in the United States. Their assumption has been that the Black church was little more than a somewhat more noisy and colorful facsimile of the white rural Baptist and Methodist churches and that Black religion had nothing in particular to offer over any other "folk religion" in the Protestant tradition. The few whites who have attempted to study and write about Black religion in America, unlike those who have done research on the religions of Africa, have never lived deeply enough nor been accepted long enough in the Black rural slum or the urban ghetto to have come into a sufficient knowledge of Black religion and the Black church "from the inside." Today African scholars are also questioning whether their own religions have been understood by white investigators.

This book intends to be a modest contribution to these studies. In a sense, it is an introduction to the bibliography of Black religion in the United States with the implication, by the admittedly scanty inclusion of certain material from overseas, that it is impossible to make a comprehensive study of the Black church and religion without cognizance of the triangular relationship between the United States, Africa and the Caribbean. Black religion began in Africa, was mixed with European Christianity in the Caribbean and in Latin America, and was further molded by, and recoiled *from*, American evangelical Protestantism on the slave plantations of the South and among the tiny communities of free Negroes in the North. It is hoped that the readers of this book will be impelled to explore these relationships and fill in the interstices of this rather cursory survey of the field with the rich source material still to be found, but rapidly passing into oblivion.

An exceedingly elastic but tenacious thread binds together the contributive and developmental factors of Black religion in the United States as one distinctive social phenomenon. It is the thread of what may be called, if properly defined, "Black Radicalism." Black religion has always concerned itself with the fascination of an incorrigibly religious people with the mystery of God, but it has been equally concerned with the yearning of a despised and subjugated people with the freedom of man—freedom from the religious, economic, social and political domination which white men have exercised over Black men since the beginning of the African slave trade. It is this radical thrust of Black people for human liberation expressed in theological terms and religious institutions which is the defining characteristic of Black Christianity and of Black religion in the United States, from the preacher-led slave revolts to the Black Manifesto of James Forman and the 1970 "Black Declaration of Independence" of the National Committee of Black Churchmen.

Despite the inseparable connection between Black religion and the struggle for freedom, in no place in the world today, with the possible exceptions of Red China and the Soviet Union, is the institution of the Christian religion and its official representatives more roundly criticized than in the Black community in the United States. Leading this attack upon the Black church are militant students, the young "street people" and the Black professional class, itself only recently drawn into the vortex of Black Power and Black awareness. The criticism is not misplaced. One of the continuing paradoxes of the Black church as the custodian of a great portion of Black culture and religion is that it is at once the most reactionary and the most radical of Black institutions, the most imbued with the mythology and values of white America, and yet the most proud, the most independent and indigenous collectivity in the Black community. In order to appreciate Black religion and the Black church—indeed, in order to understand Black radicalism anywhere in the world—one must delve into the nature and meaning of this paradox of the religious experience of African people—both on the African continent and in the diaspora. The radicals who deprecate the Black church, the Black professionals who avoid it, and the Black television comedians who mimic it, need to know how facilely they have absorbed the white man's ignorance and how they have sewn themselves up in his bag. Black pride and power, Black nationalism and Pan-Africanism have had no past without the Black church and Black religion, and without them it may well have no enduring future.

Black Religion and Black Radicalism

CHAPTER I

The Religion of the Slave

Perceiving from the readiness of these answers that the subject had been a familiar one with him, I immediately asked: "The black people talk among themselves about this, do they: and they think so, generally?"

"Oh! yes, sir; dey talk so: dat's wat dey tink."

"Then they talk about being free a good deal, do they?"

"Yes, sir. Dey—dat is, dey Say dey wish it was so; dat's all dey talk, master—dat's all, sir."

FROM: *A Journey in the Seaboard Slave States,* by Frederick Law Olmsted, 1856

THE RELIGION of the descendants of the Africans who were brought to the Western world as slaves has, from the very beginning, been something less and something more than what is generally regarded as the Christian religion. It could not have been otherwise. The religious beliefs and rituals of any people are inevitably and inseparably bound up with the material and psychological realities of their daily existence. Certainly those realities for the slaves were vastly different from those experienced by the slavemasters. In a way, the slavemasters understood this better than the missionaries and were never so sanguine as the latter about the possibilities of master and slave sharing the same religion.

The Reverend James Ramsay, an indefatigable and pious slaveholding preacher who spent eighteen years preaching the gospel to the slaves in the West Indies, wrote in one of his essays:

> Master and slave are in every respect opposite terms; the persons to whom they are applied, are natural enemies to each other. Slavery, in the manner and degree that it exists in our colonies, could never have been intended for the social state; for it supposes tyranny on one side, treachery and cunning on the other. Nor is it necessary to discuss which gives first occasion to the other.[1]

Such uncommon good sense ought to precede every serious discussion of what characterized the religion of the African slaves once the controversy about manumission after baptism was over and they had become the objects of Christian evangelization. The most immediate and determinative reality in the life of most slaves was their bondage in a strange land, thousands of miles from the sacred earth in which were interred the bones of their ancestors and upon whose bosom the gods of their fathers walked and talked with men. The religion of the white man, first Roman Catholicism and later Protestantism, could make an effective affiliation with the slave's religious experience in Africa, but the consequences were never so deferential to the European version of the true faith as the missionaries hoped for and believed.

The religion of Black people in the United States today, and in parts of the West Indies, Central and South America, is unquestionably predisposed to the beliefs and practices associated with the Judeo-Christian tradition. But the Christianity which had been developing for more than four hundred years among the descendants of the first slaves brought to this part of the world is a different version of the religion that is professed by the descendants of the slavemasters. In recent years, particularly in the United States, Black theologians and historians of religion have been uncovering this aboriginal "Black Religion" and have sought to indicate the points at which it not only differs from what most white people believe, but where it may illuminate some of the depths of man's most elemental religious consciousness which have been obfuscated by secularism and the technological development of Euro-American civilization.

On the other hand, Black churchmen—in both the historic Black churches and the predominantly white denominations —are attempting to recover the distinctive attributes of the religion of an oppressed people who never surrendered their humanity under the most exasperating circumstances of their enslavement or lost sight of the freedom and justice which they believed to be their due. It should be noted also that other Black religionists are similarly involved in this search for meaning and renewal in the spiritual life of those who feel themselves to be inextricably bound to an African past and caught up in the possibilities and promises of an African future.

In Africa itself, especially in the ecumenical centers and universities, African scholars—of both Christian and Islamic persuasion—have for several years been inquiring into the meaning and significance for the future of the continent when Christianity, Islam, the traditional religions, and the new African nationalism encounter one another at *Orita*, the Yoruba word for "where the ways come together." Today the urgency of that task is accentuated by the belated termination of the missionary enterprises of the historic Christian churches of Europe and America in Africa, and a new, indigenous form of African Christianity, unabashed by its differences from white Christianity, taking root among the African peoples.

Meanwhile, in the United States, the nation of Islam which produced one of the great Black martyrs of our time, Malcolm X; the quasi-religious communities which have gathered around Maulana Ron Karenga and other Black prophets of contemporary urban America; and the Reverend Albert B. Cleage's Shrine of the Black Madonna, are continual reminders that Black religion is a complex concatenation of archaic and modern belief systems, mythologies, symbols and attitudes, none of which can be claimed as the exclusive possession of any one religious tradition. Today in the United States, Black poets and preachers, academicians and charismatic leaders of the masses in the ghettos of the rural South and the great metropolitan areas, are all excavating the meaning of Afro-American history and culture and finding that the deepest roots of the Black experience in the New World, as well as in Africa, lie in the variegated religious and philosophic acquirements of Black people. The broad consensus is that it is through these doors that modern-day Black people may have to walk, if they are to find their true identity and destiny.

It is the purpose of this book to continue this search for meaning and direction, which is already in process on both sides of the Atlantic, by an analysis of the development of Black religion in America from the period of slavery to the emergence of the new theological currents which have impelled Black churchmen into the center of the civil rights movement of the last decade, and now into what has been called the Black Power movement. The analysis is both historical and theological. Its basic theoretical postulation is that, notwithstanding the well-known elements of evangelical conservatism in the mainstream of Black Christianity in this country, there was, from the beginning, a fusion between a highly developed and pervasive feeling about the hierophantic nature of historical experience, flowing from the African religious past, and a radical and programatic secularity, related to the experience of slavery and oppression, which constituted the essential and most significant characteristic of Black religion. The dialectical relationship of these two predominant elements of the Black religious consciousness was institutionalized in the historic Black churches and in the communal and associational groupings which grew up around and have, by no means, severed their connection with the churches. The profound cultural shock and revolution which occurred in the Black community at every historical moment when an inveterate white racism backlashed to check progress toward liberation, drew upon the resources of this distinctive religious tradition to interpret the meaning of the Black experience and to find a saving strength for meeting the crisis.

What we may call "White Christianity" in Europe and the United States has made a deep and lasting impression upon Black people everywhere, including Africa, but Blacks have used Christianity not as it was delivered to them by segregated white churches, but as its truth was authenticated to them in the experience of suffering, to reinforce an ingrained religious temperament and to produce an indigenous religion oriented to freedom and human welfare.

Most sociologists of religion will agree that religion does much of the same thing for all sorts and conditions of men. But it is a matter of serious debate whether a specific religion of a specific people can be transmitted *in toto* to another people—even in the same geographical area—without certain differences arising on account of ethnicity, nationality, social structure and many other factors. Especially is this true in the case of one people who are free and another people who are in slavery.

The questions that existence presents to the religious intelligence and imagination of a person who is relatively free to determine his own style of life and vocation are existentially different questions from those which the religious introspection of a slave predicates and seeks to answer. The matter seems almost too commonplace to belabor. And yet, many people express astonishment and not a little vexation at the suggestion that there has been in the past, and to some lesser but significant extent continues to exist today, important discontinuities between the Christian religion among white Americans and that same religion as it is practiced in the segregated Black communities of the United States and the West Indies.

Newbell Niles Puckett, in commenting upon the similarities and differences between Negro and Anglo-Saxon folk religion, writes:

The mere fact that a people *profess* to be Christians does not necessarily mean that their Christianity is of the same type as our own. The way in which a people interpret Christian doctrines depends largely upon their secular customs and their traditions of the past. There is an infinite difference between the Christianity of the North and South in America, between that of city and country, and between that of whites and colored, due in the main to their different modes of life and social backgrounds. Most of the time the Negro outwardly accepts the doctrines of Christianity and goes on living according to his own conflicting secular mores, but sometimes he enlarges upon the activities of God to explain certain phenomena not specifically dealt with in the Holy Scriptures.[2]

It is true that the first independent Black churches, the Baptists and the African Methodist denominations, patterned their creeds and orders of worship after the white churches from which they had separated in the latter half of the eighteenth century. But it is also true, and perhaps even more significant, that these racial churches, especially in the South, developed out of that "invisible institution," the slave church, and soon produced a "Negro style" of devotion and orthodoxy. Whatever those first gatherings of the slaves for religious purposes outside of the supervision of white people may have been like, it seems inaccurate to think of the religious institution that made its first appearance among them as "a church" in the sense of the European or American model. According to Du Bois:

It was not at first by any means a Christian Church, but a mere adaptation of those heathen rites which we roughly designate by the term Obe Worship, or "Voodooism." Association and missionary effort soon gave these rites a veneer of Christianity, and gradually, after two centuries, the Church became Christian, with a simple Calvinistic creed, but with many of the old customs still clinging to the services.[3]

Later we will examine this relationship between Black religion and Voodoo, but at this point we must concede that the precise manner in which the earliest teachings of Christianity by the colonial preachers impinged upon the religions which were brought from Africa and the West Indies is now extremely difficult if not impossible to reconstruct. We have a few slave narratives and the reports of missionaries, but we lack written descriptions by priests and medicine men of their accommodation to Christianity and the methods by which they and their fellow slaves were induced to accept a system of belief which contained elements of both faiths. Moreover, complete freedom of expression by those slaves who had previously been religious leaders would have necessitated the absence of any white person, since the whites would have been offended by any corruption of Christian worship as they understood it. Accordingly, we have few records of such meetings held in the absence of whites, though it cannot be doubted that they were held, before the establishment of the great plantations, in those areas where several slaves were together in one place and sufficiently isolated to hold independent services.

It is not certain how much exposure any individual slave had had to Christianity prior to the systematic mission inaugurated in 1701 by the English through the Society for the Propagation of the Gospel in Foreign Parts. Slavery had actually existed since about 1505 under Roman Catholic auspices in the Spanish West Indies and in Latin America. By the middle of the sixteenth century some African slaves from the coasts of Guinea had been introduced to Protestantism by Captain John Hawkins, the English privateer and adventurer.[4] Since most of the first slaves to be brought to the American colonies came from the Antillean subregion, it is possible that some of them had already made a partial transition from their native religions to Christianity prior to any systematic evangelization on the mainland. Brawley tells us that some of the slaves brought to the West Indies after 1517 had been educated as Mohammedans or as Catholics, and that in 1540 in Quivira, Mexico, there was a Negro who had taken holy orders. By 1542, the Roman Church had established three brotherhoods of the True Cross of Spaniards, two of them given to the mission to the Negroes and Indians.[5]

These facts leave open the possibility that when the American colonists began to turn from their earlier indifference to the Christianization of their slaves and began to give them religious instruction in earnest, there was not only a readiness for more thorough indoctrination among some, but a few who had already begun to emerge as religious leaders, having made some kind of earlier transition to Christianity or an assimilation of Christianity and African religion. But in the absence of solid historical evidence, we are obliged to move cautiously with this kind of speculation.

We do know that many of the early underground preachers to the slaves were not white men, but African priests who possessed unusual gifts of leadership and persuasion. One known source of such leaders was Dahomey, where dynastic quarrels produced persons who were then sold to white traders as slaves. Some of the victims were not only the defeated chiefs and their families, but also his priests and diviners. Herskovits points out that the most intransigent among the people conquered by the Dahomeans were the local priests of the river cults. While compliant priests were retained in order not to incur the wrath of their gods, those who resisted, such as the priests of the river gods, were sold to the slavers and probably ended up in the New World.[6] Herskovits comments on the implication of this for the incipient development of resistance among the slaves:

> What, indeed, could have more adequately sanctioned resistance to slavery than the presence of priests who, able to assure supernatural support to leaders and followers alike, helped them fight by giving the conviction that the powers of their ancestors were aiding them in their struggle for freedom.[7]

Whatever leadership roles they may have played, it is certain that by the beginning of the eighteenth century there were a few Black church members in all of the colonies—most of them worshiping in the same churches with their masters, or if freedmen, with their white neighbors—albeit under conditions of segregation.[8] It was not until after the Revolution that Black preachers began to be licensed by the denominations, but before that time they were recognized by their own people and exercised "jack-leg" ministries whenever opportunity was given and the slaves were able to assemble for their own meetings.

What do we know about the main features of this religion prior to the establishment of the first "aboveground" and organized Black churches during the period of the American Revolution? The famous statement by Du Bois that slave religion was characterized by "The Preacher, the Music and the Frenzy" is one way to summarize the matter.[9]

The late E. Franklin Frazier recognized the presence of these elements, but emphasized also the importance of the Bible in the development of early Negro Christianity. It is true that despite the illiteracy of the slaves, they were greatly attracted to what they considered "the sacred book" and they gave rapt attention to its recitation by missionaries and the Black preachers, many of whom had learned the Bible "by heart." In the Biblical stories, psalms and accounts of miracles they found the conviction and hope that a better life was available for them in this world and, with even more certainty, in the world beyond. Frazier writes:

> It was from the Bible that the slaves learned of the god of the white man and of his ways with the world and with men. The slaves were taught that the God with whom they became acquainted in the Bible was the ruler of the universe and superior to all other gods. They were taught that the God of the Bible punished and rewarded black men as well as white men. Black men were expected to accept their lot in this world and if they were obedient and honest and truthful they would be rewarded in the world after death.[10]

In the slave autobiographies and descriptions of religious services some evidences can be seen of the importance of

Scripture, even though it was more often than not rendered in accordance with the personal predilection of the preacher. But even more prominent are the highly charged emotionalism of the services, the "mourners' bench," the shouting, handclapping and holy dancing, and the picturesque imagery of the sermon and the spirituals.[11] The slave made an adaptation to Christianity that rendered it something more than a dispassionate system of belief and a code of pious behavior. He did accept the spirited, revivalistic interpretation of the impassioned Methodist and Baptist missionaries and imitated them, but he also went far beyond their understanding of Christianity to fashion it to his own social and recreational, as well as personal, spiritual needs.

One of the outstanding white missionaries in the South during the first part of the nineteenth century was a Presbyterian, the Reverend Charles Colcock Jones. With true Calvinistic concern for purity of doctrine, Jones complained of perversions of the Gospel among the newly converted slaves and was particularly exercised over their propensity to antinomianism, the belief that the moral law is of no effect to one who has come under the dispensation of the Gospel. Jones observed about the religious practices he witnessed:

> True religion they are inclined to place in profession, in forms and ordinances, and in excited states of feeling. And true conversion, in dreams, visions, trances, voices— all bearing a perfect or striking resemblance to some form or type which has been handed down for generations, or which has been originated in the wild fancy of some religious teacher among them.[12]

Jones describes the slave's concept of the Supreme Being and of the Person of Christ as indefinite and confused. It is interesting to note, in this connection, that the spirituals rarely express Christological interest, nor is their subject matter particularly theistic in emphasis. As far as Christ is concerned, some of the slaves had heard of someone by that name, but did not know who he was or were inclined, said Jones, to identify him with Mohammed, the prophet of Islam:

The Mohammedan Africans remaining of the old stock of importations, although accustomed to hear the Gospel preached, have been known to accommodate Christianity to Mohammedanism. "God," say they, "is Allah, and Jesus Christ is Mohammed—the religion is the same, but different countries have different names."[13]

It was reported that in Georgia some slaves had a religion of their own based on their own experiences, the experience of God with them, and upon various visions and revelations.[14] Even though "churched Negroes" respected the Bible and learned to read it before they could read anything else, among many slaves there was a contempt for "book religion," not merely because they had to depend upon oral instruction, but because they possessed great self-esteem and confidence in their own manner of believing and worshiping God. For them, "the Spirit within" was superior to the Bible as a guide to religious knowledge. One informant discovered that the slaves on his plantation were adverse to the Bible because they had been told by their masters that it upheld slavery.[15]

An incident that happened to C. C. Jones, who was evidently an industrious missionary but always "the agent of the masters," was reported in the Tenth Report of the Association for the Religious Instruction of the Negroes in Liberty County, Georgia:

I was preaching to a large congregation on the Epistle to Philemon; and when I insisted on fidelity and obedience as Christian virtues in servants, and upon the authority of Paul, condemned the practice of running away, one-half of my audience deliberately rose up and walked off with themselves; and those who remained looked anything but satisfied with the preacher or his doctrine. After dismission, there was no small stir among them; some solemnly declared that there was no such Epistle in the Bible; others, that it was not the Gospel; others, that I preached to please the masters; others, that they did not care if they never heard me preach again.[16]

The togetherness of the slaves in the mystique of the Black Christian community is another aspect of the style of religious life that many of the white missionaries could neither understand nor appreciate. Members of the same church were sometimes sacrally bound not to reveal each other's sins. One need not suspect some profound theological aberration for such conspiracies, particularly in view of the fact that, for the slavemaster, by far the most heinous sins were rebelliousness, stealing, sabotage and malingering. Jones, however, has a keen smell for what he considered to be a heretical antinomianism among his charges. He found all kinds of degradation and immorality among those who had been baptized and professed to be Christians. In one place he remarks: "That which would be an abominable sin, committed by a church member with a worldly person, becomes no sin at all if committed with another church member." The brethren must "Bear one another's burdens and so fulfill the law of Christ."[17]

Joseph B. Earnest also supports the idea of antinomianism among the slaves, observing that "frequently sins are committed during, or immediately after, a religious service."[18] This may be an exaggeration, but one can believe the story he tells of an old Negro who testified in church that he had cursed some, stolen some, drunk whiskey some and had certainly committed other sins during his life, but thank God, he had never lost his religion.

In his monumental study *Folk Beliefs of the Southern Negro*, Newbell Niles Puckett holds that the African concept of sin, which survived to some degree in the early Negro church, had to do with a broken relationship with the gods rather than an offense against another person. It was an offense, a neglect, or an ill-advised act against the spirits that was judged a sin—whether committed consciously or accidentally. Hence, he concludes that, following the West African practice, there was resident in the Christianity of the southern Negro almost no connection between religion and morality. He writes:

> An Arkansas Negro considered it all right to conjure inasmuch as he had "'surrance er salvation," and most of

the conjure-doctors with whom I have come in contact
are unusually religious and ostentatious in their church
obligations—some of them even being ministers.[19]

Puckett's observation concerning African religions, like some
of his other comments about Black folk, reveals his own prejudice. Certainly we know that there are definite and sometimes elaborate codes of morals in African societies, and many
of them are assumed to have been instituted by God. Therefore, they are inseparable from religion. It is true that in many
African religions sin is regarded in terms of its corporate, external significance and consequence, not in terms of its personal, inward meaning or lack of conformity with a set of *a
priori* moral principles. Thus, the sinfulness of an act, according to Professor Mbiti, is judged by its consequences, not
by the act itself.[20] The practical religious attitude of the
slaves could have easily assimilated this concept from their
African past and found in the antinomianism unwittingly
fostered by the manner in which the missionaries taught the
doctrine of the perseverance of the saints a theological ration-
alization for what they already believed. But this is a far cry
from assuming that religion and morality have nothing to do
with one another.

Actually, something more important for our discussion is at
issue here. What Jones, Earnest and others fail to understand
is how the slave looked upon and evaluated the hypocrisy
of white Christianity, how the frequent refusals to be disci-
plined by the moral strictures of the slavemasters' religion
suggest the depth of a moral integrity and a protest which
would not have been tolerated in any other area of plantation life. The missionary was looking for purity of doctrinal
belief and daily life in accordance with the accepted standards of Christianity. Nothing could have been further from
the existential situation in which the slave found himself or
from the basic religious orientation that situation invoked.

The slaves had little concern for doctrinal fidelity not because there was no theological or philosophic content in the
religions of Africa, or in the African adaptations of Roman
Catholicism which took place in the French and Spanish col-

onies. The hierarchical structure and utilitarian quality of the polytheistic African religions which were carried over into the Voodooized Catholicism of Saint-Domingue, Cuba and the coastal areas of South America maintained the basic ontology and soteriology that are still present in the traditional religions and separatist cults of many parts of Africa today. The absence of theological interest among the slaves was due, first of all, to the pragmatic and experiential nature of slave religion in which the existence of a Supreme Being, the reality of the spirit world and the revelatory significance of symbol and myth were all taken for granted and required no explicit theological formulation. Indeed, what the African slave already believed about nature, God and man was more firmly corroborated by his experience than by any catechetical instruction that was obliged to conform to the requirements of the institution of slavery.

The slaves were uneducated, by Western standards, but they were not fools. Almost immediately they recognized the gross inconsistency between the allegation that this all-powerful God of the white man cared so much about their eternal salvation, and the fact of his indifference to the powerlessness and wretchedness of their present condition. Even though they adopted the outward appearance of Christian conversion, they took from it whatever seemed efficacious for easing the burden of their captivity, and gave scant attention to the rest. They were fully aware that the God who demanded their devotion and the spirit that infused their secret meetings and possessed their souls and bodies in the ecstasy of worship, was not the God of the slavemaster, with his whip and gun, nor the God of the plantation preacher, with his segregated services and unctuous injunction to humility and obedience.

Well into the early nineteenth century, the slaves relied upon the most elemental presuppositions of a primitive religious consciousness to give consolation and meaning to their existence. Whatever the specific beliefs that had been salvaged from Africa, or from their sojourn in the West Indies they came under the most vigorous assault by the Protestant missionaries. The polytheistic aspect of African spirituality had to be surrendered under great duress, but the spirits of the ancestral gods, disembodied and depersonalized, invaded the interstices of the objectified world and impregnated the imagination with an interminable variety of the ghosts, witches, talking animals and supernatural experiences which comprise the antebellum folklore of the southern Negro. The harsh, oppressive conditions of daily life, especially for the field hands, rendered this animated, divinized environment generally hostile in the mind of the slave, for it could scarcely be more than the subconscious manifestation of the nightmarish reality of almost every waking hour. The disorganization and dehumanization of the social situation in the slave quarters was caused largely by the unnatural requirements forced upon it by the economics of the slave system. The living situation itself, after working hours were over, served to fortify the fatalistic and demonic character of existence.

The question was continually one of survival, mental and physical, and whatever the slave could appropriate from the conjure man, or later from the charismatic Christian preacher, to deal with the aleatory aspects of his situation and to ward off the evil influences all around him, was seized upon as a gift of power from "de Lawd," who had not seen fit to extricate him from his plight, but nevertheless, provided the means of temporarily preserving health and sanity.

The foregoing is not to suggest that the slaves did not find joy and consolation in religion. Slave religion did indeed address itself to the serious problems of existence and survival in an alien land by falling back into some of the more malevolent traditions of the past. But there was another side. The grim determination and sanctimonious punctiliousness with which most Protestant missionaries went about the business of saving the souls of the heathen from eternal damnation was foreign to the basic nature of the slave's religious sensibilities. Reverence toward the Supreme Being was, for the slave, first of all, the joyous affirmation of his presence and protection. Once the gods had come near, one opened himself to them with a vivaciousness and abandon that were expressed most satisfactorily in song and dance. The secular and the sacred met and embraced each other in the bodily celebration of the homologous unity of all things—the holy and the profane, the good and evil, the beautiful and dreadful. To give oneself up with shouts of triumph and "singing feet" to this wholeness of being, to the ecstatic acquisition of one's own creaturehood, and to experience in frenzy that creatureliness taken up and possessed by the familiar God, was to imbibe the most restorative medicine available to the soul.

The brooding melancholy of some of the Negro spirituals have led many people to the belief that the religion of the slave was one of unrelieved gloom and grief—a religion of lost souls flailing hopelessly against an unbreachable wall of darkness. The slaves certainly knew sorrow, but they knew it as an inevitable part of the natural life—of creaturely life—and they lowered themselves into its depths in funeral services and in mournful songs and spirituals, not out of compulsion but as a way of *feeling*, of being more deeply nourished by the power of the tragic in finitude, without which man cannot fully realize himself and his place in the mysterious womb of the universe.

The dominant motif of slave religion was affirmation and enjoyment—even carnal pleasure. His religion bound him to the organic and vitalistic powers of the Creation—to the powers that he believed could fulfill and provide for those who joyfully acknowledge and serve the Creator.

The curious mixture of zeal and carelessness which resulted from the combination of Christianity with whatever the slaves had brought with them of the African religions, was a constant puzzlement to some of the missionaries who arduously labored to get them to contemplate the state of their souls with fear and trembling. The preachers could never understand the humor and light touch with which the slave handled sacred things, a habit which the preachers charged to heathenism, stupidity or the lack of refinement. The shouts of a Saturday night over the spirits from a bottle of rum and the shouts of a Sunday morning over the Holy Spirit sounded suspiciously

alike to the white missionaries, and they shared their un-
easiness about it with one another, although they would never
concede it to the slaveowners. How could one enjoy the form
and ceremony of Christianity so much, on the one hand,
while, on the other, taking in such tongue-in-check fashion
the solemn moral requirements of the faith? And if such
moral gymnastics as the slaves exhibited were permitted,
how were the sober preachers to judge whether such persons
had experienced a genuine Christian conversion?

Many of the missionaries confessed that they did not know
how to deal with this dilemma. The Methodist William Capers, in a letter to Wilbur Fisk, complained of nursing the
slaves through a probationary period for church membership
only to have them fall away into their old habits because, as
he said, "the prevalent conceit that sin is sin for white men
not negroes . . . [held] a fond control over them."[21] Back-
sliding, jumping from one denomination to another in accordance with the personal advantage gained, and distorting
Christian teachings to fit their own personal predilections,
were reported by the white preachers as proof of the religious immaturity and childishness of their Black converts.
Their extreme excitability in prayer and praise, often exhibited with subtle traces of sensuality, their exaggerated
imitation of white piety—which in the next moment would
slip into boisterousness and lighthearted disregard of the
sanctity of worship—gave some missionaries the general impression that the Negroes were "playing at religion" and were
innately incapable of Christianization by the standards of
white people.

But it seems incontestable that what the whites regarded
as incapacity and childishness was more often a completely
different approach to religion, a different view of the world, a
studied avoidance of autocratic control, and a clandestine protest against the hypocrisy of a system of belief that taught
Black men to be the virtuous and obedient slaves of men
who themselves lived lives of indolence and immorality in
full view of those they purported to serve as examples. The
Reverend Charles C. Jones did well to warn inexperienced

white missionaries who were naïve enough to assume that the slaves had swallowed all their teachings, and thus—"beholding their attention to the preaching of the Gospel, adapted to their comprehension, and hearing the expressions of their thankfulness for the pains taken for their instruction, come to the conclusion that they are an unsophisticated race."[22]

The preacher, said Jones, could take nothing for granted in the outward manifestations of Christian conversion if he did not want, in the end, to be frightened away from the mission field in disgust and disappointment.

> He discovers deism, skepticism, universalism. As already stated, the various perversions of the Gospel, and all the strong objections which he may perhaps have considered peculiar only to the cultivated minds, the ripe scholarship and profound intelligence of *critics and philosophers!*[23]

For all its deficiencies and excesses, the religion that the slave practiced was his own. It was unmistakably the religion of an oppressed and segregated people. It had, of course, common features with white Protestantism and, in the French and Spanish areas, with Roman Catholicism. But it was forged not in the drawing rooms of the southern mansions, nor in the segregated balconies of the northern churches. It was born in Blackness. Its most direct antecedents were the quasi-religious, quasi-secular meetings which took place on the plantations, unimpeded by white supervision and under the inspired leadership of the first generation of African priests to be taken in slavery. It was soon suppressed and dominated by the religious instruction of the Society for the Propagation of the Gospel in Foreign Parts and the colonial churches—especially the Baptists and Methodists. But the faith that evolved from the coming together of diverse religious influences was a *tertium quid*, distinctly different from its two major contributors.

What both the slave churches of the South—"the invisible institution"—and the free churches of the North developed was a religion suffused with a sublimated outrage that was balanced with a patient cheerfulness and boundless confidence in the ultimate justice of God. As the religion of a subjugated and suffering people, it had both positive and negative effects upon those who participated in its cultus. Black religion served, in formal and informal ways, to order and interpret an existence that was characterized, on one hand, by repression, self-abnegation and submissiveness, and on the other, by subterfuge, rebelliousness and the joyous affirmation of life in the face of tribulation.

It would be helpful at this point to examine in somewhat more detail the African religious background which provided a rapidly disintegrating but persistently influential base upon which the religious institutions of the slave were erected. It is not the purpose of this discussion to make a comparative analysis of Christianity *vis-à-vis* the traditional religions of West Africa and the Caribbean islands during the slave period. Such a task belongs to the fields of cultural anthropology and the history of religions. Melville Herskovits, Newbell Niles Puckett, W. E. B. Du Bois, and in more recent years Janheinz Jahn, Lorenzo D. Turner, LeRoi Jones, Charles Long, and others, have adequately demonstrated, at least to this author's satisfaction, that Black religion in America has roots in Africa and the West Indies as well as in the evangelicalism of the Great Awakenings.[24]

What many European and Americans once regarded as a lower form of primitive animism and pagan superstition in Africa is increasingly being recognized as sophisticated, complex ontological and ethical systems, as African scholars themselves begin to examine their traditional religions without the earlier undue deference to Western scholarship. We know that the Africans who were imported to the New World could not have been completely divested of belief systems. Whatever was the precise nature of their religions, we know today that they were not unenlightened and preposterous. The native religions of West and Central Africa had a single dominating characteristic which, in an attenuated form, survived for many years among Black religionists in the United States: a profound belief that both the individual and the community had a continuous involvement with the spirit world in the practical affairs of daily life.

African religions know of no rigid demarcation between the natural and the supernatural, the sacred and the profane. All of life is permeated with forces or powers which exist in some relationship to man's weal or woe. Man is, therefore, required—for his own sake and that of the community—to understand and appreciate this spirit world which merges imperceptibly with immediate, tangible reality. He must, in some prescribed way, enter into communion with it in order to receive its benefits and avoid its condemnation. The Supreme Being, departed ancestors, spirits resident in or associated with certain lakes, trees, and animals, and living human beings who possessed mysterious gifts of healing or of making mischief, were all united in one overarching, invisible world that has its own laws and conventions which sustain and order the visible world.

Considerable injustice has been done to our understanding of the true quality of these traditions by the writings of the early missionaries, anthropologists and historians of religion, who could only regard them as "ignorant superstitions" and "dark and cruel fetishism." Even Du Bois, in commenting upon Obi, or Obeah, worship, which he attributes to the Africans who were transported to the West Indies, identifies this form of belief uncritically with nature worship and witchcraft. What is suggested by such identification is that we are dealing with a crude and demonic perversion of the natural revelation of God, little more than the weird concoction of aboriginal religious fanatics and charlatans. A somewhat more sophisticated analysis assumes that these systems were basically animistic and manifested themselves primarily as sorcery and magic. These terms are used pejoratively by most people, Black as well as white, and the implication, with respect to the religion of the American slaves, is that they were ignorant and misguided people; that insofar as the vestiges of African religions survived, they were responsible for the hysteria, degradation and destructive elements in Negro religiosity.

Recent work by African scholars on the religions and philosophies of Africa has thrown a different light on these structures of belief and, therefore, on what may have been the true meaning of the religious background that the slaves brought with them to the New World.[25] While the critical questions are still debatable, it is possible to correct some popular presuppositions about the barbarity and inferiority (as compared, let us say, to American Christianity during the systematic extermination of the Indian) of what the Africans believed in the past and, among traditionalists, what they believe today.

Formerly the major emphasis has been upon the assumption of a strong predisposition for animism and nature worship. It is interesting to note that when American and European anthropologists did not understand what they were observing in a primitive religion, the term "animism" always cropped up. In the case of Africa, it implied that the people found their gods in the sun, moon, stones, rivers and in countless other natural objects or phenomena which, for a long time, have been desacralized in Western civilization. The missionaries, both in America and Africa, assumed that this was an idolatrous practice that had little soteriological or ethical meaning that could be related in any feasible way to the religion of Jesus. The Protestants, much more than the Roman Catholics, were horrified by the native religions reported by visitors and traders to the "Slave Coast." By the seventeenth and eighteenth centuries the Reformation was still a relatively recent occurrence, and Protestantism, especially the churches strongly influenced by Puritanism, was still reacting to what it considered the idolatry and paganism of Roman Catholicism. Both Catholicism and Islam were less intolerant of the religious practices of the Africans, but the Protestant missionaries saw nothing in them vaguely representing a preparation for the Gospel. The use of charms, magic, ghosts and witches was deplored as nothing less than Satanism and superstition. No religion that was basically polytheistic, that countenanced polygamy and made so much of ancestors, spirits and the phenomena of nature, could provide an acceptable ground for Christianization. It had first to be stamped out.

But the religious systems of Africa, for all their exotic peculiarities and strangeness to the European mind, were by no means crude and unenlightened superstitions. Professor John Mbiti has shown, for example, that the widespread assumption that the Africans worshiped nature and venerated animals as gods, is a gross misunderstanding. While the heavenly bodies and such animals as lizards and snakes have a place in some African religions, they are only two of several categories of Being and are, in a way, symbolic representations of the living, pulsating environment in which man subsists and through which he is related to the spirits of supernatural beings and the ancestors, but pre-eminently with the Supreme Being, the God who is above all gods and who is Creator, Judge and Redeemer.[26]

Concerning "nature worship," Mbiti considers, in several places in his recent work, the central place of the sun for such peoples as the Ashanti and the Igbo, two West African nations from which many slaves were brought to America. At one point he observes:

> Among many societies, the sun is considered to be a manifestation of God Himself . . . There is no concrete indication that the sun is considered to be God, or God considered to be the sun, however closely these may be associated. At best, the sun symbolizes aspects of God, such as His omniscience, His power, His everlasting endurance, and even His nature.[27]

By far the most familiar criticism of African religion has been what Westerners have regarded as the inordinate reliance of its devotees upon "medicine men," "conjurers" and other strange practitioners who are supposed to dabble in magic or to possess supernatural powers. The popular opinion has made such specialists to be little more than religious imposters and racketeers who make their living off the fears and anxieties of primitive peoples. Actually, not a few of them were among the shipments of slaves from Dahomey and Togo, and it is they who must have formed the original cadres out of which the earliest Black preachers (not those who were designated as such by the slavemasters and missionaries) began to emerge as the leaders of the slave society. This partially explains the low estate in which most Black preachers were held by the American colonists before they became dependable representatives of the white man's religion.

It is true that all kinds of religious workers were included among the slaves—from high priests and priestesses to diviners and root doctors. It is necessary, however, to differentiate among the various roles of these persons and to evaluate the contribution each made to the survival and, ultimately, to the resistance of the African to slavery. It is important to note that it is not at all certain that "conjurer" and "medicine man" are terms which can be employed to comprehend both good and bad magic indiscriminately. The term "medicine man," as it is used by Mbiti and others, must be reserved for what we would call "good magic." The conjurer, or witch doctor, plied his trade more frequently for antisocial purposes and was the object of fear among most African peoples. Such persons were sought out by those who wished to harm or destroy others, and since it was possible for bad magic to be turned back against the one who desired to use it for his own purposes, the conjurer was hated as well as feared. He was usually blamed for whatever went amiss in the natural course of life and in the tempestuous interpersonal relationships which were particularly exacerbated under the conditions of slavery. In Africa, a witch, or conjurer, was sometimes driven physically from the village, if not hunted down and slain.

On the other hand, the medicine man in African societies is a source of help and healing for the community in which he lives. Mbiti speaks of him as "the greatest gift" to the community and as "both doctor and pastor." He not only made use of plants, herbs, minerals, etc., in his healing art, but was called upon for priestly ministrations. He gave such advice and counsel as the people needed to make themselves more productive and effective in the various situations of daily life—whether as warriors, farmers, husbands or wives. He was, in other words, the precursor of the slave preachers or "exhorters," who, with and without the certification of the white churches, became the first religious leaders of Black community. In a summary description of this religious specialist, Mbiti writes:

> In short, the medicine-men symbolize the hopes of society: hopes of good health, protection and security from evil forces, prosperity and good fortune, and ritual cleansing when harm or impurities have been contracted. These men and women are not fools; they are on the average intelligent and devoted to their work, and those who are not simply do not prosper or get too far.[28]

He is, of course, describing the medicine man in contemporary Africa, but here is a considerably more accurate picture of the religious practitioners and priests who were occasionally mentioned by the missionaries than the one we have from popular prejudice. This is not to deny that there were slaves who were the operators of a fraudulent "mumbo-jumbo" and who made a good living from the fear and credulity of their neighbors. Any casual glance today at the classified section of the *New Amsterdam News* and other Black newspapers in the United States, will attest to the fact that, among certain segments of the community, this kind of business is still carried on and profitably. But most of the so-called conjure men" and "Voodoo doctors" who rose to stature and leadership in the secret plantation meetings of the slaves, were men of ability and integrity who took their vocations with the utmost seriousness. They were really "medicine men" who came to be called "Reverend" and were sought out for spiritual counsel and healing by both Black and white in the South.[29]

Originally, the prophets and preachers who evolved out of the class of African medicine men among the slaves attempted to direct the propitious, health-giving forces of nature into the lives of those who, despite the devastation of their native culture, still believed in the efficacy of the spirit world and the protecting gods of their homeland. Often they sold amulets, charms, "gre-gre bags" or "hands" (small parcels containing bits of paper, bones or potions that hung around the neck or were carried in some other way for protection and good luck). But their services were by no means confined to the use of magic. They also interpreted the meaning of events, with some coaptation later of Biblical prophecy, and called the people to a sense of pride, solidarity and the first stirrings of resentment against slavery. Herskovits, in discussing the probability that a certain group of priests from Dahomey were among the slaves brought from West Africa, writes:

> It is apparent that here is a mechanism which may well account for the tenaciousness of African religious beliefs in the New World, which . . . bulk largest among the various elements of West African culture surviving. What could have more effectively aided in this than the presence of a considerable number of specialists who could interpret the universe in terms of aboriginal belief? What, indeed, could have more adequately sanctioned resistance to slavery than the presence of priests who, able to assure supernatural support to leaders and followers alike, helped them fight by giving the conviction that the powers of their ancestors were aiding them in their struggle for freedom?[30]

The point that needs to be stressed here is that the early spiritual leaders among the slaves in the West Indian and American colonies were the representatives of the traditional African religions we are beginning to understand and appreciate today. What they brought to Christianity, which they were ultimately to adopt as their own, were attitudes and perspectives fundamentally at variance with the passivity of missionary teaching. For all of what has seemed to us to have been weird and outlandish practices, these men retained from Africa an instinctive intelligence about existence, about the presence in life of that which is radically antagonistic to man and irreconcilable with the best interests of the community. They already had a concept of a Supreme Being who was deeply involved in the practical affairs of man's life, but in a different way than the Christian God. This Being was approachable through many intermediaries, but he was known to them also as Father—as one who loved and protected his children and whose power was available against the elemental spirits of the universe. It was not only in the identification of the healing properties of plants and minerals or in the exorcism of demonic influences that these "medicine-men preachers" contributed to the security of the uprooted slave. What became most relevant and significant for a later time was the fact that they recognized the relationship between "bad magic," as the white man practiced it, and the dehumanizing situation in which Black people found themselves.

In attempting to describe the corruption of African religions in the New World, several writers have settled upon the term "Voodooism" as the one that best sums up the various strains of deteriorating African religions which were residual in the transplanted African society of the American plantations.[31] Whether or not this expedient is permissible depends, to some extent, on how one defines "Voodoo." It is, however, widely accepted that the beliefs and rituals that cluster around the idea of Voodoo—if, indeed, not the cult itself— were vestigial remains of African religions which mixed early with Roman Catholicism in the French and Spanish colonies. There are undeniable affiliations between the traditional mythologies of West Africa, particularly of Dahomey and Nigeria, and the *vodu* invoked in the temples of Haiti today, as well as during slavery.[32] We know that for the first thirty-five or forty years of slavery on the mainland, practically all of the slaves brought to American ports came from the West Indies—particularly from the Island of Dominica (Haiti, Dominican Republic), where we begin to trace the development of Voodoo, and that many continued to come from the Caribbean as long as the external slave trade persisted.

According to Parrinder, the term "Voodoo," or *vodu,* originated with the Ewe origin (a tribe from the area of what is now Ghana) and is derived from *vo* (apart) which has roughly the same meaning as our word "holy" (set apart) or "sacred." The word we mentioned earlier as used by Du Bois in his description of slave worship, *Obe* or *Obeah,* refers to the use of charms or fetishes for the purpose of bewitching others or shielding oneself from harm. It is sometimes associated with the practice of Voodoo. The slaves from Dahomey and Togo went mainly to Haiti and San Domingo, and it is to them that the Voodoo religious tradition is mainly ascribed. Those who were brought to Jamaica came mainly from the Gold Coast, and Parrinder finds the Jamaican Obeah a derivative of the Twi *obayifo,* which he translates simply as witchcraft and does not associate with snake worship as others do Voodoo.[33]

Voodoo, however, was and is more than ophiolatry and trickery. Its devotees "believe in one supreme God, too good to get angry," and they find in him the same succor and help that others find in the God of the so-called higher religions. What remains in the slums of Port-au-Prince and Kingston today, being exploited both by pretenders and tourists, can be only an impoverished relic of original Voodoo. But during slavery, Voodoo had close affinities with the theologies and rituals of West Africa. Metraux finds that the most important of its divinities still belong to the West African peoples, who have shrines for them in the towns and villages of Ghana, Dahomey and Nigeria. He writes further:

> Moreover . . . the main divinities [of the Voodoo pantheon] are still classified according to the tribe or region from which they originate. Thus we have Nago gods, Siniga [Senegalese], Anmine [Minas], Ibo, Congo and Wangol [Angolese] gods. Some gods even carry as an epithet the name of their African place of origin: for instance, Ogu-Badagri [Badagri is a town in Nigeria] and Ezili-Freda-Dahomey [Ezili of Whydah-Dahomey].[34]

Voodoo should be understood as a conglomeration of half-remembered, partially "dereligionized" beliefs and rites which came out of the West Indies in the seventeenth and eighteenth centuries. It had its antisocial and destructive aspects, to be sure, but it was not the morbid, menacing superstition that is attributed to cannibalism, the criminal use of poison and sexual cohabitation with snakes, which is the way it is so often pictured in lurid motion pictures and comic books. The French and English travelers and missionaries of the period who were exposed to Voodoo practices in Africa and the islands of the Caribbean, were terrified by what they regarded as its blood-curdling and diabolical character. But modern investigation has thrown light on its fundamentally religious nature, its proximate relationship to the traditional religions of Africa and the way it has been both functional and dysfunctional, like all religions, in the lives of individuals and society. The Voodoo that was extant by the end of the eighteenth century, at least among the West Indian slaves, was close to, if not in fact, an organized church—with its temples, its *Bokono* (magicians) and *vodu-no* (priests) who had been trained in Africa, its elaborate ritual, ceremonial dancing and hymnody. It had probably already been infiltrated by Roman Catholicism and, in turn, was recreating out of Christianity, a religion with a distinctively Afro-American flavor, much more sensitive to the reality and immediacy of the supernatural and more aware of the nebulous demarcation between the secular and the sacred.

As the American slaves must have known it, Voodoo was the worship of "an all-powerful and supernatural being," symbolized by a serpent, but also personified in a hierarchy of gods closely resembling those of Dahomean mythology.[85] It was, in substance, a religion of the people, explaining for them the nature of the world in which they lived, the terrifying experiences of their captivity in a strange land, and the means by which they could, under the skilled guidance of medicine men and priests, protect themselves from the ever-present evil. They sought deliverance from evil that was seen and unseen, through faithfulness to the great Voodoo and due reverence to the lesser *loa* who surround him and who eventually were identified with the saints of the Roman Catholic Church. Rather than merely a vengeful stratagem to punish those one hated (although, as we shall see, that was not without its utility in insurrection), Voodoo was as much a moral religion as the Christianity of the plantation owners and missionaries. The Voodoo was a god of goodness, not of satanic evil, and as Metraux points out regarding its modern version (which he believes has changed little from earlier days), the spirits do not engage in criminal acts, but behave in conformity with the normative mores and conventions of the society.[36]

For the purposes of this discussion, however, it is necessary to understand Voodoo, to some extent, as a response to the demoralizing conditions of slavery and one means by which the slave made some adjustment to his actual situation, while also finding in this religion a secret inspiration for resistance. What we know about the revolutionary proclivities of those West Indians who practiced Voodoo in Haiti and elsewhere raises a question about whether it had anything to do with what we noted earlier as radical and obstreperous elements in the religion of Protestant slaves on the mainland. We know, of course, about its continuation in Louisiana, but it went far afield from Creole culture. Many students of Negro folklore find it in many places throughout the South before and after the Civil War. Indeed, it found its way into the storefront cults and occult shops of Harlem and other Black ghettos of the North and, probably with the aid of more recent immigrants from the Caribbean, can be found in American cities today. We know also that Voodoo has always been adaptive to the anti-white feelings of oppressed Black people. Wherever we find it converging with pneumatoscopic elements in Black religion in America, as in the earliest days, we can expect to find a militant, religiously inspired rejection of white values and white control.

People who today speak disparagingly of Voodoo, Shango worship and other forms of African religion among Blacks, usually express concern about the terroristic aspects of these beliefs, the unending spiral of fear in which people seem to be caught, and the feeling of having to turn to magic to defend themselves and to exact retributive justice from others. This may well be. All societies provide more or less socially acceptable, but frequently devastating ways for people to deal with their fears, prejudices and petty jealousies. There are no laws against snubbing your mother-in-law at a party, refusing to answer the telephone, selling jet fighters to a friendly nation or defoliating the forests of an enemy. But all of these represent negative and sometimes psychotic reactions to interpersonal and international problems and frustrations. Where social situations are fraught with conflict and tension, whether in an affluent suburban enclave or in an overcrowded slum, the techniques for survival and self-gratification become ruthless and destructive, no matter how natural or genteel they may seem in terms of accepted cultural norms.

In a "primitive" society, the same conditions obtain for "dealing with" or "gettting back at" someone, and the fetishistic or conjural instrumentalities that are employed seem to those who use them to be no more exotic and no more or less effective than those which are used by a supposedly enlightened and civilized society. Consider, for example, what Professor Mbiti has written concerning the difficult human conditions under which sorcery and witchcraft developed in an African village:

> The environment of intense relationship favors strongly the growth of the belief in magic, sorcery, witchcraft, and all the fears, practices and concepts that go with this belief. I do not for a moment deny that there are spiritual forces outside man which seem sometimes to function within human history and human society. But the belief in the mystical power is greater than the ways in which that power might actually function within the human society. African communities in the villages are deeply affected and permeated by the psychological atmosphere which creates both real and imaginery powers or forces of evil that give rise to more tensions, jealousies, sus-

picions, slander, accusations and scapegoats. It is a vicious cycle. Let us illustrate this by moving from the academic to the practical.

Within this intensely corporate type of society, there are endless manifestations of evil. These include murders, robberies, rape, adultery, lies, stealing, cruelty especially toward women, quarrels, bad words, disrespect to persons of a higher status, accusations of sorcery, magic and witchcraft, disobedience of children and the like. In this atmosphere, all is neither grim nor bright. It is hard to describe these things: one needs to participate or grow up in village life to get an idea of the depth of evil and its consequences upon individuals and society. A visitor to the village will immediately be struck by African readiness to externalize the spontaneous feelings of joy, love, friendship and generosity. But this must be balanced by the fact that Africans are men, and there are many occasions when their feelings of hatred, strain, fear, jealousy and suspicion also become readily externalized. *This makes them just as brutal, cruel, destructive and unkind as any other human beings in the world.*[37]

If this can be said about people under the relatively quiescent conditions of village life in West Africa, what can be expected of them, or of any human beings, under the conditions of slavery as experienced in the New World? Here whole villages were sold into bondage. Black people were uprooted from ancestral lands and transported across the Atlantic Ocean to be set down on sugar plantations where men, women and children were treated worse than beasts of burden. It was in this bitter and inflammatory situation that Voodooism and Obeah flourished as the African slaves strove with one another and the slavemasters over color, status and the brutality of forced labor. The intimidation and hatred which conjuration and witchcraft often represented came to be part of a religion that sought to deal with the enigmatic questions of good and evil, life and death, and the cause of unprovoked suffering at the hands of white strangers. This was the inevitable consequence of slavery, and it could be only a matter of time and opportunity for the violent impulses released by such a religion to be turned against the real enemy in a struggle for revenge and liberation.

That is what eventually happened in Haiti. When the slaves revolted in 1791, sending tremors of hope and excitement for Blacks throughout the world, all of the powers of Voodoo were invoked. The leaders of the revolution later tried to make it the state religion, holding that it was the mystical powers of the Voodoo priests that gave the Black soldiers the feeling of invincibility and drove the English, Spanish and, finally, the army of Napoleon, into the sea. Although Toussaint L'Ouverture himself was a staunch Roman Catholic, before his career as a guerrilla he had been a medicine man, or "root doctor." Once, on the arrival of the French expeditionary forces under Leclerc, Toussaint sought divination from a Voodoo priest at the fort of Crête-à-Pierrot.[38] Dessalines, his successor, had been a plantation slave, and tradition has it that he knew Voodoo better than his predecessor and deliberately incited the Congolese and Guinean slaves to practice it on the eve of battle as a means of obtaining invulnerability. The doubt that some historians cast over whether Dessalines, who was deified in the Voodoo pantheism, had real sympathy with the cult, because he later attempted to stamp it out, seems not well-founded merely on that account. Christian princes were known to have been great patrons of the Church during times of war, but feared and suppressed the papacy and the radical leaders of the Reformation once peace had been won and their political problems solved.

The fact is that the Haitian nationalists found in Voodoo a spiritual force that could not be separated from their yearning for liberation. The "maroons," or fugitive slaves, who held out in the mountains and spurred the slave rebellions of 1758 and 1790 had their priests with them and faithfully practiced Voodoo rites. About 1758, a Voodoo prophet or magician named Makandal began to preach the destruction of the whites by poisoning. He was later burned at the stake at Limbé in northern Haiti, but legends about his escape from the fire continued for years. The name of Makandal, along with that of Toussaint L'Ouverture and Jean Jacques Dessalines, was traditionally invoked by members of the cult to inspire anticolonial resistance.[39] Dantes Bellegarde, in his *Historie du peuple haitien,* writes that "the slaves found in Voodoo the ideal stimulus for their energy—since Voodoo had become less of a religion than a political association—a sort of 'black carbonaro.' "[40] As we shall see, this transmutation of spiritual energy into a political movement for freedom has been an inherent capacity of Black religion from the earliest period of slavery. It played an important part in slave insurrections in the United States and in the militancy of a significant sector of the Black church down to the civil rights movement of the twentieth century.

Notwithstanding the efforts of the early missionaries in the American colonies to introduce the slaves to a religion which demythologized the elemental powers of the primitive consciousness, encouraged escape from the world and submission to slavery in the hope of paradise when earthly life was over, the fact remains that religion had a much more practical and immediate role to play among the slaves. Whether the missionaries desired it or not, Christianity had to provide *some* aspects of faith and practice that were continuous with the African experience—as with Voodoo in Haiti or the Santeria in Cuba—and the most notable were those that dealt with the curative, shielding, self-gratifying powers of the deity. As much as he might have quoted John 3:16 as the cornerstone of the true faith, the missionary could not evade the fact that this "only begotten Son of God" performed miracles, cast out demons, waged a continuous struggle against Satan, and gave to those who trusted in him the power to do the same. All this was translated into a religious pragmatism by which the slave dealt with the most destructive and threatening aspects of his real situation. Moreover, the missionary could not, in good conscience, depreciate the presence and mysterious work of the Holy Spirit in the life of the believer. This work could readily be interpreted by the slave as identical with conjuration and the Orisha-possession of his ancestral religion. Even with the exclusion of other factors, this alone assured a measure of freedom and continuity with the past while, at the same time, it diverted certain Biblical and theological conceptions of Christianity into structures of belief and practice that more adequately served the needs of the slaves. Those needs had to do with physical survival, psychic stability, and ultimately with liberation.

The implications of "the freedom of the Christian man," basic to the New Testament and the theology of the Protestant Reformation, had no difficulty being recalled by the churches during the War of Independence. It was, however, assiduously avoided by most missionaries in their instruction to Negroes. Having convinced the dubious slaveowners that the conversion of his human property would not result in a capital loss, but greatly increase his profits, the missionary reduced Christian theology and ethics to their most simplistic and inoffensive affirmations. A favorite text was, of course, the passage from Ephesians 6:5—"Servants, be obedient to them that are your masters according to the flesh, with fear and trembling, in singleness of your heart, as unto Christ." By the middle of the nineteenth century several catechisms were available for oral instruction, such as Charles C. Jones's catechism for Presbyterian slaves and Capers' "A *Catechism for little Children and for Use on the Missions to the Slaves in South Carolina.*"[41] Most of these outlined the basic tenets of orthodoxy with suitable ethical injunctions calculated to inculcate the virtues of monogamy, honesty, industriousness, and to discourage the temptations to insurrection. One such document inquired of the slave: "What did God make you for?" The answer: "To make a crop." "What is the meaning of 'Thou shalt not commit adultery'?" Answer: "To serve our heavenly Father, and our earthly master, obey our overseer, and not steal anything."[42]

While all the missionaries deplored what they regarded as obstinacy and superstition among the slaves and gave their major effort to the dethronement of heathenism, a few early

Quakers and Methodists made an abortive attempt to make their slave converts aware of the implications of Christianity for human equality and justice. Like George Fox and Bishop Asbury, these men at first sought voluntary manumission from the slaveowner as an expression of the genuineness of his own conversion and his repentance from the sin of trafficking in human flesh. When this method proved to be of no avail in the face of the sheer economic advantage of the institution, more radical itinerant white preachers actually instigated slave uprisings on religious principles, and a few of them were apprehended in the process. The consequence throughout the South was the fear and suspicion of strange white men who came upon the plantation with the professed purpose of evangelizing. In most cases, such unsolicited preaching was strictly forbidden, or if permitted, carefully regulated and kept under surveillance. All in all, it is fair to assume that the opening up of the whole issue of human equality in the context of the Gospel and the moral right, under the Christian religion, of the slave to escape or to resist enslavement, was due in no small measure to the agitation of a few intrepid whites who transmitted the egalitarian spirit of the American Revolution and radical Christianity to the secret gatherings of the plantation slaves. These early abolitionists helped to fan the winds of prophecy that broke over Denmark Vesey and Nat Turner in the tumultuous period of protest and rebellion that preceded the Civil War. Even the most conservative teachings of the missionaries could be exploited, in a negative way, to turn the religiosity of the slaves and the organizational potential of the slave churches, such as they were, to the intrigue of insurrection. The fears of the slaveowners were essentially well-founded. Instinctively, they knew that any attempt to educate or indoctrinate the slave would, in the long run, change the precarious relationship between master and slave. For this reason, many of them opposed any kind of religious instruction, preferring to maintain law and order by brute force rather than by a paternalistic form of Christian education.

In this determination the planters were assisted by the

colonial governments. As early as 1715, North Carolina passed an act declaring that any master or slaveowner who permitted "Negroes to build . . . any house under the pretense of a meeting-house upon account of worship, shall be liable to a fine of fifty pounds."[43] In 1723, Maryland voted to restrict independent religious meetings among Negroes, and by 1770, Georgia had forbidden slave assemblies under the penalty of "twenty-five stripes, with a whip, switch or cowskin." Thus, the American colonies, prior to the Revolutionary War, kept the overt religious life of the slaves under severe restrictions. Du Bois writes, however:

> Whether or not such acts tended to curb the really religious meetings of the slaves or not it is not easy to know. Probably they did, although at the same time there was probably much disorder and turmoil among the slaves, which sought to cloak itself under the name of the church.[44]

In summary, we can say that despite the deliberate distortion of Christian doctrine and stringent restrictions upon religious activity and the ministry of Black and white preachers, a distinctive, African American form of Christianity—actually the new religion of an oppressed people—slowly took root in the Black community. This Black folk religion contained within its perspectives a definitive moral judgment against slavery and a clear legitimation of the slave's, and later the freedman's, struggle against the forces of injustice and inequality. White abolitionism contributed to the rising militancy of Black Christians and to the spirit which created the independent Black churches, but it was a great deal more than abolitionism among a few radical white clergymen that made religion among the slaves something different from the conventional Christianity of the American churches. It was the slave's African past that did the most to influence his style of religion, his rejection of the spiritual and political despotism of the white man, and made the most important contribution to his coming struggle for freedom.

This is to say that the essential ingredient of Black Christianity prior to the Civil War was the creative spirituality of the African religions. The defining characteristic of that spirituality was its spontaneous fascination with, and unself-conscious response to, the reality of the spirit world and the intersection between that world and the world of objective perception. Such an ontology called for the release of the human spirit, as the sacred vessel in which the vital forces of the universe coalesce, from every power—whether of man or the gods—that would seek to exercise tyranny over it. Those who profess such a religion cannot be bound by any-one or anything indefinitely. Freedom is intrinsic to its very nature.[45] The African attitude literally created the image of the pre-existent God in the freedom of the religious imagina-tion and opened the life of man to the influence of divinity which flowed to him from his ancestors and from the natural world. The liberation of the whole man—body, mind and soul—from every internal and external restraint that was not deliberately and purposely chosen was the first re-quirement for one who would be possessed by the Spirit. God alone had the authority to command, to invoke life and death, blessing and cursing, although it is clear that he cus-tomarily exercised this power though many kinds of inter-mediaries. But the indispensable condition for life and human fulfillment in the religious and philosophical tradition of Africa is freedom—the untrammeled, unconditional free-dom to be, to exist, and to express the power of Being fully and creatively for the sheer joy and profound meaning of *Muntu*, man.

We have seen that it was against this background that the slave made his adjustment to Christianity when he had re-ceived the Gospel. The influences of the African religious past extended into his new life, first in the West Indies and later in the United States, and were culturally conditioned—without being completely obliterated, by the circumstances of his en-slavement. Slavery, as a matter of fact, only served to drive them beneath the surface by the force of terror and brutal-ity. But instead of decaying, the African residuum was en-hanced and strengthened in the subterranean vaults of the unconscious from which it arose—time and time again—during moments of greatest adversity and repression—to subvert the attempt to make the slave an emasculated, second-class version of the white man.

Christianity alone, as it was usually presented to the slaves, adulterated, otherworldly and disengaged from its most radical implications, could not have provided the slave with the religious resources he needed for revolt. It had to be enriched with the volatile ingredients of the African religious perspective and, most important of all, with the profound human yearning for freedom that found a channel for expression in the survivals of African religions resident in the early Black churches of the South.

Joseph R. Washington, Jr., made a signal contribution to the contemporary discussion about Black theology when, in 1964, he reminded us that:

> Born in slavery, weaned in segregation and reared in discrimination, the religion of the Negro folk was chosen to bear the roles of both protest and relief. Thus, the uniqueness of black religion is the racial bond which seeks to risk its life for the elusive but ultimate goal of freedom and equality by means of protest and action. It does so through the only avenues to which its members have always been permitted a measure of access, religious convocations in the fields or in houses of worship.[46]

But this Black religion, as the religious common sense, sagacity and style of life of the folk, went far beyond "religious" convocations in fields and churches. It permeated the wit and wisdom, the music and literature, the politics and prophecy of a wide spectrum of Black life in the highly secularized urban areas of the North, as well as in the rural communities of the Bible Belt. It was the soil out of which grew the syncretistic, militant Black nationalism and the African culture interests of many a store-front cult in the ghettos of Harlem and Southside Chicago. It erupts intermittently, like an underwater volcano, in the music of the late Mahalia Jackson and Duke Ellington and in the writings of people who are otherwise as far apart as James Baldwin and LeRoi Jones. It inundated the Black churches of the South, and many in the North, during the height of the civil rights movement, when Martin Luther King, Jr., was its high priest, and the Southern Leadership Conference, its institutional "church." In a later chapter we will examine the contribution of Black folk religion to the social radicalism of that sector of the church which embraces the concept of Black Power. It suffices, at this point, simply to note that those strains of Black religion that have been least influenced by white Christianity are intrinsic to the Black struggle for liberation and inseparable from Black culture as a whole.

But we must go on now to see how this substratum of the religion of the slaves affected the long struggle of Black people against slavery and the role it played in three of the best-known and most important slave revolts in the nineteenth century.

CHAPTER II

Not Peace,
But the Sword

The slaveholders of the present generation,
if cloven down by God's judgment, cannot
plead that they were *unwarned* . . . well may
the God of the oppressed cry out against them,
"because I have called and ye have refused
. . . Therefore will I laugh at your calamity
and mock when your fear cometh. When your
fear cometh like desolation and destruction
like a whirlwind, then shall ye call but I will
not answer."

Theodore Weld to Angelina Weld, Feb. 6, 1842

WITH THE publication in 1938 of Joseph C. Carroll's *Slave Insurrections in the United States, 1800–1865,* a new interest began to develop in what had been a neglected area of Black history. Some attention had previously been given to the matter in a few monographs and in larger works on the general moral and social conditions of the slaves. It was left to the radical abolitionists and a few Black preachers like Henry Highland Garnet and Henry M. Turner to make the American public aware of the fact that the Black man had never been satisfied in his bonds and from the beginning of slavery had made a persistent effort to free himself from them. Nevertheless, even to this day most white Americans have a picture of the slave as a rather good-natured coward. The popular view has been that the slave who came from Africa, unlike the American Indian, did little to secure his freedom except beg for it, purchase it occasionally by years of brutish labor, or pray for it with manacled hands uplifted to God in heaven to the accompaniment of "Swing Low, Sweet Chariot."

One of the reasons for the widespread misunderstanding about the true situation of the slave with respect to organized resistance was the paucity of available information due to the suppression of facts which would serve to stimulate hope and trigger more uprisings. The trials of conspirators by self-appointed or even legitimate authorities were often conducted in secrecy, although in the immediate neighborhood the grisly remains of a lynching party were sometimes put on display to remind others what they might expect from such adventures. But by and large, there was little inclination on the part of the slaveholding establishment to ignite the fires of freedom—particularly among the class of free Negroes in the South—or to encourage the collaboration of northern abolitionists by broadcasting the true extent of insurrectionary activity. Undue publicity could only risk sending out the long-awaited signal that at last the situation in the slave states was ripe for revolution.

The result was that, even given the numerous revolts that we know about, there must have been many more that have never come to light.[1] The widespread fear of slave insurrections that is manifest in all of the public and private records of the period seem out of all proportion to the actual number of events that have been recorded. It now seems clear that, notwithstanding the suppression of information, the whole issue of slave insurrections has been underplayed, partly because of that peculiar racist predisposition of many Americans to prefer to remember the Negro slave as a docile, accommodating collaborator in his own misery waiting for the white man to give him his freedom.

If there was little systematic treatment of this subject before Carroll's work, there is today even less on the role of religion, and specifically of Black preachers, in slave plots and

rebellions. It is, of course, well known that white abolitionists
—many of them motivated by Christianity—stirred up discontent and instigated some of the desperate attempts to run
away or to foment revolt that followed upon their visits to
the plantation country. Quaker and Methodist attacks on the
institution of slavery were no secret to the slaves. James Redpath of Malden, Massachusetts, who wrote a book on his travels through the South, said frankly that the slaveholding class
ought to be abolished and the overseers driven into the sea,
"as Christ once drove the swine; or chase them into the dismal swamps and black morasses of the South . . . I would
slay every man who attempted to resist the liberation of the
slave."[2] Among white northerners, Redpath was rare, but not
unique. There were a few such persons among the Baptist
and Methodist missionaries, and they left a legacy of secret
rebelliousness among the slaves with whom they shared their
inner feelings. But there has been almost no sustained inquiry
into the question of the slave preachers themselves, or the religiously motivated slave leaders. To what extent were these
men the instigators and executors of insurrections? And how
did they put to the service of slave resistance, the resources of
religion—Christian or otherwise?

The relationship between Black religion and the slave insurrections deserves much more study than has been given to
it. This chapter does not pretend to be a full treatment of the
problem. What is intended here is a reminder of the religious
background of the slave's discontent and an examination of
the religious orientation of some of the major propagandists,
some of the most important conspiracies about which we
have some knowledge. More extensive and detailed research
on this matter must be left to the church historians, who
know a great deal about the relationship of the churches to
the American Revolution, but almost nothing about the role
of Black religion in the slave revolts which occurred in the
United States, the Caribbean area and in Latin America.
While it is not accurate to say that every Black congregation
was a seedbed of revolution and every Black preacher a Nat
Turner, there is good reason to believe that religion was con-

siderably more involved than the most accessible records reveal.

White preachers and missionaries to the slaves protested too much that their charges would never countenance such "gross immorality" as rebellion. Needless to say, they would have been painfully embarrassed if the matter proved to be quite the contrary. They labored among Negroes at the behest of the slaveowners, and the slightest indication that their ministries were sowing seeds of rebellion, consciously or unconsciously, would have brought immediate dismissal, if nothing worse. There were frequent enough occasions when white men were known to be collaborators in slave uprisings to make any white man suspect when trouble broke out among seemingly well-disciplined slaves. And this would be even more true when the white man was a fire-eating Baptist or Methodist evangelist who had such lack of common sense as to "love niggers" so much as to attempt to make silk purses out of sows' ears. As the editor of the Baton Rouge *Gazette* wrote in 1841:

> We need not wonder if deeds of blood and murder should take place if incendiary preachers are allowed to hold forth with impunity at camp meetings and other places where our slaves congregate, and baldly make appeals to the worst passions of human nature.
>
> A stop must be put to the ranting and raving of these wolves in sheep's clothing.[3]

As early as 1723, Governor Drysdale, in a message to the Virginia House of Burgesses, remarked on the difficulty the colony was having in detecting and punishing slave insurrections. That year the Virginia legislature passed new laws concerning the control of slaves, since the regulations then in effect were "found insufficient to restrain their tumultuous and unlawful meetings, or to punish the secret plots and conspiracies carried on amongst them."[4] These "tumultuous and unlawful meetings" were, in all probability, church or other religious meetings where the emotions of the slaves, whipped to a frenzy by some slave preacher, rose to such an intensity that they were extremely vulnerable to an appeal, in the context of a sermon or one of the typically long prayers, to throw off their chains in a bloody revolt.

White missionaries were not infrequently suspected of being implicated in slave plots. That some of them had serious religious objections to slavery as early as the period preceding the Revolutionary War and encouraged insurrection is evident. For example, the charge was made by the Charles Town, South Carolina, grand jury on March 17, 1741, that a journal of "enthusiastic prophecys" of the destruction of the town and the liberation of the slaves contained the signature of one Hugh Brian. Under the influence of this white man, according to the record, "great bodies of Negroes have assembled together on pretense of religious worship."[5]

In the Archives of Virginia, *Executive Papers,* dated September 5, 1789, appears the complaint of one Holt Richardson, of King William County, of certain insurrectionary activities related to religion going on in that vicinity:

I have appointed Paterrolers to Keep our Negroes in order & to search all Disorderly houses after night & unlawful Meetings & where they find a large quantity of Negroes assembled at night to take them up & carry them before a justice which has been done, but we have a sett of disorderly People who call themselves Methodists and are joined by some of those who call themselves Baptist, who make it a rule two or three times every week to meet after dark & call in all the Negroes they can gather & a few whites & free mulatoes who pretend under the clock of Religion to meet at a School house where no one lives & there they pretend to preach & pray with a sett of the greatest Roges of Negroes in this County & they never break up till about two or three o'clock in the morning & those Negroes who stays with them goes through the neighborhood & steele everything theat they can lay their hands on & our Negroes are not to be found when we are in want of them, but are at some such meetings and I have ordered the Patterolers to go to such unlawful meetings & to take up all Negroes that they should find at such places.[6]

The Nat Turner revolt greatly heightened the suspicion that religion was a primary factor in the slave uprisings. Governor John Floyd, in his message to the Virginia legislature on December 6, 1831, expressed the opinion that the spirit of insubordination and insurrection among the slaves had its origin in "Yankee pedlars and traders" who taught that "God was no respecter of persons—the black man was as good as the white" and "that the white people rebelled against England to obtain freedom, so have the blacks a right to do so." He further blamed the Turner revolt on the Negroes' reading of the Bible, David Walker's and William Lloyd Garrison's writings and the turning of this knowledge into conspiratorial purposes through the instigation of "black preachers."[7]

The reason for the relative paucity of information on this aspect of the slave revolts is not difficult to surmise. In the first place, little is known about the actual content of slave preaching when whites were not in the congregation. Secondly, what writers like Olmsted and the early historians have given us about the conservatism and otherworldliness of the Black preacher and the slave church, they received from the Negroes themselves who were not about to tell white people all they knew about the complicity of their preachers in revolutionary activity. It is known that many plots were aborted because of the betrayal of some house slave who had been promised his or her freedom for the information. But such disclosures usually came at the time the insurrectionists were moving from talk to action—almost on the eve of an attack. There must have been considerable "rapping," in churches and elsewhere, that never produced a plan that people were willing to act on and was never reported to the masters. The very fact that rebellion and religion were associated with one another in the minds of many Black preachers—particularly those who had run away and returned to preach secretly— means that the religious atmosphere was charged and would have exploded many more times, by the incitement of some

Black preacher or devout layman, had not the odds been so heavily weighted against the possibility of success.

In the third place, a considerable amount of our knowledge of Black preachers and of Black churches of the antebellum period, is from the reports of white missionaries, who usually went to great pains to prove to the sending churches that Christianity was good rather than bad for the slaves. The original objection of the slaveowners to the conversion of the slaves and the toleration of religious services on the plantation was that itinerant abolitionist ministers or excessively enthusiastic Black "exhorters" would take advantage of the situation and distort the message of the gospel into a summons to secular freedom. White pastors and missionaries, having difficulty enough in persuading the white population to accept Christianity, were not in the habit of revealing to the slaveowners the strange and devious transmutations their teachings were subjected to in the hearts and minds of the slaves. There was, in fact, a constant longing for deliverance and a seizing upon every rumor that might suggest that it was at hand.

Successful insurrections do not occur without planning and organization. People must come together at some time. What better time than on Sundays, when there was some leisure available for most slaves, when they could visit one another on nearby plantations, and when the white people were in their own churches? What better place for the slave than a religious gathering to talk about freedom? In church a sense of personal worth and dignity was most complete, and the passion for being delivered from the bondage of sin easily slipped over into a desire to be delivered also from the sin of white people, who flourished like the green bay tree while they treated their Black brothers like beasts of the field.[8]

The slaveowners constantly suspected that this kind of thing was going on in clandestine church meetings, at feasts and burials. There is good evidence to prove that they were not mistaken. Enough mischief seeped out of meetinghouses and field worship services for them to have tightened security around them by the middle of the eighteenth century. In the

Carolinas and Virginia night patrols were on the prowl to interrupt church services held in some part of the plantation that was out of the sight and earshot of white people. Slaves who were caught at such meetings had to use every artifice not to be taken to the authorities or have their Bibles confiscated. Black preachers could expect to be severely whipped for leading such meetings, no matter how harmless in fact they may have been.

Slave discontent, to some degree, was due also to the various kinds of resistance literature which was disseminated from the Revolutionary period to the Civil War. Before considering specific conspiracies related to religious ferment, it is necessary to understand the supportive role that this literature—slave petitions, antislavery tracts and pamphlets—played in awakening the religious consciences of both slave and free, setting the stage for insurrection.

From 1688, when the Quakers of Germantown, Pennsylvania, issued their famous protest against slavery, to 1829, when the Appeal of David Walker made its first appearance, a steady stream of pronouncements and pamphlets—many of them religiously inspired—circulated throughout the country. Although the vast majority of Negroes were illiterate, many who had learned to read, both slaves and freedmen, eagerly absorbed the nutriment of freedom that flowed from the pages of this prolific literature. Many who could not read for themselves heard it read aloud or discussed by others, for such material—although suppressed in the slave states —was secretly distributed by Black freedmen and sympathetic whites. The period immediately preceding and following the American Revolution produced a climate of opinion generally favorable to the expression of ideas concerning the rights of man and the legitimacy of revolution against tyrannical authority. By the end of the century, the Haitian and French revolutions had added fuel to the bright burning. For a time the atmosphere was electric with the militant declarations of Patrick Henry, Tom Paine, the antislavery polemics of Freeborn Garretson, one of the early Methodist missionaries, and Bishop Asbury. The famous Methodist conference of 1784, which viewed slavery as "contrary to the golden laws of God," struck a responsive chord among many evangelical Protestants in the South as well as the North. Voluntary manumissions became for some churchmen an expression of religious conviction. Antislavery tracts and pamphlets began to multiply toward the end of the eighteenth century when it became clear that Negro slavery—now made profitable by the mechanization of cotton production—was becoming what appeared to be a permanent fixture in the American economy.

Actually, fewer Negroes were drawn to the Methodists, who were forced to suspend the authority of the 1784 declaration in less than twelve months, than to the Baptists. Among the latter, a splinter group that rallied against slavery became known as the Emancipating Baptist. One of them, the Reverend David Barrow of Virginia and, later, Kentucky, published a pamphlet entitled "Involuntary, Unmerited, Perpetual, Absolute, Hereditary Slavery, Examined on the Principles of Nature, Reason, Justice, Policy and Scripture," which became a part of the arsenal of incendiary materials used by the early Baptist emancipationists.[9] In addition to these, between 1773 and 1779 in the wake of the libertarianism accompanying the war, a series of public petitions written by single individuals or groups of slaves set forth the Negro's own disputation against his bondage in terms of both Natural Law and the Scriptures. In ungrammatical English, but with perfect clarity of meaning, one such slave petition was sent in 1774 by a group in Massachusetts to the colonial legislature. An example of the way in which such statements employed religious arguments for the abolition of slavery is apparent in the following excerpt from the Massachusetts petition:

> There is a great number of us sencear members of the Church of Christ, how can the master and the slave be said to fulfill that Command Live in love, let Brotherly Love contuner and abound, Beare yea onenothers Bordenes. How can the master be said to Beare my Bordon when he Beares me down with the Have chanes of slav-

ery and operson against my will and how can we fulfill ou parte of duty to him whilst in this condition and as we cannot serve our God as we ought whilst in this situation.[10]

A similar petition was forwarded in May 1779 to the General Assembly of Connecticut by the slaves of the towns of Stratford and Fairfield. A fragment contains these words:

We perceive by our own Reflection, that we are endowed with the same Faculties with our masters, and there is nothing that leads us to a Belief, or Suspicion, that we are any more obliged to serve them, than they us, and the more we Consider of this matter, the more we are Convinced of our Right (by the laws of Nature and by the whole Tenor of the Christian Religion, so far as we have been taught) to be free; we have endeavored rightly to understand what is our Right, and what is our Duty, and can never be convinced that we were made to be Slaves. Altho God almighty may justly lay this, and more upon us, yet we deserve it not, from the hands of Men. We are impatient under the grievous Yoke, but our Reason (sic!) teaches us that it is not best for us to use violent measures, to cast it off; we are also convinced that we are unable to extricate ourselves from our abject State, but we think we may with the greatest Propriety look up to your Honours, (who are the fathers of the People) for Relief.[11]

The majority of these documents from the pre-Abolitionist period, and many which resulted from the organized activity of Negroes in the North, indicate the extent to which the slaves appealed from their most profound religious convictions to the obdurate conscience of white churchmen. Some of the earliest statements from Black people were voted upon and distributed by the African Societies in the North, which were offshoots of the Free African Society organized in Philadelphia in 1787 by the Reverend Richard Allen, about whom more will be said later. The antislavery pronouncements of the first independent Black churches, the sermons and addresses against slavery of northern Black preachers, belong to this literature. Also included are the speeches of Christian laymen like James Forten of Philadelphia and the articles and editorials of the first Black newspaper, *Freedom's Journal,* published in New York by the Reverend Samuel E. Cornish and John B. Russwurm, beginning in 1827.[12] All, or certainly a large amount, of this evocative witness against slavery from the pens of Black men, at one time or another, fell into the eager hands of the slaves—even in the Deep South, where restrictions against such propaganda were more assiduously enforced. Such material was often smuggled into the coastal cities of the South by sailors and commercial agents. Despite the fact that many of the slaves could not read it with facility, they "read" it nevertheless (in the mysterious manner by which many Negroes learned how to read the Bible before they knew the alphabet). They were able to glean from it the knowledge that other people, Black as well as white, far away from the scene of their humiliation, were condemning the institution of chattel slavery and calling upon the resources of the Christian faith and the principles of American democracy to abolish it forthwith.

In February 1829, there appeared an unusual pamphlet by one Robert Alexander Young, a free Negro of New York, entitled "The Ethiopian Manifesto, Issued in Defense of the Blackman's Rights, in the Scale of Universal Freedom." In this work and others of a similar genre it is possible to see what is essential to an understanding of early Black religion in its relationship to the freedom struggle—a deep-lying African spirituality, an almost God-madness, a latent enthusiasm for dream interpretation and prophecy. These proclivities were unfettered and enhanced when the Black man, in the groaning and travail of his spirit, attempted to understand and deal with his oppression in Biblical categories. With a mystical, theopathetic sense of prophecy and divine intervention, the Black preacher or devout layman found in the Bible—especially in the apocalyptic writings— a power for resistance that required no human justification and gave them license to become oracles of retribution for the white man and resurrection and vindication for the Black. Under the sanction of this kind of religious intuition and in the flowery language of mysticism, Young appealed to Black people of all nations to take stock of the injustices visited upon them by the whites and to prepare for the revelation of God's judgment. It was an unmistakable call to militancy, if not to Black revolution. Young placed the responsibility for freedom squarely on the shoulders of Black people themselves. As he wrote, God by his power had decreed to man "that either in himself he stands, or by himself he falls." To the slaveowners he prophesied that destruction would be the consequence of their own evil work, even as their own consciences condemned them.

> Weigh well these my words in the balance of your conscientious reason, and abide the judgment thereof to your own standing, for we tell you of a surety, the decree hath already passed the judgment seat of an undeviating God, wherein he hath said, "surely hath the cries of the black, a most persecuted people, ascended to my throne and craved my mercy; now, behold! I will stretch forth mine hand and gather them to the palm, that they become unto me a people, and I unto them their God."[13]

One of the striking differences between the Black church of the early nineteenth century as compared with today is the thorough knowledge of the Scriptures it possessed—particularly of the Old Testament—which is evident in the writings and speeches of both the laity and the clergy. The Bible was, of course, universally regarded by Black and white as the inspired Word of God. Quotations, poetic allusions and literary devices from the King James Version made up much of the stylistic embroidery of many erudite writings of the period. But the Black Christian, under the influence of educated Black clergy and gifted laymen like Young and David Walker, felt a particular affinity to the people of the Old Testament. The God of Israel was the Lord of Hosts, the God of battle who swept the enemies of his people before him.

The great prophets who had struggled against the idolatry, hypocrisy and social injustice of Israel and Judah in the pre-Exilic period were familar allies in the crusade against American slavery. The maledictions of the psalmist against his tormentors and his cries to God for vindication perfectly suited the religious sentiment of the slaves.

But the pre-eminent relevance of the Old Testament for Black people, as many of the most famous spirituals bear witness, was found in the story of the Exodus. The Egyptian captivity of the Jews, their miraculous deliverance from the hands of the Pharaohs, and their eventual possession of the land promised by God to their fathers—this was the inspiration to which the Black religionist so often turned in the dark night of his soul. Whenever the Judeo-Christian tradition has been accessible to oppressed peoples, this scenario of election, captivity and liberation has captured the imagination of religious leadership. The story of the deliverance of the Jews from slavery has always been understood as the prototype of racial and nationalistic redemption—the divine revelation of the transhistorical meaning of historical experience. In the pre-Civil War days, Black prophets avidly seized upon this revolutionary hermaneutic and bore home upon white America its foreboding implications. The Ethiopian Manifesto makes the message clear:

> Ah, doth your expanding judgment, base slaveholder, not from here descry that the shackles which have been by you so undeservingly forged upon a wretched Ethiopian's frame, are about to be forever from him unlinked. Say ye, this can never be accomplished? If so, must indeed the power and decrees of Infinity become subservient to the will of depraved man. But learn, slaveholder, thine will rests not in thine hand; God decrees to thy slave his rights as a man.[14]

Robert Alexander Young's mystical vision in 1829 was that a Black Messiah who would champion the cause of "the degraded of this earth" was to come. He would call the slaves to a life of adamantine asceticism, including a prohibition against cohabitation, until freedom was attained or racial suicide came in preference to the ignominy of slavery. The theme of the Black Messiah has occurred periodically in Black religion in the United States, the West Indies and Africa ever since. Young's challenge to Black people throughout the world is certainly one of the earliest expressions of militant Pan-Africanism, which was not to come to full bloom until the Fifth Pan-African Congress, held in Manchester, England, in October 1945. His prophecy of a Black Savior was one of the many messages to "the Ethiopians" which he claimed to have read in "an instructive Book" which he does not describe further. The Savior, however, has—in view of the preparation made for his coming—a certain resemblance to the New Testament Christ:

> As came John the Baptist, of old, to spread abroad the forthcoming of his master, so alike are intended these our words, to denote to the black African or Ethiopian people, that God has prepared for them a leader, who awaits but his season to proclaim to them his birthright. How shall you know this man? By indubitable signs which cannot be controverted by the power of mortal, his marks being stamped in open visage, as equally so upon his frame, which constitutes him to have been particularly regarded in the infinite work of God to man.[15]

The most powerful piece of antislavery propaganda to be written by a Black man was the famous "Appeal to the Coloured Citizens of the World" by David Walker, which appeared in 1829, later in the same year as Young's Manifesto. Walker's pamphlet attracted wide attention among both friend and foe of abolition and was published in three editions, the first in September 1829 with seventy-six pages, and the third with eighty-eight pages in the next year. It is not known how many copies of the Appeal were distributed, but hundreds must have found their way into the South, where there were several notices of their being circulated among the slaves.[16]

Even more than Young's Ethiopian Manifesto, Walker's Appeal is steeped in Biblical language and prophecy. It is certainly one of the most remarkable religious documents of the Protestant era, rivaling in its righteous indignation and Christian radicalism Luther's "Open Letter to the Christian Nobility of the German Nation," published in Wittenberg in 1520. A comparative study of these two documents reveals striking similarities. Both men were addressing themselves to their own oppressed and beleaguered people out of a last-ditch, desperate situation which called for the most basic alteration of the religious and civil order. Both believed that God had commanded them to pronounce judgment against powers which seemed almost as indestructible as they were corrupt. Both men were aware that such audacity might cost them their lives. The pugnacious German reformer, of course, has been univerally recognized as one of the great religious leaders of all time and one whose work resulted in what was the most important "detour" in the history of Western Christendom. David Walker, on the other hand, a Black man—the son of a slave—has been shamefully neglected by church historians in the United States. Yet his genius as a lay theologian and prophet of radical Black religion is indisputable. His critique of the congenital corruption of the American church and society is unparalleled in American literature, and it is impossible to calculate the influence it had in quickening the passion for revolt among Black abolitionists in the tumultuous decades immediately preceding the Civil War.

We learn from Henry Highland Garnet's brief sketch of Walker's life that he was born in Wilmington, North Carolina, on September 28, 1785. The son of a free mother and a slave father, as a boy he developed a deep hatred for slavery and determined to quit the South for some part of the country where it did not exist. Vowing to "be avenged for the sorrow which my people have suffered," Walker left North Carolina and settled in Boston, where he learned to read and write. In 1827 he entered the clothing business on Brattle Street.[17] According to one report, he kept a "slop shop" that was frequented by sailors who pawned their clothing for drinks.[18]

Walker married in 1828 and began the scholarly study that is everywhere reflected in his writings. His house in Boston became a refuge for fugitive slaves and "the home of the poor and needy." He became the Boston agent of *Freedom's Journal,* the first Black newspaper, and spoke frequently on the subject of slavery to small, informal groups. By 1828, his speaking had gained considerable notice, and he was just beginning to lecture to large audiences before his untimely death.[19]

From Boston, Walker probably made the several extensive excursions through the South which are mentioned in the Appeal. After its initial publication his life was in great danger from the enraged slaveholders, whose network of spies and informers extended as far north as New England. Garnet, whose information came from Mrs. Dewson, Walker's widow, writes that when Walker was advised to flee to Canada for his life, he refused to leave Boston, saying: "I may be doomed to the stake and the fire, or to the scaffold tree, but it is not in me to falter if I can promote the work of emancipation."[20]

The cause of his death at the early age of forty-four, on June 28, 1830—possibly while the third edition of his work was just beginning to be distributed—remains shrouded in mystery. Garnet tells us that many people believed that he was poisoned, but expresses no opinion of his own except that "he died in Bridge Street."[21] It is more than probable that he was murdered, and it would not be far afield, under the circumstances of those days, to surmise that he could have been betrayed by some misguided person of his own race, even as the Christ to whom he had dedicated his life and work.

David Walker's fierce excoriation of Christianity is the most devastating since Voltaire's *Catéchisme de l'honnête homme.* And yet Walker was far from being an atheist. He never surrendered his faith to cynicism. For him, the truth of the gospel and the mission of Christianity in the world was being hindered by the system of slavery, and it was his purpose to call all true believers to its defense. Until his death he was a faithful member of the Methodist Church in Boston. In the Appeal, he held in highest esteem the venerable Bishop

Richard Allen and the work of the African Methodist Episcopal Church. The book itself is a religious document. Not only is its theme of sin and retribution based on a Biblical understanding of the justice of God and the redemption of human history through the power of love, but the entire work is "dedicated to the Lord,"[22] and to this dedication Walker adds the following observation:

> Some of my brethren, who are sensible, do not take an interest in enlightening the minds of our more ignorant brethren respecting this BOOK, and in reading it to them, just as though they will not have either to stand or fall by what is written in this book. Do they believe that I would be so foolish as to put out a book of this kind without strict—ah! very strict commandments of the Lord?—Surely the blacks and whites must think that I am ignorant enough.—Do they think that I would have the audacious wickedness to take the name of my God in vain?[23]

In the first article of the Appeal, "Our Wretchedness in Consequence of Slavery," Walker compares slavery in the United States with slavery in ancient pagan civilizations and advances the argument that in the history of the world no people have been as degraded and dehumanized as the Negro in America. In this context this crowning example is the way in which the Jews fared under Egyptian captivity, and he traces the Biblical story from Joseph, who was sold into slavery by his brothers, to Moses in order to demonstrate that through all their trials in Egypt the Israelites were never subjected to the "insupportable insult" that they were not to be regarded as men and members of the human family. Racism unprecedented in history and the deliberate attempt to strip every vestige of humanity from Black flesh is the biting accusation Walker hurls into the faces of the white Christians of America. His conclusion is that they must surely be afflicted with some innate devilishness ("acting more like devils than accountable men") that they would not hesitate to put themselves in the place of the Creator himself. Thus, he writes, with an ironic swipe at Thomas Jefferson's well-known postulate of Black inferiority:

Now suppose God were to give them more sense, what would they do? If it were possible, would they not *dethrone* Jehovah and seat themselves upon his throne? I therefore, in the name and fear of the Lord God of Heaven and of earth, divested of prejudice either on the side of my colour or that of the whites, advance my suspicion of them, whether they are *as good by nature* as we are or not. Their actions, since they were known as a people, have been the reverse, I do indeed suspect them, but this, as I before observed, is shut up with the Lord, we cannot exactly tell, it will be proved in succeeding generations.[24]

Article III, entitled "Our Wretchedness in Consequence of Ignorance," is the condemnation of whites for withholding enlightenment from the slaves, a sharp attack upon the ignorance and treachery of Black men against one another in the interest of the oppressor, and an appeal to Black people to educate themselves. Article III is a frontal assault on "the preachers of the religion of Jesus Christ" in which Walker, in some of the harshest language of his work, declares the patent falsity of white Christianity and the impending fate of the church of the slaveholders.

They have newspapers and monthly periodicals, which they receive in continual succession, but on the pages of which, you will scarcely ever find a paragraph respecting slavery, which is ten thousand times more injurious to this country than all the other evils put together; and which will be the final overthrow of its government, unless something is very speedily done; for their cup is nearly full.—Perhaps they will laugh at or make light of this; but I tell you Americans! that unless you speedily alter your course, *you* and your *Country are gone!!!!!!* For God Almighty will tear up the very face of the earth!!![25]

The final section, entitled "Our Wretchedness in Consequence of the Colonizing Plan," begins with a repudiation of Henry Clay and the whole scheme of Negro colonization which had been advanced as a solution to the race problem since 1713. In the third edition, Walker supplements the original version of Article IV, the concluding section, with additional material dealing wih legal prohibitions against Negro education, the acceptable alternative to forced colonization—Black migration to parts of the British Empire or to Haiti, and a list of "the cruelties inflicted on us by the enlightened Christians of America." Here as elsewhere he speaks of white Americans as "our natural enemies"—a designation which arises from his interpretation of the history of American civilization. He believed that God had given up that civilization ("they have got to be hardened in consequence of our blood") because of its unremitting brutality. But he clarifies what he means by the natural enmity that he sees between the Black and white races.

> I say from the beginning, I do not think we were natural enemies to each other. But the whites having made us so wretched, by subjecting us to slavery, and having murdered so many millions of us, in order to make us work for them, and out of devilishness . . . Consequently they, themselves, (and not us) render themselves our natural enemies, by treating us so cruel.[26]

The Appeal is a summons to Black manhood. It is a call to rebellion, to throw off the chains of slavery and fight in self-defense for freedom and dignity in the name of the Lord of Hosts. The strategy for battle is as direct as it is sanguinary:

> If you commence, make sure work—do not trifle, for they will not trifle with you—they want us for their slaves, and think nothing of murdering us in order to subject us to that wretched condition—therefore, if there is an *attempt* made by us, kill or be killed . . . Look upon your mother, wife and children, and answer God Almighty! and believe this, that it is no more harm for

you to kill a man, who is trying to kill you, than it is for you to take a drink of water when thirsty;—in fact, the man who will stand still and let another murder him, is worse than an infidel, and, if he has common sense, ought not to be pitied.[27]

Walker cannot understand how it is possible for white men to expect Black men to do anything less than reject their proffered friendship until they repent of their sins before God.

But Americans, I declare to you, while you keep us and our children in bondage, and treat us like brutes, to make us support you and your families, we cannot be your friends. You do not look for it, do you?[28]

As stridently militant as it is, Walker's Appeal does not represent unmitigated hostility and hatred of all white people. The spirit of the document strains toward some kind of resolution of the problem of race without violence—if white America will have it so. In that sense it is consonant with the dominant mood and motif of Black militance in the United States from the earliest slave petitions to the writings of Eldridge Cleaver. In Walker the theme of reconciliation arises again and again, but always out of a solemn recognition of the inevitability of whites reaping what has been sown, of facing the necessity of true repentance for the sins of the past and of bringing racism and oppression to an end without further delay. Walker even acknowledges those whites who have been the friends of freedom and believes that only their faithfulness has sustained the nation in the past and will save it in the future.

What would have become of the United States of America, was it not for those among the whites, who not in words barely, but in truth and indeed, love and fear of the Lord . . . Remove the people of God among the whites, from this land of blood and it will stand until they cleverly get out of the way.[29]

Through all the blood and fire, an ultimately hopeful Christian spirit breathes as Walker calls upon white Christians to count the cost of racial peace and to humble themselves before God in order that friendship and brotherhood can bless the land that otherwise must be soaked in blood. Toward the end of the book, in a plaintive, almost wistful change of mood, he addresses himself to those whites who may read it.

> Throw away your fears and prejudices then, and enlighten us and treat us like men, and we will like you more than we do now hate you . . . Treat us then like men, and we will be your friends. And there is not a doubt in my mind, but that the whole of the past will be sunk into oblivion, and we yet, under God, will become a united and happy people. The whites may say it is impossible, but remember that nothing is impossible with God.[30]

David Walker's Appeal struck fear into the hearts of the white people of the South, and the authorities immediately sought its suppression. The mayor of Savannah, where sixty copies were discovered, wrote to Mayor Harrison Gray Otis of Boston and demanded that something be done to restrain the publication and distribution of this "highly inflammatory work." Otis replied that he was powerless to stop it under the law. He did, however, issue a warning to captains of vessels putting out from Boston harbor to be careful to see that they were not carrying it aboard their ships.[31] The editor of the *Columbian Sentinel* of Boston called it "one of the most wicked and inflammatory productions ever issued from the press" and said that its ban in Georgia was more than justified in order to secure "the immediate safety of the whites."[32]

It is not certain that Nat Turner read or was directly influenced by Walker's Appeal, but it is not inconceivable that he knew the work of both Walker and Young. We do know that the publication of the Appeal sent warning signals throughout the eastern seaboard states. Although

many people opposed its bellicose call for the violent overthrow of slave power, others secretly welcomed the way it
narrowed the issue to immediate emancipation or slave revolt.
Black preachers in the North pretended to be shocked by its
ferocity, but made good use of it for their own purposes.
Among whites it was the subject of much thought and discussion in antislavery circles. Actually, it marked the beginning of the increased militancy of Garrison, Weld and Birney
and the martyrdom of Reverend Elijah Lovejoy and John
Brown.[33]

Literature of this character played a significant role in
reminding the slaves that it was not only against the Law of
Nature and the principles of democracy that they should
forever be patient under slavery, but more than that—it was
contrary to the will and purpose of God. Through the distribution of such tracts and pamphlets in their churches
they came to know that there were Black brothers in the
North who were prepared to join them with brains and
brawn if ever the blow for freedom would be struck. Many
of those men, like Richard Allen, Daniel Coker and David
Walker, were known among Black people as deeply religious
leaders who shared a common hatred of slavery and were
ready to push the whole institution over the precipice of
a physical struggle against the slaveholders. Black ministers
could not openly sanction violence and retain either their
own personal safety or continue to cultivate helpful contacts
with white abolitionists who deprecated such tactics, like
Garrison and the Tappan brothers, but they kept their own
counsel and few of them were attracted to the pacifist movement. Most of them vacillated back and forth between
violence and nonviolence, but in their most discouraging
moments could say with Samuel E. Cornish, a Black Presbyterian preacher, that "offensive aggression" could be "indispensable to . . . personal liberty and rights."[34]

We turn now to some of the slave insurrections. To what
extent did religious factors, such as the agitation of religious
leaders, have to do with violent resistance? Detailed investigation into the precipitants of the revolts would be re-

quired to give a complete answer to that question. Such research into each instance of conspiracy or rebellion if outside the limits of this study. It is possible, nevertheless, to isolate some of the linkages between religion and those revolts for which the most data are now accessible. Needless to say, it is not possible at every point to differentiate between the role played by the religion of the slaves, or what we are calling Black religion, and white Christianity as it was understood and practiced by the religiously motivated white abolitionists. In one sense the two traditions are imperceptibly merged in the religion of antislavery itself, which brought Blacks and whites together in many societies and conventions of the early nineteenth century. Black and white abolitionists who went into the South to agitate and to organize the Underground Railroad were generally informed by the same Biblical texts and infused with the same Christian spirit. But there were some notable differences.

In the application of religion, as such, to the struggle for freedom, few white men were as radical in their interpretations of Scriptural injunctions to resist tyranny in the name of the Lord as were Denmark Vesey, David Walker and Nat Turner. Few white Christians were able to take interracial brotherhood so seriously as to be willing not only to free the slaves, but to accept Black people as their equals.[35] Few white abolitionists understood or were prepared to accept the role of what they considered pagan religious practices and superstitions, and most of them deplored the complicity of this kind of religion—no matter what affinities it might have to Black Christians—in the slave revolts in Haiti, Jamaica or Southampton County, Virginia.

Aptheker, in his discussion of some of the causes of the insurrections, points out that it was the general assumption that they were brought about primarily by the activity of Methodist and Quaker missionaries, and that without this instigation Negroes would not have become infected with the fever for revolt.[36] He goes on to point out that while this popular view may be true, it is impossible to substantiate it with fact. His own conclusion is that the fundamental factor provoking rebellion "was that social system itself"—the system of slavery and—"the degradation, exploitation, oppression, and brutality which it created."[37]

There is no doubting that any inquiry into the role of religion in fomenting and guiding insurrections must give considerable credit to the fact that radical white Christians taught the Negroes how to read the Bible in such a way as to discover the relevance of their faith to the question of liberation. That assumption, however, should not lead us to believe that Black religion was so insubstantial and Black preachers so lacking in righteous indignation that only the ethical revivalism of the main white denominations and the inspired teachings of "white ministers and religious ladies" could have provided Blacks with a theology of revolution and the spiritual impulse to act it out. We have already taken note that white men were involved in some of the conspiracies, but even the most radical abolitionists among them were quick to deny that they had any part in violence, and there is certainly no discernible causative relationship between them and the slave insurrections.

To the extent that religion is at least *one* important factor, among others, in some of the major slave insurrections or conspiracies, it must be said that it did not emanate from the white churches of the South or the North, or even from the disreputable Methodist circuit riders and the Christian anti-slavery societies of the North. It sprang rather from the creative religious imagination of the slaves themselves and from those former slaves who pastored churches or sat in the pews of the new independent Black congregations of Baltimore, Wilmington, Philadelphia, New York and other cities of the North. W. E. B. Du Bois, whose understanding of the origin and nature of Black religion is incomparable, tells us that for the transplanted African, slavery represented the dark triumph of evil over him. He therefore called up all of the resources of his primitive religion to express and activate the spirit of revolt that was in his heart.[38] As for the free Negroes of the North in this regard, Du Bois writes:

The free Negro leader early arose and his chief characteristic was intense earnestness and deep feeling on the slavery question. Freedom became to him a real thing and not a dream. His religion became darker and more intense, and into his ethics crept a note of revenge, into his songs a day of reckoning close at hand. The "Coming of the Lord" swept this side of Death, and came to be a thing hoped for in this day . . . this desire for freedom seized the black millions still in bondage, and became their one ideal of life . . . For fifty years Negro religion thus transformed itself and identified itself with the dream of Abolition, *until that which was a radical fad in the white North and an anarchistic plot in the white South had become a religion to the black world.*[39]

It was this overarching character of Black religion in the late eighteenth and the nineteenth centuries that gave it an ethical base more pliant and consequently more easily adapted to the exigencies of a one-sided struggle than either the evangelical Protestantism of the major white churches or the Christian abolitionism of Lewis and Arthur Tappan and other white friends. There were, of course, exceptional men like the radical Methodist evangelist Orange Scott, and later Lovejoy, Theodore Parker, the Unitarian minister, and the redoubtable John Brown. But while these men were looked upon as mutants in the evolutionary process of white Christianity in America, Black churchmen have, for the most part, regarded the leaders of the slave insurrections as exemplary heroes of the race.

One of the earliest conspiracies which we may suspect of having been connected with religious fervor occurred in the Northern Neck region of Virginia in 1687.[40] Suspicion of the true character of the incident, which is said to have involved a large number of slaves, arises from the fact that the plot developed in connection with mass funerals which the slaves were then permitted to hold. Such funerals were, of course, religious events. They were intensely emotional experiences in which charismatic Black preachers whipped the mourners into a frenzy that could readily be turned against the masters.[41] The reports of the Northern Neck rebellion are extremely sparse. Few books and no newspapers were published in North America prior to 1700.[42] But we know that the leaders were arrested and executed and the authorities placed a ban upon public funerals. Prohibitions against funerals, holiday feasts and other types of slave gatherings where religious excitement could provide an excuse for conspiracy became the common law in many parts of the South and in the West Indies. In this connection it is worth noting the comment by Joseph C. Carroll on another Virginia insurrection involving some two hundred Blacks which took place on a Sunday, not far from the scene of the Northern Neck rebellion, in October 1722, near the mouth of the Rappahannock River:

> Sunday was a favorite day on which the slaves often planned outbreaks, because it was easy to get together on Sunday . . . the slaves were given a deal of liberty in assembling for religious worship. Hence the religious services were the great incubators where Slave Insurrections were hatches. Fortunately for the ruling class this plot (in October 1722) was discovered just in time to be nipped in the bud.[43]

In 1712 an insurrection broke out in New York City which was thought to be related to a school for young Negroes founded in 1704 by Elias Neau, an agent for the Society for the Propagation of the Gospel in Foreign Parts.[44] The plot was actually brewed by Negroes of the Carmantee and Pappa tribes of West Africa who, "with the aid of a conjurer, believed that they had made themselves invulnerable."[45] The slaves, early in the morning of April 7, set fire to the house of Peter van Tilburgh and fired on the whites who came to extinguish the blaze—a not uncommon practice in ghetto rebellions. They were finally subdued and the incident ended with eight or ten white persons killed and eighteen or more Negroes executed. It is clear that witch doctors were involved in the plot, and the rebels, in keeping with an African custom, sucked the blood of each other's hands as a bond and pledge of secrecy.

The uprising seems to have been in some degree related to Neau's religious instruction. The French catechist conducted classes in Christian education and was at first accused of having encouraged a desire for freedom as a part of his instruction. While a formal inquiry into the matter exonerated Neau and his catechumens, one eyewitness account acknowledged that at least one of the Black students was in the plot. Another was condemned on "slander evidence," and two Roman Catholic Blacks were implicated, but saved at the last moment. Later investigation ascertained that the African witch doctor and the recent arrivals from the Slave Coast were the chief conspirators.[46]

The governor apologized to Neau and attempted to protect him from the hostility of the still unconvinced whites. Nevertheless, the fact that some members of his class, together with Black Roman Catholics, were on the edge of the circle of those who plotted and carried out the insurrection under the incitement of an African witch doctor, leaves justifiable suspicion that some volatile combination of Christianity and African religion was one of the precipitants of the revolt. The white population continued for some time to associate the school with the uprising, and it was not safe for Neau to be seen on the streets until white tempers were cooled.

Rumors of freedom were rife in slave country and were frequently the cause of rising expectations, only to be followed by dismay and conspiracy to rebel when hopes were dashed. Such was the case in 1730 in colonial Virginia, where the word spread among the slaves that the newly arrived Colonel Spotswood had been empowered by the King of England to free all slaves who had received baptism. This custom was first introduced by the Portuguese in Africa, but it had never been made mandatory in America.[47] In the eighteenth century, however, the fact that the matter was debated in church and civil courts caused considerable confusion, and many slaves desired to be baptized with the hope that their status would thereby be improved. Most of them received it, however, with little or no religious instruction. The relationship that was thus established between religion, baptism and freedom had a continuing effect in the further mystification of the sacrament among the slaves and in convincing them that their adoption of the master's religion made them as good a man as he was. In 1730, Virginia authorities found many gatherings and meetings among them with "loose Discourses" on the topic of liberty.[48] The leaders were arrested and soundly whipped, but six weeks later two hundred slaves in Norfolk and Princess Anne counties assembled on Sunday and, according to a letter of Lieutenant-Governor Gooch to the Bishop of London, chose new officers to lead their intended revolt.[49] The plot was discovered and four of the leaders were tried and executed.

Throughout the 1730s, slaveowners had serious difficulty with their slaves escaping to St. Augustine, Florida, where the Spanish were in control. Hostility against the Roman Catholics ran high in the towns along the Atlantic Coast. Although it was never proved, it was generally believed that a Roman Catholic priest was involved in a slave insurrection planned for Prince George County, Maryland, in 1739.[50] The enmity between the English and the Spanish made the latter encourage the slaves to escape to Florida, and a royal decree of October, 1733—which secret informers brought to the attention of the slaves—promised them safe residence and their freedom. During 1739 and 1740 there were at least three insurrections in South Carolina believed to have been instigated by Catholic priests. Many of the slaves in that colony were from Angola and had already been converted to Catholicism. By religious conviction they associated freedom with the Roman Catholic Church and were strongly drawn to the Catholic establishment in St. Augustine.[51]

The most serious insurrection during this period occurred in South Carolina, where seventy-five or eighty slaves burned buildings and killed whites as they marched toward St. Augustine shouting slogans of liberty and with colors flying and drums beating. They were met ten miles south of Stone, South Carolina, by a better-armed detachment of militia and defeated after a sharp engagement in which at least twenty-five whites and fifty slaves were slain.[52] Two years later, in September 1741, fires broke out in Charles Town that were attributed to Blacks who were said to have been on the brink of revolt. The complicity of religion in this incident is found in a report to the grand jury of the town concerning a book signed by Hugh Brian, a white man, which contained "sundry enthusiastic Prophecys, of the destruction of Charles Town, and deliverance of the Negroes from their Servitude, and that by the Influence of ye said Hugh Brian, great bodys of Negroes have assembled together on pretense of religious worship."[53]

It is difficult to know what role to assign to religious influences such as inflammatory preaching and conjuration in the strange conspiracy of Negroes and four disreputable whites that created a sensation in New York City during the same year. An extended description of the plot by Carroll from contemporary newspaper accounts indicates that a man named John Ury, identified as a Roman Catholic priest but who claimed to be an Anglican clergyman, and another, John Romme (who told Blacks that he possessed a charmed life), were involved in a plan to set fire to the town and plunder its inhabitants. Punishment was exacted indiscriminately as far as the Blacks were concerned, and thirty-one slaves were hanged or burned at the stake "amid prayers, imprecations and shrieks of agony" from the victims.[54]

We will have occasion later to examine the role of Black churchmen in the increasing disposition to abandon the "moral suasion" and nonviolence of the white abolitionists in aiding fugitive slaves and supporting slave conspiracies in the West Indies and nationalistic uprisings in Africa. The point that must be made at the close of this chapter is that even in the numerous slave revolts prior to 1800, religious factors of one sort or another are not to be discounted. Sometimes visionary white men, marginal to their own society's norms and customs, were involved. At other times, African conjurers or witch doctors who had received their basic training in the Caribbean were somewhere in the background. At still other times, Black "jack-legged" preachers—some of them undoubtedly practiced in the lore of African and West Indian religions—men of extraordinary intelligence and influence over their fellows, kept the pot boiling by relating slavery with the white man's immorality, and freedom with the Black man's eternal salvation.

If fewer of these Black religionists came forward in the United States than in Africa in the latter part of the nineteenth and the early twentieth century, it is only because slavery in America, especially in those areas where Blacks were in the majority, was highly institutionalized. The slaves had no strong, uniform religious tradition to fall back upon, and their practice of the new religion they were developing was under closer surveillance than any other activity of their leisure time. What Black preachers in America did to foment discontent and insurrection, they did not so much by example and exhortation as by the same subtle use of suggestion and innuendo as we find in such spirituals as "Steal Away," "O Mary, Don' You Weep" and "Joshua Fit de Battle of Jericho."[55] They were able, for the most part, like Shakespeare's Iago, to stay in the background and watch their mischief do its work of undermining the American system of chattel slavery.

The popular assumption is that revolts, like Turner's in Virginia or Chilembwe's in Nyasaland, were seldom led by Black religionists in the United States, because their religion was conservative and otherworldly and Black preachers were generally kindly, ignorant, foot-shuffling clowns. Nothing could be further from the truth. These men were not the fools and buffoons they are often made out to be by the "cultured despisers" of Black religion. Their restraint in leading open slave rebellion had nothing to do either with the otherworldliness of their faith, or the cowardice of their personal lives. They knew the power of their own charisma and they knew what to expect from the slaveholders if rebellion should break out among the inexperienced and unarmed slaves. A few religious men, as we shall see, even dared to risk insurrection under these circumstances, but the majority moved with caution and decided to let white people fight the matter out among themselves in the great war they knew had to come in God's own time.

The slave preacher understood the awe-inspiring power of the Spirit. For him it was not only the source of personal freedom, it also represented the judgment, the holy vengeance of God, who required the blood of sacrifice as the propitiation of mortal sin. Like Moses with the serpent, he held this great power in his hands when he stood before his people. His lineal relationship to the shaman, the witch doctor and the medicine man, who communed with the nature spirits and the ancestors on the banks of the Niger and the Congo, made him deeply sensitive to the dynamic mysteriousness of religion and its capacity to take possession of men and drive them to frenzy. The exorcism of the demonic spirits which lie beneath the surface of the human soul, as the New Testament bears witness, is never completely predictable in its results. The full power of primitive religion can bring forth uncontrollable forces of good and evil, intertwined and inseparable. In African religion the line of demarcation between such forces is sometimes barely discernible.

It is difficult for persons accustomed to an orderly, intellectual religious experience to understand the immediate, involuntary propensity to surrender oneself wholly to these elemental powers when they are called forth by the emotional intensity of messianic preaching in the context of deprivation and oppression. The Black slave preacher approached these powers boldly, but with deep respect and caution. With one phrase, one word or gesture, he could transform a church meeting into a boiling caldron of emotion that would send his hearers pouring out of the woods and into the house of the slavemaster to kill, burn and lay waste. Black preachers were fully aware of this possibility, and only on rare occasions did they permit the hysteria to advance to such a degree that the boiling point of antislavery fanaticism was reached.

In recent times white civil rights workers who labored in the various campaigns in the South which were led by Dr. Martin Luther King, Jr., and his cadre of Black, grass-roots preachers, came to know and appreciate this power of Black religion. Men like James Bevel, Hosea Williams and Jesse Jackson demonstrated their ability to use religion to reach the masses even more effectively than Dr. King himself. Many times they could have closed the switch that would have transformed the singing, shouting throng of poor Blacks into a violent mob that would have swept out of the churches, out of the Black ghetto of some southern town and into the white neighborhoods with the torch and the gun. The civil-rights preachers restrained themselves and the people by restraining the spirit. Every Sunday in the Black churches of the rural South and in the northern city ghettos, old-style preachers exercise that same restraint, bringing their congregations to the penultimate expression of religious fervor with "the gravy" of homiletical peroration and at the climax— "sitting down in the storm." The traditional Black preacher knows when the danger point has been reached—when another swell of emotion might do physical harm to those who were inundated by it. Such floods of the spirit have been known to lead worshipers to throw themselves against hot stoves, to rip and tear their clothing, to break up chairs and literally to pull, like Samson, the foundation of the temple down upon their heads.

If one can speak of the slave preacher as "conservative," it was this tremendous power and the recognition of its dangerous potentiality that made him so. But he was certainly not conservative in what he desired and hoped for his people. He knew the injustices and brutalities they suffered. He knew how defenseless they would be against the patrols, the militia and the soldiers who would be instant in response to the first indication of insurrection. Many of them must have thought that one day the sign would be given by God to release "the Power" and let it do its will. But they bided their time. They prayed for the Day of the Lord that is not light but darkness—perhaps more often in their solitude than in public. And they looked for a sign. That sign, indeed, was given to Vesey and to Nat Turner and to other visionaries and prophets on both sides of the Atlantic who led their people into revolt in the name of the God of liberation.

Most of the slave preachers stopped short of insurrection. They lived and worked in the time between the recognition of grievances and the revolution to cast them off—the time for Black unity and for understanding the purposes of God on the wilderness side of the Jordan. In this interim period they turned to the vision of what lay on the other side of victory. The golden streets, the rivers of milk and honey, the melodious harps and trumpets of the angels, the golden crowns and shining robes that awaited those who shall overcome. The Black preacher's imaginative rendition of the eschatological passages of the Old and New Testaments became his second option—a means of drawing back his people from the precipice of doom that he knew was just beyond the pinnacle of Black rage which their religion masked, but at the same time, nourished against a day of reckoning. He continued, therefore, to preach what in his own situation he considered to be the pragmatic implications of the message that Christ had made all men free and that the day would surely come when the truth of the gospel would be manifest.

The "otherworldliness" of slave preaching was nothing less than an interim strategy. It was the deliberate choice of the preacher to give his people something to which they could attach their tumultuous emotions—something to substitute for the immediate, uncontrollable and probably ill-fated decision to experience, then and there, the freedom which Christ had promised. He gave, thereby, relief from the tragedy of life in slavery, a modicum of comfort in the presence of the overwhelming reality of defeat and despair. Black religion may have been otherworldly, but it was not *otherworldly-quietistic,* —it was *otherworldly-disruptive.* The oppressors have never been able to relax in the presence of this kind of otherworldliness. During slavery it was a way of living already in that *other* world of transcendent freedom, and its purpose and meaning have not greatly changed in the traditional churches and fundamentalistic sects and cults of the Black community today. To let "this little light of mine" shine in the dark corners of the white man's world meant that whatever the Black Christian did received a transcendent meaning, not from the present world of injustice which the whites ruled, but from a future world of truth, justice and divine retribution which was already breaking in upon the present world in many hidden deceptive ways. Subterfuge, sabotage, fraud, trickery, foot-dragging and other behavior patterns of resistance were insinuated into the daily intercourse with white people in the guise of stupidity and obsequiousness, as a tactic of simple survival.[56]

But the effect was a sense of divine vindication and self-righteousness in foiling the oppressor and getting the satisfaction of seeing him writhe in his frustration without knowing why, or being able to do very much about it. In the absence of the opportunity and the means of fomenting successful insurrection, this attack on the flanks and from the rear of the enemy—a kind of psychological guerrilla warfare—was the conspiratorial response of Black preachers to white oppression. It was justified not by the imitative theology of the Black church, but by the realized eschatology of Black preaching, its mastery over the absurdity of the Black condition, and its appropriation of a radical ethic of underground resistance which produced inarticulate and concealed norms for interracial contact and confrontation.

CHAPTER III

Three Generals in the Lord's Army

Up, Afric, up; the land is free
It sees no slave to despot bow.
Our cry is Liberty—
On; strike for God and vengeance now
Fly, tyrants fly,
Or stay and die.
No chains to bear, no scourge we fear;
We conquer, or we perish here.

By V. Supposed to have been sung
by slaves in insurrection.
The Liberator, July 23, 1831.

ONE OF the most important slave revolts in the United States occurred in 1800, the year Thomas Jefferson was elected President, beginning a new emphasis on popular democracy in the nation. In Haiti, Toussaint L'Ouverture had completed a successful revolution against slavery. The great Black liberator defeated the invading English army and had assumed command of the entire colony of Santo Domingo as general-in-chief. Slaves throughout the New World were emboldened by these events, and rebellion was in the air as never before.

A young man of twenty-five named Gabriel, slave of Thomas Prosser, whose plantation was just outside of the City of Richmond, Virginia, was moved to strike the first blow for liberty in the new century. A man of impressive physical and mental capacities, Gabriel was also a student of the Bible and was strongly drawn to lead an insurrection among the slaves by religious convictions. His favorite Biblical hero was Samson, and in imitation of the great leader of the Israelites, Gabriel wore his hair long, recalling Judges 16:17—"There hath not come a razor upon mine head; for I have been a Nazarite unto God from my mother's womb: if I be shaven, then my strength will go from me, and I shall become weak, and be like any other man." Gabriel believed that from his childhood God had marked him as a deliverer of his people.[1] At frequent meetings throughout the summer of 1800 he made this divine election known to several men who were associated with him and interpreted to them the various parts of the Scripture which he believed referred to the condition of Negro slavery and the necessity of rising up against the Philistine slaveowners. The exploits of Samson in Judges 15 had a particular significance for Gabriel as he laid careful plans to sow destruction throughout Henrico County and lead the slaves to the establishment of a new Black kingdom in Virginia, with himself as king. The passage from Judges reads:

> And when he came unto Lehi, the Philistines shouted against him: and the Spirit of the Lord came mightily upon him, and the cords that were upon his arms became as flax that was burnt with fire, and his band loosed from off his hands. And he found a new jawbone of an ass, and put forth his hand, and took it, and slew a thousand men therewith . . . And he judged Israel in the days of the Philistines for twenty years.
>
> Judges 15:14-15, 20

In this passage Gabriel saw his own name as the new Black Samson who was called to bring down the kingdom of slavery and institute on the American shores what Toussaint was able to create in the Caribbean—a nation of free Black men. His plan was to kill all the whites who were accosted, seize arms and ammunition from the arsenal in Richmond, loot the state treasury and, if possible, strike an agreement with the remaining slavemasters for the liberation of all slaves. Various estimates have been made of how many were involved. According to the official report, about one thousand actually rendezvoused outside the city, but because of a great storm which struck on the evening of August 30, when the attack was to be launched, they did not enter Richmond but disbanded in confusion—possibly believing that a sign from heaven had been given in the great storm that the time was not ripe or that the plan, as devised, was unacceptable to God.[2] According to Gabriel's own testimony, he had about ten thousand men ready to go into battle. Other witnesses at the trial gave estimates of two thousand and six thousand. The Governor of Mississippi Territory said that fifty thousand slaves were involved.[3]

The Gabriel plot was probably the first well-planned, consciously revolutionary attempt in a long history of slave revolts on the mainland. The slaves were well-organized. There was to be a cavalry and an infantry. Gabriel himself was given the title of General. Undoubtedly, the Haitian revolution was the model, but religious factors played a more important role in the Gabriel insurrection than in the uprising led by Toussaint L'Ouverture. If the revolt failed, the plan was to retreat into the mountains and carry on a protracted warfare as a guerrilla band. But even before the storm broke on the night of August 30, two slaves, Tom and Pharaoh, revealed the plot to their master, Mosby Sheppard of Richmond. Guards were posted at the penitentiary arsenal and cavalry was dispatched on a patrol of all roads leading from Prosser's plantation to the city. An attack might well have been put into effect during the next two or three days, but because of some failure in logistics—perhaps the problem of communicating new orders to all of the dispersed groups—the conspirators began to be apprehended by the state militia and the patrols early in September. Governor Monroe secured all strategic points in the Richmond area during the next several days while continuing to arrest suspects. On September 12, five slaves were executed. Three days later, five or six more met the same fate. All in all, thirty-five were finally hanged, one com-

mitted suicide, and four escaped from prison.[4] Gabriel himself had attempted escape. Despairing of trying to reorganize
his scattered force, he went aboard a schooner lying in Norfolk Harbor and lay in hiding for eleven days. In the end he
was once again betrayed and was arrested on September 24
and executed on October 7.

General Gabriel, despite his failure, had reminded the
people of Virginia and the nation as a whole of the fact that
the temper of the times—the spirit of Jeffersonian democracy,
the Haitian revolution, French egalitarianism spreading out
from the Revolution of 1789, and the increasing agitation of
abolitionists—made it impossible for Blacks not to demand the
application of the so-called Rights of Man and the principles
of Christian democracy to themselves. As one Virginia journalist of the time wrote: "This doctrine of equality cannot fail in
producing either a general Insurrection or a general emancipation."[5] Because of their support of emancipation, Gabriel
had ordered that all Methodists, Quakers and Frenchmen be
spared by the rebels. Thereby, his own deep religious commitment to freedom reached out to the two Christian groups
that he believed to be on God's side against slavery and to the
government which had recognized the legitimacy of the new
Black nation in the Caribbean.

The immediate reaction of the slaveholders to these events
was fear and suspicion. Restriction on the movements of slaves
were tightened and a public guard was organized in Richmond as a precaution against future outbreaks. They came
hard upon the Gabriel affair, for slave revolts occurred frequently after 1800 in South Carolina, North Carolina, Georgia,
Louisiana and Mississippi. In the latter two states agitation for
restrictions on religious activities among the slaves became
prominent after several attempted rebellions prior to 1812.[6]
For months, slave discontent flared throughout Virginia.
Insurrectionary plans were laid and uncovered and several
local attempts were carried out, all without success. There
were instances of use of poison in connection with some of the
plots. This practice was undoubtedly related to the complicity
of Voodoo religion. In 1802 a slave named Dick, of Mecklen-

burg County, was convicted of conspiring to poison his master, "and believed he could accomplish his purpose by beating up leaves with snake heads and leaving the combination at the door of his master."[7] In 1805 there was an insurrection in Wayne County, North Carolina, where the method of poisoning was attributed to the influence of West Indian Blacks among the slaves.[8] Richard Byrd of Smithfield, Virginia, wrote on May 30, 1810, to Governor John Tyler about an insurrectionary plan for Whitsunday in North Carolina. A Negro boy, after flogging, revealed that operations were to begin in North Carolina and that the insurgents were to come into Virginia to help the slaves there. Such information was usually transmitted from church to church by itinerant preachers who went back and forth among them. Indeed, Byrd was confident that slave preachers were involved and were using religious meetings for the purpose of organizing the scheme. He referred particularly, in this regard, to a "General Peter" on the Isle of Wight, who had been communicating with the slaves of North Carolina.[9]

Another instance of the use of religion in slave uprisings is recorded for 1816 in Spottsylvania and Louisa counties, Virginia, where a white man named George Boxley, a proprietor of a country store, led the slaves—although it is not clear who had the most influence over whom in the beginning of the plot. Carroll writes concerning Boxley:

> He was a visionary character, somewhat like John Brown. He participated in the religious gatherings of the Negroes and told his experiences along with the rest, as Negroes are accustomed to do on such occasions. Among other things that the Lord had done for him, Boxley told the Negroes that a little white bird had brought him a holy message, which was that he was to deliver his fellowmen from bondage. On the basis of this religious superstition he enlisted many Negroes in his project for an insurrection.[10]

Here again we see the openness of the slaves for revolt when they were convinced that divine sanction had been given to a charismatic leader. Slave preachers used the church meeting as a place where the Blacks could most easily be persuaded to join in conspiracy against the system. Although some of these men were self-serving opportunists who manipulated credulous minds, many of them, like General Gabriel, were serious, sincere believers who knew that the great leaders and prophets of the Bible set themselves unswervingly against injustice of every kind and called down the wrath of God upon those who victimized the poor and defenseless. They had not the slightest doubt that this same God brooded over the captivity of the African and commanded them to lead these new Israelites to freedom and independence.

Denmark Vesey, the great leader of the famous slave insurrection in South Carolina, purchased his freedom in 1800, the year of General Gabriel's plot, from a Captain Joseph Vesey who had acquired Denmark on one of his voyages as a slave trader. As a result of his travels as the personal cabin boy of Captain Vesey, Denmark had become a cultured and sophisticated man by the time he planned to lead the slaves in revolt. After leaving the service of his former master he decided to settle down in Charleston and work as a carpenter. For the next twenty years he studied everything he could get his hands on and became a respected leader in the little community of free Negroes which had grown up in Charleston. Actually, his influence extended beyond Charleston. His travels to the Sea Islands and into the interior brought him into contact with Black people in various communities in the state, and everyone esteemed him as a man of extraordinary intellectual proportions and one who had a future as a leader of the race.[11] Among the things which interested Vesey and engaged him in many informal talks and conversations with individuals and groups were the several inflammatory pamphlets on slavery that were brought into the Charleston area from the North, including one said to have been published in Sierre Leone.[12] It is a matter of interest that the Black Methodists with whom Vesey was closely involved had been in that British colony since 1820, and Black Baptists from the United States had been working there since 1792. A rebellious

Black religion had already begun to be communicated back and forth across the Atlantic.

The great absorbing interest of Vesey was this Black religion. Like Gabriel Prosser, he was engrossed in the study of the Bible and brought to his reading of the Scripture some interpretations that were decidedly unorthodox by white standards and possibly of African or West Indian origin.[13] He particularly applied himself to the study of two passages from the Old Testament. The first, from Zechariah 14:

> Behold, a day of Jehovah cometh, when thy spoil shall be divided in the midst of thee. For I will gather all nations against Jerusalem to battle; and the city shall be taken, and the houses rifled, and the women ravished; and half of the city shall go forth into captivity, and the residue of the people shall not be cut off from the city. Then shall Jehovah go forth, and fight against those nations, as when he fought in the day of battle.

The second passage bears closer examination. It was from a part of the Bible the slave preachers often turned to in their sermons and it inspired one of the best known of the Negro spirituals—Joshua's siege of the Canaanite city of Jericho. The story itself is strongly suggestive of the conspiratorial requirements of a slave insurrection. A man like Denmark Vesey, with his mystical intuition and knowledge of Scripture, could see many parallels between the children of Israel, after they had crossed the Jordan and stood before the cities which barred their way to the Promised Land, and the situation of Black men brought across the Atlantic Ocean to the New World by the rich and powerful cities which now stood between them and the attainment of freedom.

Even before the crossing from Shittim, Joshua had sent spies into the land to ascertain the weaknesses of the enemy. They were befriended in Jericho only by a harlot, Rehab—one of the least respected of the inhabitants. When the city was taken, she and her family were spared. The utmost secrecy had to be maintained, but when the time was ripe terror had to be struck into the hearts of the defenders. Evidently, the children of Israel, though highly organized for the battle, were poorly armed for it. Joshua 6:9 speaks of "armed men" preceding the seven priests who were to blow on trumpets of rams' horns; immediately behind the priests was the ark of the covenant, followed by all the people, who had only their voices to raise against the Canaanites. The Lord himself, in the form of an angel with a drawn sword in his hand—"prince of the host of Jehovah"—came before Joshua and consecrated the ground on which he stood. Like all the battles of the Israelites, this was a holy war, and without the God of their fathers they could accomplish nothing. Denmark Vesey was convinced that the same was true for the slaves he had been called to lead to freedom.

During the six days in which the Israelites encompassed the city, Joshua commanded the people: "Ye shall not shout, nor let your voice be heard, neither shall any word proceed out of your mouth, until the day I bid you shout; then shall ye shout." (Joshua 6:10) On the seventh day and on the seventh turn about the city walls, when the priests blew on the trumpets, Joshua ordered the people to shout.[14] The pertinent verses read:

> So the people shouted, and the priests blew the trumpet: and it came to pass, when the people heard the sound of the trumpet, that the people shouted with a great shout, and the wall fell down flat, so that the people went up into the city, every man straight before him, and they took the city. And they utterly destroyed all that was in the city, both man and woman, both young and old, and ox and sheep, and ass, with the edge of the sword.
>
> Joshua 6:20–21

There is no record of how Denmark actually treated this dramatic story when he related it to the slaves, but we know that he was fascinated by it and used it often in addresses to the Blacks of Charleston and environs. At these religious meetings he enlisted his followers and used stories from Greek mythology, such as Hercules and the wagoner, as well as Bible stories to give them self-respect and fearlessness.[15] He also held up the example of Toussaint L'Ouverture and the rebels of San Domingo as examples. One of his most trusted companions was Gullah Jack, the slave of Paul Pritchard, who worked through a group known as the Gullah Society, which met regularly and whose members were bound to Jack "by a shrewd combination of magic and discipline."[16] Jack himself was a native African sorcerer who had the reputation of being invulnerable. He instructed those who joined the conspiracy to eat nothing but parched corn and ground nuts on the fateful day and to keep a piece of crab claw in their mouths as a protection against harm during the attack. Whatever may have gone on in the religious meetings held during the months of planning, it is clear that Denmark Vesey and Gullah Jack, each drawing upon the reservoir of his own religious convictions, were able to work together in preparing the hearts and minds of those who were to participate in the insurrection.

Church meetings again provided the opportunity for indoctrination and planning. In 1800, South Carolina had passed a law forbidding all Negro religious meetings between sunset and sunrise.[17] But in response to a petition of the Charleston Baptist Association this prohibition was mended in 1803 to permit class meetings until 9 P.M., providing a majority of white people were present. In 1819 this requirement was also dropped and religious gatherings of Blacks were considered lawful if at least one white man attended to make sure that no conspiracy was in process. Actually, as Woodson and others point out and as was the case in other parts of the South, these laws against religious assemblies were honored more in the breach than in the observance. The slaves met with their own preachers, and behind closed doors, whenever things were relatively quiet. As soon as the rumor of an insurrection was noised abroad or some misconduct resulted from a meeting, the white people were terrified and regulations were again stringently enforced.

In his excellent book on the Denmark Vesey insurrection,

John Loften quotes from a writer in *The Times* of Charleston who in 1816 wrote:

> Almost every night there is a meeting of these noisy, frantic worshippers . . . Midnight! Is that the season for religious convocation? Even allowing that these meetings were conducted with propriety, is that the accepted time? That the meeting of numerous black people to hear the scripture expounded by an ignorant and (too frequently) vicious person of their own color can be of no benefit either to themselves or the community is certain; that it may be attended with many evils is, I presume, obvious to every reflecting mind.[18]

It is important to note in connection with the Denmark Vesey plot that the Black Methodists, recently organized as the African Methodist Episcopal Church following Richard Allen's departure from white Methodism in Philadelphia, were involved in the 1822 conspiracy and in almost continuous difficulty with the Charleston authorities from 1817. Denmark Vesey was a member of the Hampstead church, one of several Black congregations which broke away from the white denomination that year. The class system of the independent African Methodist Association of Charleston was used as a recruiting and indoctrination vehicle as well as a communications network for the revolt. All of the leaders were members of the new independent Black church. Many of them were class leaders, and at least one was a preacher.[19] The Reverend Morris Brown, after whom one of the Black colleges in Atlanta is named, was a secret counselor to the group.[20] Brown was away on church business when the insurrection took place, but was forced to leave the state upon his return. He later became a bishop of the A.M.E. Church.

The Black Methodists of Charleston provided an excellent pool of dissidence and conspiracy. In 1817, as a result of complaints from white Methodists who were incensed with the schismatic tendencies of their Black brethren, 469 members of one of the separated congregations were arrested. In 1818 the Hampstead church itself was said to be in violation of the law prohibiting assembly, and on a June Sunday 140 members were arrested. The next day the City Council sentenced a bishop and four ministers to one month in prison or exile from the state. Eight ministers were sentenced to ten lashes or ten dollars each.[21] Vesey, who was an influential member of the most troublesome congregation, must have been as bitter about this interference as anyone. It can only be a matter of conjecture how much this continuous harassment confirmed him and others in their determination to strike not only for ecclesiastical freedom, but for political freedom as well. In any event, the Hampstead congregation was strongly implicated, and the church was destroyed by the white backlash which followed the attempted insurrection.

Vesey had done his work well. Between three and nine thousand Blacks were ready to move on signal. The area of operation was to extend for eighty miles from Charleston. The date was originally set for July 14, 1822, but was later changed to Sunday, June 16. Having only homemade weapons to complement a few guns and swords, a key aspect of the plan was for the several groups to supply themselves with arms from gunshops and the arsenal shortly upon entering the city. According to carefully laid plans, once the attack had been mounted it was anticipated that not only many other slaves would join in, but also "several white men of low character"—symbolic of Rehab and her household.[22] Monday Gell, one of Vesey's lieutenants, had even written to President Boyer of Haiti, informing him of the intended "stroke for liberty" and seeking his cooperation.[23]

Vesey insisted, against the protests of some of his followers, that the Lord had commanded that not a soul was to be spared, with the exception of the white men already mentioned. The white people were to be totally destroyed and the city to be set on fire simultaneously in several places. It is a mark of the determination of these men and the ultimate nature of the commitment they had made, that they did not shrink from this extreme violence to property and this indiscriminate slaughter. They were property themselves, and they were prepared to destroy everything, including themselves, if they could not be free. As for killing—not only did they have the Biblical precedents before them and believed themselves to be the instruments of God's terrible judgment upon unrighteousness, but they also knew, as David Walker pointed out later, that once they had begun, only total extermination, as lamentable as it may be, could hope to succeed in such an impossible situation. They could expect no mercy from the whites if the insurrection failed.

On the afternoon of May 25, 1822, a slave of Messrs. J. and D. Paul, named William, approached another slave, Devany of Colonel Prioleau, and told him what was about to happen. William offered to take Devany to one of the leaders, who would take his name down and give him an assignment for the great day. Devany, a house servant, could not contain himself. When his master Prioleau returned to town from a trip to the country, he revealed the secret to him and all was lost. By five o'clock on May 30, both Devany and William had been arrested and were being interrogated for further information, the whole business being kept as secret as possible. The official record continues:

> Things remained in this state for six or seven days, until about the 8th of June, when William, who had been a week in solitary confinement, beginning to fear that he would soon be led forth to the scaffold, for summary execution, in an interview with Mr. Napier (one of the committee appointed to examine him) confessed, that he had for some time known of the plot, that it was very extensive, embracing an indiscriminate massacre of the whites, and that the blacks were to be headed by an individual, who carried about with him a charm which rendered him invulnerable. He stated, that the period fixed for the rising, was on the second Sunday in June. This information was without delay conveyed to his excellency the Governor, and a Council forthwith convened.[24]

By ten o'clock on the Sunday night of June 16, Charleston was surrounded with a strong force of militia and police. The plan of Vesey and his compatriots could not be put into effect without certain disaster. By June 18, ten slaves were under arrest. Among them were Peter Poyas and Mingo Harth, two of Vesey's trusted lieutenants. On June 28, Ned and Rolla Bennett (slaves of Governor Thomas Bennett of South Carolina and the first men who had been approached by Vesey, Batteau Bennett, Peter Poyas, Jesse Blackwood and Denmark Vesey were summarily sentenced to death. On July 2, all of them were executed. An attempt was made by those who were still at large to rise up on Sunday night, June 16, and again on July 2—the day of the execution of the six—but it was much too late. The town by this time was thoroughly prepared, and when Gullah Jack, the Angolan conjurer, was arrested on July 5, the leadership was decisively shattered. Within thirty days, 131 persons had been arrested, 37 were executed, 43 transported out of the state or banished from the United States, and 48 whipped and discharged, there being no evidence against them.[25] Vesey and most of the doomed men died in silence, following the counsel of Peter Poyas, the highly intelligent vice-commander who had warned against including "house niggers" in the plot. At the end he said to the others: "Do not open your lips; die silent as you shall see me do."[26]

As happened following the Gabriel plot, the Charleston conspiracy—rather than dampening the ardor for revolt—encouraged plots in other communities of the state and elsewhere in the South.[27] For example, fires of an incendiary origin broke out in several places during the next few years. When the slaves were unable to do anything else, they frequently turned to the torch and to poison to carry on their resistance. Once again an attempt was made by the whites to intensify suppression by actions forbidding the hiring out of slaves, forcing free Blacks over fifteen years of age to have a guardian to control their behavior, prohibiting the congregating of slaves or their instruction in reading and writing, and forbidding any Black person from Mexico, the West Indies or South America to enter the state.[28] Negro crew members of ships entering the harbor of Charleston were required to remain on their ships or suffer imprisonment.

After the wholesale execution of the Blacks, Northern news-papers began to write about how South Carolina justice was meted out to slaves, about the "bloody sacrifice" and "the great sacrifice of human lives" which had taken place without any white man having been struck a blow. An editorial debate ensued between the Charleston *City Gazette* and papers in New York, Philadelphia, Boston and other cities. Antislavery sympathies and discussions about the administration of south-ern justice were the results, in other parts of the country, of the Charleston insurrection. The dismal failure and the terrible consequences were evidently the price that had to be paid by Black men, who could not erase from their minds the con-viction that God had aligned himself with them against the iniquitous system of the slaveholders. They came to believe that the blood of slave martyrs was destined to soak the red clay of Dixie for another generation before white men, in a tragic and cataclysmic struggle, would have to pay with many more lives for the blasphemy of holding their brothers in chains.

Before the tremors of the South Carolina earthquake that was the Vesey revolt had died away, the ground was being prepared for a new and more serious insurrection farther north in Virginia. Second only to John Brown's raid on Harper's Ferry in 1859, the Southampton, Virginia, insurrection of Nat Turner is the most famous in American history. Despite the contemporary reports of the incident and the official record of Turner's Confession, which has been republished several times since 1831, the melancholy truth is that most white Americans to whom the name is familiar today, became ac-quainted with the great slave preacher, turned revolutionary, through the highly fictionized version of his life in the best-selling, Pulitzer prize-winning book *The Confessions of Nat Turner* by William Styron.[29]

The misfortune is that Styron completely distorted the known facts about Turner in the interest of producing a sensational and unusually marketable "historical novel" during one of the most critical periods of race relations in the history of the United States. That misfortune is exceeded only by the extravagant praise from some of America's leading literary critics which greeted the publication of *The Confession of Nat Turner* and commended it to an overcredulous reading public. There is little question but that the popularity of Styron's work was in large measure one to the fact that the white community in the United States was still reverberating from its backlash against the Black Revolution of the 1960s. The young militants of the Black Power movement, which came into prominence in 1966, were not only nagging reminders of the guilt of white America, but also represented an inexplicable and frightening departure from what most white people had come to regard as a paradigm of the Negro's struggle for human rights—the nonviolent direct-action program of Martin Luther King, Jr. Many white Americans who read Styron's book could imagine that he had brilliantly perceived something about the other side of Black militancy—its paradoxical love-hate syndrome, its bestial lust for power, and its futility—which others lacked the courage to disclose. This most recent commentary on the life and exploits of Nat Turner was, therefore, not only a travesty of history, it was also a contributor to the sociological gullibility and miscalculation of the white liberal community in a time when Black Power ought to have been seriously regarded and understood, if not appreciated, by white Americans.

In the introduction to *William Styron's Nat Turner*, an anthology of the critical response of ten Black writers, John Henrik Clarke makes a telling query about the effect of Styron's work upon white people when he asks: "Why had the book received so much applause from the established press and a large number of well-known scholars who, in praising this book, display their ignorance of the true story of the Nat Turner revolt? Have they failed to see Nat Turner as a hero and revolutionist out of fear that they might have to see H. Rap Brown and Stokely Carmichael the same way?"[30]

In any event, it is necessary for anyone recalling the crisis in Southampton County, Virginia, during the summer of 1831 to correct the degrading image of Nat Turner that has been thrust upon an already miseducated American public by

Styron's novel. The picture of Turner as "a fanatical black man who dreams of going to bed with white women, who holds nothing but contempt for his fellow blacks, and who understands, somewhat, the basic human desire to be free, but still believes in the basic humanity of some slaveholders"[31] must be replaced with what we actually know about Reverend Turner from historical evidence and what a sensitive and rational examination of such evidence might surmise about what manner of man he was and what were the forces which drove him and others to take violent reprisal against their oppressors.

The most important thing to know about Nat Turner is that he is the prototype of an important group of slave preachers who discovered a secret about the Judeo-Christian faith that white Christians had attempted to conceal from the slaves for more than two hundred years. Nat Turner, like others before him whose names are buried forever under the debris of the citadel of slavery, discovered that the God of the Bible demanded justice and that to know him and his Son, Jesus Christ, was to be set free from every power on earth. Nat Turner discovered his manhood by unveiling the God who liberates. His fanatical attempt to authenticate that manhood in blood was the inevitable consequence of the fanatical attempt of white men to deny it. Styron's frequent Biblical quotations and references to his inner life never lifts this essential fact about the man to the level of significance.

Even a casual reading of the 1831 text of Turner's Confession to Thomas R. Gray will make clear that his conversion and development as a slave preacher are basic to any true understanding of what motivated him to insurrection. He was born on October 2, 1800, as the slave of Benjamin Turner of Southampton County, Virginia. At a very early age it was obvious to everyone who came into contact with him that Nat was a precocious child. This belief was fortified in the mind of his mother and father by certain birthmarks which, according to African custom, indicated the unusual mental capacities associated with a "witcheh-man."[32] Throughout his childhood they strengthened Nat in the belief that he was intended for some great purpose. It was his paternal grandmother, however, who had a decisive religious influence on him. She was a member of the Methodist church called Turner's Meeting House, where slaves of the Turner family worshiped with their masters from the late colonial period. Benjamin Turner believed in promoting religion on his plantation and conducted prayer meetings for the family in which the slaves were included. It was in this atmosphere of evangelical piety that Nat came into a knowledge of the faith and was supported in his belief that God had ordained him for a special vocation. Surrounded by such influences, his childhood was unusual for a slave, and opportunities were given to him that were denied to others. He astonished his master and others in the household by the facility with which he learned to read and write. As a boy, much of his free time was spent in meditation and prayer. Sometimes he stole off to carry on various experiments with paper and gunpowder.

Nat's superior ability partly separated him from the other slaves, but not entirely. Even though he was "marked to be a preacher," the Blacks in the neighborhood took him with them when, as he says, "they were going on any roguery." He, apparently, did not participate in the stealing that occurred on such occasions, but had the confidence of his fellows as one who could help them plan their forays. The fact that he participated at all in this activity is an interesting commentary on what the slaveholding class considered a common fault among their Negroes. What it actually constituted was day-to-day resistance to the system, no matter how benign it may have been in Southampton County at the time. It is unthinkable that an intelligent slave like Turner, during his frequent meditations, had not considered the moral implications of this behavior. His recollection of it in the Confessions shows no sign of remorse, for he says plainly: "Growing up among them, with this confidence in my superior judgment, and when this, in their opinion, was perfected by Divine inspiration . . . became the subject of remark by white and black."

The text of Luke 12:31, "But rather seek ye the kingdom of God; and all these things shall be added unto you," struck Nat Turner as having peculiar relevance during this period of his life. We cannot know precisely what meanings he attached to these words of Jesus, but the context is highly suggestive in light of his subsequent development as a messianic figure. The nations of the world seek material things, and these indeed are needful to life, but the followers of Jesus shall not only receive them in abundance, but much more when the Kingdom of God shall come secretly, and with great power.

> Let your loins be girded about, and your lights burning . . . And this know, that if the goodman of the house had known what hour the thief would come, he would have watched, and not have suffered his house to be broken through. Be ye therefore ready also: for the Son of man cometh at an hour when ye think not . . . I am come to send fire on the earth; and what will I if it be already kindled? But I have a baptism to be baptized with; and how am I straightened till it be accomplished! Suppose ye that I am come to give peace on earth? I tell you, Nay; but rather division.
>
> Luke 12:35, 39-40, 49-51

The context of this Lucan passage, which made such an impression on Turner, tells us that the messianic vocation that ushers in the Kingdom of prosperity and power is symbolized not by peace, but by the sword. When Gray, dubious of what spirit had prompted Nat to concentrate upon this passage, questioned him about it, he replied without hesitation that it was the spirit of the prophets of the Old Testament. At the beginning of his ministry he had already perceived a close relationship, as did other slave preachers, between Jesus of Nazareth and the great prophets who had called down the wrath of God upon his disobedient people and their enemies. This is all the more remarkable when we remember that this interpretation of Jesus was far from that of the missionaries. Jesus, for them, was the meek and mild exemplar—the Lamb of God, slain from the foundation of the world, whose obedience to *his* Master, God the Father, was the accepted model for the Christian slave. In recognizing the meaning of Jesus and the Kingdom in relation to the great prophets of justice in the Old Testament, Turner's reading of Scripture adumbrated the Black theology of preachers from Henry Highland Garnet and Henry McNeal Turner to Martin Luther King, Jr., who understood Jesus as a protagonist of radical social change.

When he was a boy, Nat's father escaped from slavery by running away from the Turner plantation, never to return. The same desire possessed Nat as a young man. He had always believed that it was revealed to those who knew him that he had too much intelligence to be a slave and would never give satisfactory service to anyone. He began to tell the other slaves what he planned to do, describing his purposes as a fulfillment of divination. For thirty days he remained in the woods, but finally, to the astonishment of his fellow slaves, he returned to the plantation, saying that the Spirit had directed him to do so. Drewry comments on the passage of Scripture thought to have influenced Nat's decision to terminate his escape and to continue his ministry to the slaves of Southampton.

> The reason he returned was that he imagined the spirit appeared to him and told him that he had his wishes directed toward the things of this world and not to the Kingdom of Heaven, and that he should return to the service of his earthly master, "for," said the spirit, "he who knoweth his master's will and doeth it not shall be beaten with many stripes, and thus have I chastened you."[33]

He thus implies that Nat was harassed by the feeling of having betrayed his master and that he returned partly out of guilt for running away. That Nat would have confused his earthly master's will with the will of his heavenly master seems most unlikely for such a man. Mike Thelwell's interpretation of his return is also questionable. Thelwell credits his use of these words as a brilliant thrust of irony by which he disarms his master by using one of the slaveholder's favorite texts. The truth is that Turner feigned repentance and pretended to be "the faithful darky—well-steeped in the acceptable slave morality."[34]

There is no reason why we should not assume that "the master's will" meant nothing less than the will of Christ. Nat himself said: "the reason of my return was that the Spirit appeared to me and said I had my wishes directed to the things of this world and not to the Kingdom of Heaven." He had, in other words, been disobedient to his calling. Instead of remaining on the plantation and waiting for the Day of the Lord, when he and those he had enlisted would make their decisive move for freedom, he had yielded to impatience, to the temptation of getting away alone. He had evaded the terrible work he had been called to do and had thought selfishly of the freedom and material success that awaited a man of his capabilities in the North.

Actually, what we have is Turner's own rendition of the parable on being ready for the *parousia*—the Second Advent of Christ—which is found, interestingly enough, in his favorite part of the New Testament—Luke 12.[35] The faithful and wise steward in the parable (Luke 12:37-47) is the one who remains at his post and watches for his lord's coming. He is to be rewarded by being made ruler over the entire household.

> But and if that servant say in his heart, My lord delayeth his coming; and shall begin to beat the menservants and maidens, and to eat and drink, and to be drunken; The lord of that servant will come in a day when he looketh not for him, and at an hour when he is not aware . . . *And that servant who knew his lord's will, and prepared not himself, neither did according to his will, shall be beaten with many stripes.*

Nat Turner had wearied—waiting for the sign that the Day of Judgment had come. He had weakened under the tremendous burden that had been his as a leader of the slaves and had run away, only to have been driven back after thirty days by the relentless spirit that pursued him. His was the classical dilemma of the Old Testament prophets, from Moses to Amos, who could always find an excuse for not taking up the mantle of the prophetic office, but in the end—contary to their own preferences—were drawn irresistibly into the vortex of the awesome responsibility of being the chosen representatives of the Eternal God. It is well to note that shortly after Nat returned to the plantation, he had a remarkable vision in which white spirits and Black spirits were engaged in a great battle, with blood flowing in streams. The voice that spoke out of that vision reminded him that the lot had fallen to him to suffer what had to be suffered to obedience to his calling. "Such is your luck," said the voice, "such you are called to see, and let it come rough or smooth, you must surely bare it." There was no escape from the Master's will. And that will was destined to be performed by Nat Turner in no other place than Southampton County, Virginia.

After 1825, a series of extraordinary experiences occurred to Reverend Turner as he redoubled his efforts to obtain true holiness. He began to see strange signs in the heavens and interpreted them as miraculous depictions of Christ's outstretched hands on the cross. During this period he believed that he had been given true knowledge of the faith and was qualified to think of himself as a minister of the gospel. From this time forward he began to preach to the slaves and to extend himself beyond the immediate neighborhood. One account has it that by 1828 he was preaching to large gatherings as far away as Hertford County, North Carolina, at the Barnes Methodist Church.[36]

One day while laboring in the fields, he tells us that he found blood on the corn, which he took to be a sign of Christ's blood "returning to earth again in the form of dew." He also reported strange hieroglyphic characters on the leaves in the woods, "and numbers, with the forms of men in different attitudes, portrayed in blood." It is impossible to say very much about these phenomena. Down through the

ages mystics have reported such amazing, unfathomable oc-
currences, leaving it to ordinary men to believe or disbelieve
as they chose. Remembering the destiny toward which Nat
Turner was moving with increasing rapidity by that time,
one thinks of Stephen (Acts 7:54ff.), who gazed into heaven
and saw the glory of God, and Jesus standing at his right
hand, before he was stoned to death. We can only say
that the great founders of religion and some of their most
renowned disciples had experiences similar to Nat Turner's
and that the power of their lives and deeds were sufficient
to convince millions that wonders which most of us are too
spiritually blind to see, were truly revealed to them.

In the absence of any indication of where he received
such information, there is certainly no reason to accept the
word of Drewry when he says that Nat wrote the hiero-
glyphics and quotations on leaves and blades of fodder,
and that "he spat blood at pleasure, but it proved to be the
coloring matter of the log-wood, stolen from his master's dye
pots."[37] Before he was hanged, Nat declared that after his
execution it would grow dark and rain for the last time.
Although he reports that it did actually rain and that "there
was for some time a dry spell," Drewry does not venture
any explanation of that particular instance.[38]

In any event, some people evidently believed that Nat
Turner was a man of God and not a practitioner of hum-
buggery. One such person was a white man named Ethelred
T. Brantley, a respectable overseer, concerning whom Drewry
writes, "after his intercourse with Nat no one would have
anything to do with him."[39] The good church people of
Southampton refused Nat permission to be baptized with
Brantley. It must have caused something of a scandal in the
community that such a highly regarded white man would
have fallen under the influence of a fanatical slave preacher,
for we learn from the Confessions that "many who reviled us"
were present when Turner and the overseer, like Philip and
the Ethiopian eunuch, with roles reversed, went down into
the water together.

This episode was followed by another vision on May 12,

1828, when Nat Turner received the unmistakable sign that he should prepare for the great work—the apocalyptic struggle with the Serpent, which symbolized the system of slavery. The white slaveholders who had made themselves first would now become last in the Kingdom. And the slaves, who had been made last, would—as the Scripture clearly prophesied—become first. In his own words:

> . . . and on the appearance of the sign [the eclipse of the sun in February 1831] I should arise and prepare myself, and slay my enemies with their own weapons. And immediately on the sign appearing in the heavens, the seal was removed from my lips, and I communicated the great work laid out for me to do, to four in whom I had the greatest confidence [Henry Porter, Hark Travis, Nelson Williams and Sam Francis are referred to here] It was intended by us to have begun the work of death on the 4th of July last—

Two years and nine months intervened before Nat felt that he had received the sign. It came in the form of a solar eclipse in February 1831. The realization that the time had come at last, and sinking deeper and deeper into that agony of spirit a man experiences when he wrestles with God over a great decision that he dare not make and yet cannot evade, brought Turner down with an illness sometime prior to the July date that had been set earlier in the year. The Fourth of July passed without incident, but the postponement served to force him and his men to review repeatedly the earlier plan. Still doubt lingered, for the Confessions mention that new schemes were formed and rejected as they weighed what was believed to be a divine necessity against the pragmatic possibility of success. Nat, the prophet of the Lord, austere and aloof, trusted the men, but long since had ceased associating intimately with them, possibly because he had more confidence in their toughness and courage than in the genuineness of their religious commitment. The men themselves, however, seem to have held him in awe. If their religion, like that of so many slaves, was not distinguished by its asceticism and the outward signs of beatitude, it was nevertheless characterized by the confidence Black people have always vested in "the preacher" who walked with God in their stead, and whose words of truth thundered against their unbelief.

Sometime in August 1831, a strange atmospheric phenomenon occurred across the broad stretch of sky over Virginia and North Carolina. It extended over a period of three days and was known as the "Three Blue Days."[40] It seemed to Nat—his sickness of July having passed, and after he had all but exhausted the discussion about alternative strategies— that this was the irrefutable sign he had been waiting for. We do not know whether or not the image of the Passover supper that Jesus had with his disciples was in his mind when he, Henry and Hark met in the woods for a dinner of barbecue and brandy on the Sunday afternoon of August 21, but with all that had gone before to bring him to that moment, he must have had a sense of re-enacting the Holy Communion. The surroundings fitted the mood. The site they chose for the meal was in the woods near the Cabin Pond, which was considered taboo because of superstitions that had grown up around the burning of a slave there for having whipped his master to death.[41]

Four others had joined Hark and Henry, the two beloved disciples. They were Sam Francis, Jack Reese, Nelson Williams[42] and Will Francis. Was Will Francis, as Styron imagines, strangely different than the others? Did Nat have an overpowering sense that this might be the Judas come to betray him? If so, he was immediately reassured. When, upon arriving late for the rendezvous, he found Will there, he questioned him sharply about why he had come. Will's reply should leave no doubt about what was uppermost in the minds of the little band that night. He answered that his life "was worth no more than the others, and his liberty was as dear to him." When asked whether he was determined to win his freedom regardless of what he might have to do, he replied that he would win it, or lose his life in the attempt.

The late nineteenth-century Black historian George W.
Williams claimed that Nat Turner gave a great speech that
Sunday night at the Cabin Pond. Among other things, he
said that God had appointed that night for the Black race
to be delivered from slavery and that the war should be
waged "upon a Christian basis."[43] No verbatim account of
what was actually said that night was recorded, as far as
we know, but the speech that Williams purports to have
come from the lips of Nat Turner is believable. Turner was
a Black preacher and he would not have failed to use the
dramatic setting of that Sunday night meeting to preach to
the little congregation as he had never preached before; to
show plainly the justice of what they were about to do, according to the Scriptures and on the basis of the revelations
that had been given to him.

Before midnight they set out, with only a hatchet and a
broadax, for the home of the man who at the time was
Nat's own master, Joseph Travis. There they slaughtered
everyone in the house—Travis, his wife, and five others. They
took what guns and ammunition they could find and, dressing
their lines like infantrymen, they marched off to perform the
bloodiest slave insurrection in American history. By Tuesday
morning, August 23, at least seventy slaves were involved in
the killing of fifty-seven whites in a twenty-mile area of
the Boykins District of Southampton County.[44]

There is no need to go into the gory details, which are
recounted with amazing coolness and without remorse in
the Confessions. The plan was ultimately to take the county
seat of Jerusalem (now Courtland, Virginia) and to furnish
themselves there with weapons and ammunition. Somewhere
on the main road between Cross Keys and Jerusalem, in a
field before the dwelling of a prosperous planter named
James W. Parker, Nat and his men met their first resistance
from a group of militia commanded by Captains Alexander
P. Peete and James Bryant. The poorly armed Negroes
were dispersed after forcing the whites to retreat, and during
the night and throughout the next day, Nat was unable to
regroup his forces in sufficient numbers to engage the alarmed

white people, who were being rapidly reinforced by militia from neighboring communities as well as soldiers from Fort Monroe.[45] Indeed, the whole Eastern Seaboard was galvanized into action by the news of the insurrection, and aid was offered to the Southampton people from New York, Philadelphia, Baltimore and New London.

In the end, Nat despaired of continuing to fight with the few men he was able to keep together. He made his escape and hid in the woods near the cabin Pond—the scene of the last supper. For six weeks he eluded the posses that scoured the area and was only discovered accidentally by two slaves whose dog, foraging for food, was attracted by the smell of meat from a cave where Nat was concealed. The slaves probably reported that they had seen him, but for ten days longer Nat managed to baffle his pursuers by hiding out on the Salathul Francis plantation.[46] He dug a hole under a fallen tree and remained there until Sunday, October 30, when a white man, Benjamin Phipps, happened upon the hideout and, being armed, was able to apprehend him. On the following day he was taken into Jerusalem, tried and convicted in the course of five days, and on November 11 was hanged. After his full confession to Gray, Nat told the court just before he was sentenced that he had nothing more to say. He made no appeal for mercy and showed no sign of penitence. Gray reports in the Confessions that when he asked the prisoner if he did not find now that he was mistaken, the reply was simply, "Was not Christ crucified?"

Thus ended the great Southampton slave insurrection. Fifty-three blacks were arrested and tried, 21 were acquitted, 12 transported out of the state and 20 hanged. Carroll estimates that more than 100 slaves were killed before the back of the movement was broken, but it is more than likely that at least half of those were summarily lynched by the white people during the first few days, when they marauded through the countryside looking for suspected insurgents.[47] Drewry's earlier account, following Gray's statistics, says that 17 blacks were executed. He adds that the body of Nat

Turner was delivered to doctors, who skinned it and made grease of the flesh.[48]

The Southampton revolt caused a paroxysm of fear and panic throughout the South. It also inspired slaves everywhere to a restive yearning for liberty. Evidence is available that Nat Turner was not the only Black preacher during this period who thought of giving leadership to a rising against slavery. Governor Floyd of Virginia wrote: "From all that has come to my knowledge during and since this affair—I am fully convinced that every black preacher in the whole country east of the Blue Ridge, was in the secret."[49] Turner himself said that the Southampton revolt was local, but he did affirm that it was more than likely that the revelations he had received had also appeared to others and prompted them to similar undertakings. As could be expected, the effect on the free exercise of Black religion was immediate. Du Bois observes:

> A wave of legislation passed over the South prohibiting the slaves from learning to read and write, forbidding Negroes to preach, and interfering with Negro religious meetings. Virginia declared, in 1831, that neither slaves nor free Negroes might preach, nor could they attend religious service at night without permission. In North Carolina slaves and free Negroes were forbidden to preach, exhort or teach "in any prayer meeting or other association for worship slaves of different families are collected together on penalty of not more than thirty-nine lashes." Maryland and Georgia had similar laws. The Mississippi law of 1831 said, It is "unlawful for any slave, free Negro, or mulatto to preach the gospel" upon pain of receiving thirty-nine lashes upon the naked back of the presumptuous preacher . . . In the District of Columbia the free Negroes began to leave white churches in 1831 and to assemble in their own.[50]

Thus, from David Walker to Nat Turner, Black religion in the United States, strongly fortified by the Old Testament prophets and the New Testament apocalyptic, provided the slaves with the inner resources to resist oppression—with violence if necessary. The white people of the South who observed the slave preachers at close range and knew of the fierce amalgam of African spirituality and radical Christianity which infused their sometimes open, but more often secret subversion of the slave system, threw up the ramparts of repressive legislation and the lynch law against them.

To insist that these remarkable men were merely misguided fanatics and that the vast majority of humble Black Christians neither approved of nor participated in their conspiracies—preferring "pie in the sky bye and bye," is to fail to appreciate the most determinative undercurrent in the Black church. In the next chapter we shall see how this undercurrent of rebellion expressed itself in the great independence movement that gave birth to the Black denominations. The Black church in the United States has never been as militant as it was in the days of Denmark Vesey and Nat Turner, but new occasions teach new duties. Nonetheless, the prophetic zeal of Turner and others has continually erupted from the ranks of Black preachers and made itself felt in the various movements for freedom and self-determination that, in one way or another, were attributable to the action of Black churchmen. The great Negro spiritual:

> O Freedom, O Freedom,
> O Freedom, ever me,
> And before I'll be a slave,
> I'll be buried in my grave,
> And go home to my Lord
> And be free.

reveals, more than the housekeeping of General Conferences and the seven-day revival meetings, what has always been at the heart of Black religion. Even when the Black church was quiescent the seed of radical resistance to oppression was being harbored in its depths against that day when the cup of patience with white people ran over.

To say, with Drewry, that a man like Nat Turner was given to gloomy fanaticism and possessed with a "love of self-importance, encouraged by the efforts of negro preachers, who were influenced by external affairs . . ."[51] is to grossly miscalculate the impact of the gospel upon those who, in their chains, could only understand the God of love as one who demanded uncompromising justice, precisely in order for love to abound. To recoil in horror at the intention of men like Denmark Vesey and Nat Turner and to argue that for all their religion they were not Christians—that the Black church can never dignify such deranged enthusiasm—is to bargain for cheap grace to cover the sin of white America against the Black man for over three hundred and fifty years. As much as white Christians might wish otherwise, there is no escape from what Reverend Francis J. Grimke once said in a sermon delivered in 1902 on the resemblance and contrast between Israel and Black people:

> God is not dead,—nor is he an indifferent onlooker at what is going on in this world. One day He will make requisition for blood; He will call the oppressors to account. Justice may sleep, but it never dies. The individual, race, or nation which does wrong, which sets at defiance God's great law, especially God's great law of love, of brotherhood, will be sure, sooner or later, to pay the penalty. We reap as we sow. With what measure we mete, it shall be measured to us again.[52]

CHAPTER IV

The Black Church Freedom Movement

The Church having opened the way for the
development of the black man, other means
have followed, and still others will follow,
until his opportunities are equal to that of
any other race . . . The African Church will
then have accomplished its special work—*not
till then.*

Bishop J. W. Hood,
One Hundred Years of the A.M.E. Church, p. 48.

DURING THE eighteenth century there were more Black and
white Christians worshiping in the same congregations, in
proportion to their numbers in the Church, than there are
today. This fact should not, however, be taken to imply that
the American churches, prior to the Civil War, were "integrated." Black people enjoyed no real freedom or parity of
ecclesiastical status in either the North or in the slave states.
White Christians did not assume that the equality which
was denied in civil society should be available within the
Church. As a matter of fact, the pattern of relationship
between Black and white in the household of God made it
difficult for Americans to presume that there was anything
immoral about inequality in the household of Caesar. In the
South it even seemed rather a matter of good judgment on
the part of the slaveholders not to permit the slaves to

come together for worship unless some white person were present. That is the most important reason why the slaves and their masters sought the blessings of God together under the same roof for more than a hundred and fifty years before Emancipation.

Interracial worship before the Civil War did exist, but it was never intended to suggest equality. Even if a few pious slaveholders sincerely believed that they benefited from worshiping with Blacks and were willing to be reminded of their sins by Black preachers, it must be conceded that these white men were wise enough to appreciate the fact that their presence had a restraining effect upon Black religion. It was expedient that inflamed passions should not be permitted to get out of hand and be exploited by some dubious character who fancied himself a witch doctor or by some itinerant Yankee preacher. The possibility of slave uprisings was invariably associated with Black religion, despite the pains that had been taken to make Christianity an instrument of compliancy and control. Black Christians who were ardent about their religion had to be watched carefully. While the church mission headquarters received word from the field that the new Black converts were zealous in their belief and generally of good behavior, one could not be sure just how deep and lasting was this Christianization which denied full manhood rights. A religiously inspired rebellion was always a possibility.

When a few independent Black churches began to appear in the South almost a hundred years before the Civil War, there was actually more rather than less control over the situation. Unlike the clandestine meetings in the forest, these churches were religious institutions much like the white churches. They were, after all, public places, in full view of the slaveholders and often erected with their blessing and financial assistance. In the South they remained, for a time, under white control. White preachers often officiated at the services of the earliest Black congregations. It was not until Black preachers began to be called by these all-Black or predominantly Black congregations, that the fear of conspiracy began anew to gnaw at the hearts of the white ruling class and Black ministers began to be harried and persecuted until it was unmistakably clear that they would pose no threat to the community. They were warned that they had a sacred trust from the white people. If they were to enjoy the privilege of preaching and a relaxation of the prohibitions against Blacks worshiping alone, they were expected to maintain the same deportment and discipline that the master or his own preacher would maintain over Negroes. The Black preacher, however, was not so naïve. He was likely to be the most intelligent man in the community. He knew he was being watched by the whites, but he also knew how to make the best use of his opportunities to teach Black people what they ought to know about themselves and their situation. Philip A. Bruce, somewhat later than the period we are discussing, made an interesting observation about the Black preacher's role, which was fairly constant throughout the nineteenth century.

The preachers of the negroes are their most active politicians, as a rule, but even when they are not they have much political influence, for they constitute, individually, the natural leaders of their race, being elevated to their clerical position not because they are men of greater holiness of life or eloquence of tongue than the rest of their fellows, but because they have more energy and decision of character. Each one brings these qualifications to bear on all occasions of public agitation from that conspicuous coigne of vantage, his pulpit, which thus becomes a rostrum, the religious doctrines enunciated from thence, taking the color of his political principles, just as, on the other hand, his political harangues have a religious echo. The two parts of minister and orator are played so skilfully at one and the same time that it is impossible to distinguish them; and the affairs of the Hereafter and a contemporary political canvass are mixed in inextricable confusion. His church is thus converted into a political organization that is consolidated by the religious fervour that pervades it, and propelled towards a single political end by a religious enthusiasm that expects to be rewarded spiritually for the performance of partisan duties. The preacher playing alternately upon both at once, excites an emotional responsiveness that is prepared to obey his slightest injunctions; and he does not hesitate to turn this exalted state of feeling to the most useful account.[1]

White commentators who write so glibly about the "other-worldliness" of the Black church fail to understand what is really going on. The Black preacher was most relevant to this world when he was telling his people what to expect in the next one, because he was whetting appetites for what everyone knew white people were undeservedly enjoying in the here and now, and because he was talking about a just God from whom everyone gets his due—including Black folks. White preachers have never made as rich and elaborate a use of religion as Black preachers. The disestablishment of white Christianity soon after Independence removed the church from the center of public life, even though it continued to exercise a certain authority in manners and morals well into the twentieth century. But for the slaves and their descendants, a religion that could unveil the reality of another world beyond "this vale of tears," and at the same time interpret what God was doing in history to redress the wrongs perpetrated against Black people, was an absolute necessity for survival. It has never really been disestablished in the Black community. It was precisely its mystique and "other-worldliness" which gave it license to speak authoritatively to Black people about daily life, about white oppression and Black liberation. For Blacks, "going to church" was never as much a matter of social custom and convention as it has been for white people. It was a necessity. The church has been the one impregnable corner of the world where consolation, solidarity and mutual aid could be found and from which the master and the bossman—at least in the North—could be effectively barred.

Andrew Bryan was one of the pioneer Black preachers in

the South. Born as a slave in 1737 at Goose Creek, South Carolina, he was baptized by George Liele, another early Black preacher in Georgia, who escaped to Jamaica with the British during the Revolution and organized a church in Kingston. At first, Bryan preached to both Blacks and whites in Savannah, but on January 20, 1788, he became minister of the first African Baptist church in that city. As pastor of one of the earliest recognized Black congregations in the region, Bryan's reputation among the slave population grew rapidly, despite the difficulty of attending meetings due to the patrols.[2] The slavemasters feared that he was fomenting insurrection, and in addition to the dispersals from assembly and the whippings, many of his members were arrested and severely punished by the authorities. Bryan himself and his brother Sampson, a deacon in the Savannah church, were whipped, imprisoned and dispossessed of their meeting place. He was later exonerated through the intervention of their master, Jonathan Bryan, who permitted the meetings to continue in a barn on his plantation.

To have suffered such indignities in the name of Jesus Christ, as was certainly the case with both Andrew Bryan and George Liele, could only have reinforced the Black preacher's conviction that if white people so desperately sought to curb its proclamation in Black churches, this gospel had to have an uncommon relevance to the freedom and well-being of Black people. Reverend Bryan survived his ordeal and later became the most highly regarded and influential Black preacher in Georgia. When he died, in 1812, the white Baptist Association of Savannah memorialized his passing with a public statement of respect and appreciation.[3]

Did Bryan and others win white appreciation by softening their attitude toward slavery? It is difficult to know the extent to which Black preachers conformed to the repeated warnings of the white people not to stir up discontent, and to what extent they pretended to go along while actually criticizing and subverting the system of slavery and the restrictions placed upon them.[4] Certainly they were more vulnerable than the white preachers who limited themselves to a mild encouragement of manumission. Two other very early slave preachers, Henry Evans and Black Harry, like Bryan, were under constant surveillance. Their meetings were infiltrated by spies and informers, who were frequently promised their freedom for seditious information. They could say and do nothing that would not speedily be brought back to the white ministers who were their mentors and benefactors. At worst they would be reported to the civil authorities, who were in a constant state of nervousness about insurrections. The fact that many Black preachers, despite their lack of formal training, were popular among white people as well as Black, would seem to indicate that they, at least ostensibly, stayed within bounds and watched how they walked.

But these pioneers were not oblivious to the degradation of their people. They would never have been tolerated for long by Black congregations if they had favored the masters. When the lash was cutting the backs of men like Bryan and Evans, the thought was burned into their flesh with every blow, that for all their protestations, the slaveholding Christians knew that their system was doomed because it was abhorrent to the God they professed to serve. It was shame and guilt that made them want to silence the Black preacher even when the danger of insurrection seemed unreal. They knew that the argument that God had ordained the slavery of the Black man was a lie, and they knew that whatever could be done by Black preachers to hasten its demise—whether from the pulpit or in secret—was an indomitable part of their commitment to the ministry. In the North, as soon as men like Richard Allen, Absalom Jones and James Varick had established their independence from white church bodies, they began to give moral and material support to their brothers in the South who were less fortunate in winning freedom and independence for the Black church.

All of this is to say that the independent church movement among Blacks, during and immediately following the period of the Revolutionary War, must be considered, *ipso facto,* an expression of Black resistance to white oppression—*the first Black freedom movement.* It had the advantage of being car-

ried on under the cloak of ecclesiastical business rather than
as an affair of state, and as such could pass as representing the
more or less legitimate desire of Black people to have "a
place of their own in which to worship." But it was, in fact, a
form of Black insurrection against the most vulnerable and
accessible form of institutionalized racism and oppression in
the nation—the American churches themselves. It is one of the
ironies of history that these good white Christians who deplored the agitation of the Black church had long since declared that the struggle of the colonies against subjugation to
the British Crown was a holy war. Even today, white churchmen will boast that the Revolutionary War was sometimes
called "the Presbyterian Rebellion."

The fever of independence was very much abroad in the
land when the Black preachers began to lay claim to their
own independent churches. Under the general impulse for
liberty, Virginia repealed its discriminatory tax on free Negroes and mulattoes in 1769, declaring that it was "derogatory
to the rights of freeborn subjects." The first draft of the
Declaration of Independence, as is well-known, contained a
passage which laid the sin of African slavery, somewhat
hypocritically, on the doorstep of the King of England. The
Quakers, who had consistently opposed the slave trade, organized the first Abolition Society in Philadelphia, in 1775.
The abolition of slavery came in Vermont in 1777, and in
1778 Virginia prohibited the external slave trade. Restraints
on emancipation were lifted generally and manumissions in
the South as well as the North were relatively numerous.
As we have seen, in 1784 the Methodist Conference in Baltimore passed a resolution against slaveholding, and throughout
the decade prohibitive and emancipatory legislation was en-
acted in the northern states.[5]

In this expansive atmosphere Black people took measure of
the sincerity of the Founding Fathers by the only method
available to them of gaining some modicum of freedom without getting themselves exterminated—namely, by petitioning
for the independence of their churches from white control. It
was the beginning of the Black Revolution. It was the first

stirring of Black rebellion in a mass-based, organized way and on a national scale. What is more, it began—perhaps unconsciously but no less effectively—in the most respected and acceptable institution in Anglo-Saxon society. Even so, it was not an easy task to accomplish. Many white churches and judicatories were not eager to let them go, and even when separate congregations were permitted, white ministers presided over many of them, and Black congregations remained under the eyes of the civil government and the discipline of the white church bodies. Before the African Methodist Episcopal Church and the African Methodist Episcopal Zion Church finally established their unconditional independence from white Methodism, Richard Allen in Philadelphia, Morris Brown in Charleston, and James Varick and Christopher Rush in New York had to fight almost every step of the way to be properly dismissed by the Mother Church and to retain undisputed legal right to their finances and properties.[6] The Baptists, having a much less centralized jurisdiction, put fewer obstacles in the way of separating brethren, and several independent Black congregations were formed in the South and the border states before the turn of the century.

The Harrison Street Baptist Church of Petersburg, Virginia, was organized in 1776, and the first Negro Baptist Church in Williamsburg, in 1785. In the North, the First African Baptist Church of Philadelphia broke away from a conservative white congregation in 1809, and in the same year, after some conflict with reluctant white Baptists, the Blacks formed their own congregation in New York City under the leadership of Thomas Paul.[7]

One of the early Methodist churches was the African Union Church, which was incorporated in Wilmington, Delaware, in 1807, before the first General Conference of the A.M.E. Church. It united with the First Colored Methodist Protestant Church in 1866 to form the African Union First Colored Methodist Protestant Church of America and Elsewhere.[8] Once the dam had been opened by Richard Allen and Absalom Jones in Philadelphia, the flood inundated the land. Black people suddenly became aware of the fact that they no longer had to suffer the indignity of segregation and unequal opportunity in white churches, even if they had to continue to be denied freedom and equality in white secular society.

Philadelphia was a hotbed of ecclesiastical insurrection. Mother Bethel African Methodist Episcopal Church began as a protest against the racism and oppression of St. George's Methodist Episcopal Church in that city. Even though Richard Allen at first attempted to keep the dissatisfied Blacks in fellowship with the St. George congregation, he did so not because he was anxious to continue worshiping with white people, but because he believed in the evangelical theology and polity of Methodism. Inherently, Allen embraced a latitudinarian, or low, doctrine of the visible Church. He believed that sanctification came to those who lived a pious and moral life rather than through adherence to rites and dogmas of the institutional Church. In this he shared with the Wesleys, Asbury, and other white Methodist fathers of the eighteenth century a bias for personalistic religion. But Allen had something more. He had a desire for a church that would combine secular relevance with deep spirituality in a context of simplicity and informality. He saw that the formalistic churchmanship that was gaining ground among the evangelicals of the northern cities as the new educated middle class began to be attracted to churches like St. George's, was not for poor Black people. Even though he finally adopted the discipline of white Methodism, with few changes, he was interested in neither a legalistic nor a socially fashionable church. The creeds and ordinances of an ecclesiastical institution Allen saw as irrelevant to the spiritual, moral and material needs of the Black people. His vision was of a well-ordered, but flexible, spirit-filled, community-oriented church which could move immediately into the arena of the struggle for Black freedom and equality. His real affection was for Blade Willgoose's class, which met on Monday nights and was made up of poor and ignorant people who needed his help as a community leader as well as a preacher.[8]

The earliest development of Black religious independence in Philadelphia was almost co-opted by Quakerism, for at that time the Black man had no better friends than the Quakers of Pennsylvania. But Allen was not inclined to that direction as the answer to the problem of a suitable form of organization and worship for Blacks. He believed in the openness of the Christian fellowship to anyone who would consent to the simple rules of moral life, but he was not given to the gentleness and individualism of the Society of Friends. He wanted to enhance the spirited preaching and singing, the congregational participation and freedom of Black worship. It was his conviction throughout his life that Methodism came closest to that form of the church needed by Black people, and it was obvious to him that it was no longer realizable at St. George's. Therefore, when he saw "a large field open in seeking and instructing my African brethren," only a few of whom were attending public worship anywhere, he brought them together in prayer meetings in his own house.[9] When he and Absalom Jones were finally forced from St. George's as they knelt in prayer, he did not immediately establish another church, but what amounted to a Christian club—the Free African Society—including in it all sorts and conditions of Black people, regardless of their religion. The Society's preamble gives us some idea of the spirit and intention of the founders.

> Whereas Absalom Jones and Richard Allen, two men of the African race, who, for their religious life and conversation have obtained a good report among men, these persons, from a love to the people of their complexion who they beheld with sorrow, because of their irreligious and uncivilized state, often communed together upon this painful and important subject in order to form some kind of religious society, but there being too few to be found under the like concern, and those who were, differed in their religious sentiments; with those circumstances they labored for some time, till it was proposed, after a serious communication of sentiments, that a society should be formed, without regard to religious tenets, provided the persons lived an orderly and sober life, in order to support one another in sickness, and for the benefit of their widows and fatherless children.[10]

While the Free African Society generally followed the pattern of the class meeting—the distinguishing mark of early Methodism—it had a broader and more secular purpose. The closing words of the preamble indicate the concerns which were uppermost in the minds of Allen and Jones. One finds in this statement of purpose a certain ambivalence about religious and secular objectives which has been a distinctive characteristic of Black religion in America. It was not precisely the original purpose of Richard Allen to organize Blacks merely for community action and social welfare, as important as those concerns were to both men. In his autobiography he writes plainly: "I established prayer meetings; I raised a society in 1786 of forty-two members. I saw the necessity of erecting a place of worship for the colored people."[11] He never gave up his dream of a self-sustaining Black Methodist congregation in the face of resolute opposition from both Blacks and whites. And in the end, his restlessness over the failure of the Society to move in that direction caused him to look elsewhere for the realization of his dream.

The suitability of the Free African Society pattern for meeting multiple needs in the Black community is amply demonstrated by the rapidity and enthusiasm by which it spread from Philadelphia to other cities. Wherever the Societies were organized they began as protests against white prejudice and neglect and with the objective of providing not only for religious needs, but for social service, mutual aid and solidarity among "people of African descent." They were typical immigrant organizations such as have been established in the cities by every ethnic group coming to America—with one important difference. The African Societies did not only express the need for cultural unity and solidarity, but the protest and resistance of a persecuted people. Richard Allen could see that the Black man was only slightly more free in the North than in the South, and he was convinced that the whites, even in the City of Brotherly Love, would never permit their churches to serve the social, political and economic needs of Black people. Most of the members of the Society were as much, or even more, persuaded that the group should move along the lines of a community-oriented, self-improvement class meeting. The others had no intention of being affiliated with the Methodists, whom they considered prejudiced, even though Allen devoutly wished for such an affiliation.

The Society was remarkably versatile in its style of life and work. Not only did it pass resolutions regulating the morals of its members—with especial attention to marriage and family life—but it also established a Committee of Monitors whose business it was to visit the membership regularly in order that they might "increase in grace and knowledge and every Christian virtue." It became involved in abolitionist activity, and in 1790 another committee was organized to assist an abolitionist group in an effort to take a census of the number of freemen in Philadelphia. Also in that year it decided to begin regular religious services. The direction in which the Society desired to move is suggested by this decision and by the fact that the regular meeting room was considered no longer appropriate for this purpose, and a special room was assigned for worship at the Friends Free African School House, where the group met from 1788 to 1791.

Thus in many respects the Free African Society, which represented the first bid for independence among Black Methodists in the North, resembled an organized church without actually being one. Even though Allen entertained hopes of a "preaching-house" coming out of it eventually, he did not intend it to be a church, as such, and yet he wanted it to serve the religious needs of the people who joined it. It was a fellowship of the Black citizens of Philadelphia who desired independence and Christian social progress without reference to the creeds and ordinances customary in most white churches. Its interests were both religious and secular and never became exclusively one or the other. It created, therefore, the classic pattern for the Black church in the United States. A pattern of religious commitment that has a double focus—the free and autonomous worship of God in the way Black people want to worship him, and the unity and social welfare of the Black community. It was not until the Society began in its religious life to move toward the style of Quaker worship and churchmanship—under the friendly persuasion of some well-meaning white Quakers—rather than toward the spirit of primitive Methodism, that Allen raised objection and separated himself from the group. A reconciliation took place by 1790, when the Society finally decided to build a church. The result was St. Thomas' African Episcopal Church, which was dedicated, with Absalom Jones as pastor, on July 17, 1794. Twelve days later, on July 29, Bishop Francis Asbury preached the dedicatory sermon at the Bethel Church, where Richard Allen and the group which followed him laid the foundation for African Methodism.

In the public statement which was issued upon the establishment of the Bethel congregation, the founders said that they were aware that they had, by their actions, "in some measure discriminated ourselves," but regarded it necessary to declare that they "had no other view therein but the glory of God and the peace of the Church, by removing what was in a measure treated and esteemed as a nuisance, on the one hand, and an insult on the other, endeavoring through grace to avoid the appearance of evil and to seek peace with all men, especially them that are of the household of faith."[12]

The spirit of African Methodism spread rapidly in a widening circle of rebelliousness from its center in Philadelphia. In 1787, the white members of the Log Meeting House, Lovely Lane, and Strawberry Alley Societies in Baltimore refused to let Negroes occupy the same pews with them or to participate in Holy Communion. The Negroes withdrew and organized the Baltimore African Church, which joined Allen's group in 1812. Reuben Cuff withdrew the Black Methodists of Salem, New Jersey, in 1800. Forty-two Black members of the Asbury Church of Wilmington, Delaware, under the leadership of Peter Spencer, organized the Union Church of Africans and joined the Allenites in 1813. Peter Spencer and William Anderson led out the Black Methodists of Attleborough, Pennsylvania, between 1813 and 1816. Sixteen people representing these communities met in General Convention in April, 1816, and formed an Ecclesiastical Compact at the Bethel Church in Philadelphia. The following resolution was adopted:

> That the people of Philadelphia, Baltimore, and all other places who should unite with them, shall become one body under the name and style of the African Methodist Episcopal Church.[13]

By 1818, several new communities had joined, including Charleston, South Carolina, and 6748 persons were counted in the first detailed membership report. A strong ecclesiastical organization, the first Black-organized and -controlled institution in the United States, had developed out of the spontaneous proliferation of the Free African Society concept, but the new church, under Allen's leadership, never lost its basically militant concern for Black liberation and community welfare. As Richard R. Wright observed after one hundred years of African Methodist Episcopal history:

> The purpose in mind of the founding father of African Methodism . . . was, among other things, to exemplify in the black man the power of self-reliance, self-help by the exercise of free religious thought with executive efficiency. Hence, her spirit and practices have been, at all times and places, to encourage fraternal and economic organizations among the colored race; so that, upon any proper occasion, she throws open her churches and halls for funerals, anniversaries and conventions.[14]

In 1796, Bishop Asbury held an urgent meeting with a small committee of Black Methodists of New York City, who were members of the predominantly white John Street Methodist Church, to discuss, at their initiative, the possibility of their meeting separately in the interval between the regular preaching hours of the white people. At that time the John Street congregation was experiencing a problem of seating Black members, who were joining the church in increasing numbers. Peter Williams, a former slave and a respected employee of the John Street Church, had been entertaining the idea of organizing an "African Chapel" in order to minister more effectively to the needs of the Black Methodists.[15] We can safely assume, however, that the matter of strained relations between the two groups went beyond the issue of seating. In his book *The Varick Family,* Wheeler makes the interesting comment that the white Methodists of John Street "did not persecute colored people, but simply denied them certain privileges."[16] In any event, steps were taken at the meeting with Asbury to form a new church.

A cabinetmaker's shop was secured for the first meeting place, and the Chapel was incorporated as the Zion Church over the signatures of Peter Williams and Francis Jacob on September 8, 1800. The first preachers serving the African Chapel were Abraham Thompson, June Scott and Thomas Miller.[17] When the Zionites, following the example of the African Methodists of South Philadelphia and Baltimore, decided to break completely with the white denomination by forming one of their own—having rejected the idea of joining Richard Allen—the Methodist Conference declined to pass on holy orders. After two decades of exasperation due to the obstructive tactics of splinter groups and a schism in the white Methodist body, led by William L. Stillwell, a white preacher who attempted to draw the Zion Church into the controversy, the Blacks made a crucial connectional decision. At a meeting on August 11, 1820, it was agreed to form the African Methodist Episcopal Church in America (later changed to the African Methodist Episcopal Zion Church), and on June 21, 1821, the original group, together with representatives from New Haven, Philadelphia and Long Island, organized the new denomination. The Zionites, however, were still plagued with difficulties. In September of 1821, a special meeting was called to consider the problem of ordination in view of the obstacles presented by the white church. Three points of view were expressed. One group wanted penitently to return to the white denomination in return for securing ordination. Another favored receiving ordination from the Stillwellites, while a third counseled the maintenance of elected elders until ordination could be secured. The problem was finally resolved in 1822 with "the imposition of hands" from three former elders of the Methodist Episcopal Church who had separated from it in the Stillwellite schism—James Corvel, Silvester Hutchinson and William Stillwell.[18] In that year James Varick was elected its first Superintendent and the Zion Church, under his leadership and that of Bishop Christopher Rush, grew rapidly and provided a strong counterpart movement of Black Methodists in the North to the Allenites.[19]

Both the African Methodist Episcopal Church and the African Methodist Episcopal Zion Church were strongly opposed to slavery, and their laws prohibited the retention of slaveholders in membership. We have already noted the complicity of the Allenites in the Denmark Vesey insurrection of 1822. One of the conspirators in that affair undoubtedly was Morris Brown, who managed, by being out of Charleston at the time, to conceal his involvement well enough to have escaped with his life. That might not have happened had not white friends in South Carolina warned him against remaining in the state and secreted him aboard a ship leaving for Philadelphia, where he remained to become a shoemaker and later a bishop of the A.M.E. Church.[20] Bishop Payne makes it quite clear that the A.M.E.s were well-informed and supportive of the Vesey plot and that the church, because of it, was feared by the slaveholders.[21]

The Bethel Church in Philadelphia and the parsonage of Bishop Allen were well-known to fugitives as stations of the Underground Railroad. Rev. Walter Proctor, one of Allen's confidants, averred that the "house of Bishop Allen was a refuge for the oppressed, and a house for the refugee from American oppression." This spirit of "benevolence" toward those who were still in chains infused the entire church, and the denominational historians take it for granted that where the Allenites stood with respect to Black liberation is common knowledge. As Elder R. Robinson said at the General Conference in Cincinnati in 1856, "Every colored man is an abolitionist, and slaveholders know it."[22] A typical antislavery resolution of the A.M.E. Church is the following adopted by the Western Conference, meeting in Pittsburgh on September 5, 1840.

We, the members of this Conference, are fully satisfied that the principles of the Gospel are arrayed against all sin, and that it is the duty of all Christians to use their influence and energies against all systems that rudely trample under foot the claims of justice and the sacred principles of revelation. And

Whereas, Slavery pollutes the character of the Church of God, and makes the Bible a sealed book to thousands of immortal beings, therefore,

Resolved, that we will aid by our prayers, those pious persons whom God has raised up to plead the cause of the dumb, until every fetter shall be broken, and all men enjoy the liberty which the Gospel proclaims.[23]

The Cincinnati Conference is of particular interest because of the extended debate which took place over the question of revising the Discipline of the church so that it would be unmistakably opposed to slaveholding. The original version read:

We will not receive any person into our society as a member who is a slaveholder. Any person now a member, having slaves, who shall refuse to emancipate them after due notice has been given by the preacher in charge, shall be expelled.

In the South and border states there were still a few Negro slaveholders. Some had purchased them with the intention of emancipating them immediately, but others expected the slaves to "work off" their purchase price before claiming full freedom. The report of the Committee on Slavery proposed to force immediate emancipation or expulsion. It also offered for adoption the policy that no person who was a slaveholder be received into membership of the church under any condition. A minority of the committee objected that there were extenuating circumstances in some cases. It argued that in order not to penalize those church members or new converts who had bought slaves for the purpose of giving them their freedom, due notice of expulsion should be given "by the preacher in charge," as the Discipline already provided for. The minority also warned that in establishing the A.M.E. Church in a new place it was impossible to tell immediately who were slaveholders and who were not, until after they had joined and furthermore, there should be a period of "mercy" for such persons, untutored in the duties of Christians, to learn of God's will, repent and emancipate slaves acquired by themselves for whatever reason.

The matter was sharply debated. The whole issue of the A.M.E. Church's position regarding Black liberation was reopened for the first time since the Discipline of the Methodist Episcopal Church had been adopted and minor changes had been made in order to establish an expressedly antislavery position in the new denomination. While there was unanimous agreement that the Church should be antislavery and most of the Conference assumed that the *de jure* position had been maintained in fact, there were others who questioned what had happened in the Church over the years. There was wide disagreement over whether the denomination had actually cleared itself of slaveholders, whether those remaining should be summarily expelled no matter what their sincere motives were, and whether or not the Church's missionary activity and expansion in the slave states would be made even more difficult than it already was if a hard line was taken on the slavery question. Just prior to the calling for the question, Rev. A. R. Green made an eloquent address to the tumultuous Conference in which he said:

If the preachers having charge of churches in slaveholding states will not execute the laws, the fault is theirs, and not that of the Church. Where is the conscience of the preacher, with this rule in his hand, that does not exclude a slaveholder? To charge the Church with the sin of slavery under such circumstances is to charge God with the sin of Adam, who did previously transgress in the very face of the law which forbade him to eat the forbidden fruit. The Church is free from this accursed sin—standing forth as a beacon light, and as glorious as the unclouded sun![24]

The minority report, calling for the enforcement of the position against slaveholding as stated in the Discipline, was adopted by a vote of forty to twelve. Thus the Allenites in the 1850s encountered some of the same dilemmas the white Methodists had wrestled with, despite the fact that the question in Cincinnati was presented as one of strategy rather than principle.

From its founding, the African Methodist Episcopal Zion Church was engaged in the struggle of the slaves for freedom. Its congregations along the Mason and Dixon line were known as Underground Railroad stations for escaped slaves. Catherine Harris, Thomas James, Frederick Douglass, Harriet Tubman, Jermain Louguen and Sojourner Truth were all associated with Zionite activity against slavery.[25] Catherine Harris of Jamestown, New York, was a member of the Zion church whose parsonage, at 12 West Seventh Street in Jamestown, is on the site of the house she used after 1831 as a sanctuary for fugitive slaves. At one time during the 1850s she had seventeen slaves in her house at one time, caring for their needs until they could be shipped out to safety. The most famous story about her and the people of the Zion church in the Jamestown "homestead" is told about the concealment of an escaped slave in a coffinlike box in which he was taken by wagon to Dunkirk and ferried across Lake Erie to Canada.[26] Jermain Louguen was himself an escaped slave. He became a bishop of the Zion Church in 1864 after many years of abolitionist work in the North. Bradley suggests that Louguen's feverish activity as an abolitionist so overshadowed his Church affiliation that he is remembered more for fighting slavery than for his work as a bishop of the Church. Much the same could be said about many Black preachers of the period.

Thomas James, the A.M.E.Z. minister at New Bedford, Massachusetts when Frederick Douglass arrived there, was born a slave in 1804 and escaped as a young boy. While working as a schoolteacher and Zionite preacher in Rochester, New York, in 1831, he was given some antislavery literature to read which so impressed him that he launched out on a career that made him one of the outstanding abolitionist lead-

ers in western New York. It was after James had been trans-
ferred to Long Island and then to New Bedford that he met
Douglass and had a significant influence on the latter's decision to engage in full-time antislavery work. In his autobiography James makes it clear that Zionite ministers were
expected to take an active part in the freedom struggle.[27]

An incident from the life of James which illustrates the
character of the man and the involvement of his church in
antislavery agitation happened on a return journey he made to
New Bedford from a visit to New York City. In the Jim Crow
coach of the train James met a slave girl from Richmond
traveling with her master and his family to New Bedford for a
summer vacation. James invited the girl to attend the Zion
church during her stay, but when he and a friend called upon
her later to find out why she had not attended services, her
owner, one Henry Ludlam, met them at the door and informed
them: "Lucy is my slave, and slaves don't receive calls." James
applied in Boston for a writ of *habeas corpus* and took possession of the girl. It so happened that her master warned her
that she was in danger with the minister and his friend and
that she should display a handkerchief as a signal for him to
come and rescue her. James writes:

> We took the girl to a chamber on the upper floor of
> the residence of the Rev. Joel Knight, and that evening
> we prepared to lie down before the door. Lucy displayed
> the handkerchief as she had promised, and when we ques-
> tioned her about it, answered, "Master told me to do it;
> he is coming to take me home." At this we quietly called
> together twenty men from the colored district of the
> place, and they took seats in the church close at hand,
> ready for any emergency. At one o'clock in the morning
> Ludlam appeared on the scene, with the backing of a
> dozen men, carrying a ladder, to effect the rescue. The
> sheriff hailed them but they gave no answer, whereat our
> party of colored men sallied forth, and the rescuers fled
> in all directions. The entire town was now agog over the
> affair.

By the intervention of the local police the girl was finally escorted to Boston, where she appeared in court, asked for her freedom and received it the next day, despite another attempt by her owner to "rescue" her by intercepting the sheriff's posse. She later married, had children and continued to live unmolested in the North.[28]

The intrepid Reverend James was subsequently assigned to the A.M.E. Zion Church in Boston and in 1856 returned to the congregation in Rochester, where he had joined the denomination in 1823 as a runaway slave. Frederick Douglass speaks of him and other Zionite ministers he respected and admired in a testimonial preserved by Bishop Hood. It deserves quoting here not only to show the quality of the Zionite preachers, but also to demonstrate the extent to which Douglass' commitment to the cause of Black freedom was rooted and grounded in his earliest encounter with Black religion.

My connection with the African Methodist Episcopal Zion Church began in 1838. This was soon after my escape from slavery and my arrival in New Bedford. Before leaving Maryland I was a member of the Methodist Church in Dallas Street, Baltimore, and should have joined a branch of that Church in New Bedford, Mass., had I not discovered the spirit of prejudice and the unholy connection of that Church with slavery. Hence I joined a little branch of Zion, of which Rev. William Serrington was the minister. I found him a man of deep piety, and of high intelligence. His character attracted me, and I received from him much excellent advice and brotherly sympathy. When he was removed to another station Bishop Rush sent us a very different man, in the person of Rev. Peter Ross, a man of high character, but of very little education. After him came Rev. Thomas James. I was deeply interested not only in these ministers, but also in Revs. Jehill Beman, Dempsey Kennedy, John P. Thompson, and Levan Smith, all of whom visited and preached in the little school house on Second Street, New

Bedford, while I resided there. My acquaintance with Bishop Rush was also formed while I was in New Bedford.

It is impossible for me to tell how far my connection with these devoted men influenced my career. As early as 1839 I obtained a license from the Quarterly Conference as a local preacher, and often occupied the pulpit by request of the preacher in charge. No doubt that the exercise of my gifts in this vocation, and my association with the excellent men to whom I have referred, helped to prepare me for the wider sphere of usefulness which I have since occupied. It was from this Zion church that I went forth to the work of delivering my brethren from bondage, and this new vocation, which separated me from New Bedford and finally so enlarged my views of duty, separated me also from the calling of a local preacher. My connection with the little church continued long after I was in the antislavery field. I look back to the days I spent in little Zion, New Bedford, in the several capacities of sexton, steward, class leader, clerk, and local preacher, as among the happiest days of my life.[29]

After 1800, a few Black congregations were established among the Presbyterians and the Episcopalians, mainly outside of the South. But the tenor of the faith and the pattern of worship in those denominations were not amenable to most Blacks, and the white presbyteries and Episcopal bishops exercised an inhibitive and paternalistic oversight of their Black congregants. The Presbyterians had exhibited an early interest in the religious instruction of Negroes, but "could never quite bring themselves to the place where they would recognize the ability of the Negro to be a responsible agent for his own salvation."[30] A succession of General Assemblies, up to the division of the Church in 1861, passed eloquent resolutions which were generally supportive of the abolition of slavery, but the denomination compromised by refusing to withhold fellowship from slaveholders and became embroiled in interminable debates over whether or not slavery was an affair of the state and therefore outside of the competence of the Church. The first Black Presbyterian church was formed as the First African Presbyterian Church of Philadelphia in 1807 with twenty-two members. Its first pastor was an ex-slave named John Gloucester, who had worked under a white minister in Tennessee.[31]

The attitude of the Episcopalians may be deduced from the fact that, unlike the Presbyterians, the Episcopal Church did not divide North and South during the Civil War.[32] Although the Anglicans were the first to evangelize the slaves, the Protestant Episcopal Church, which succeeded it in the United States, catered to its southern constituency in the interest of preserving the peace and unity of the denomination and confined itself mainly to urging slaveholders to see that their slaves received religious instruction. The first Black Episcopal church in the United States developed from the group which separated from the Methodists with Richard Allen and Absalom Jones. It was organized as St. Thomas' Church of Philadelphia and was received into the communion of the Episcopal Church on October 12, 1794. Jones was ordained as its first deacon in 1795.[33]

Despite differences in the way they developed over the years, it is clear that the same independent spirit which impelled the Black Baptists and Methodists to separate from the whites caused the organization of Black Presbyterian and Episcopal congregations in Philadelphia and New York during the same period.[34] The first decade of the nineteenth century saw a veritable hurricane of spiritual restlessness and rebellion blow through the Negro communities of the North, and new Black churches were formed, divided and subdivided as Blacks sought to exercise their powers of leadership and control their own affairs. The decorous Presbyterian and Episcopal churches were just as affected by this restlessness as were the more evangelical denominations. The Blacks who were drawn to the former were much fewer in number and more inclined to the quiet worship service and to intellectual sermonizing than those who were first attracted to the Methodist and Baptist churches. But they too were weary of being seated by white ushers in the "African Corner," a "Nigger Pew," in seats marked "B.M." (for Black Members), or in balconies which were called "Nigger Heaven."[35]

The Black Presbyterians, Congregationalists and Episcopalians, however, did not go as far as the Methodists and Baptists in breaking fellowship with their white brethren. In the first place, Blacks in those churches, being fewer in number, did not precipitate the crisis over seating that was occasioned by the large ingathering of former slaves and freemen into the Methodist and Baptist churches of New York and Philadelphia. Secondly, there were among the Blacks who were attracted to the Presbyterian and Episcopal denominations, stronger class affinities and a greater similarity of complexion with the whites than was true among the Black Baptists and Methodists. Thirdly, the emphasis upon an educated ministry in the two former denominations kept the number of Black preachers who might have created a mass church to a minimum, made them more acceptable as pastors of predominantly white congregations, and they themselves more secure in their ability to hold their own in the judicatories and reform them from within. Albeit, they were not successful in developing truly integrated churches.[36]

The Presbyterians and Episcopalians administered their "Negro Work," or "Colored Work," separately from the rest of the Church, in somewhat the same way as the northern Methodists, who in 1870 released what is today the third largest Black Methodist body, as the Colored Methodist Episcopal Church (now the Christian Methodists). Even though the Black Presbyterian and Episcopal congregations met together in their respective unofficial Black conferences, as well as in their official white judicatories, almost continuously from their inception they have always been, technically, an organic part of the white denominations. It is fair to say that, as a whole, these Black churches have been less aggressively independent and Black-oriented than the African Methodists and Baptists. Most of their pastors depended to some extent upon the white denominations for their below standard salaries. Such arrangements rarely foster self-determination and divergence from institutional norms. The real independence movement—which took upon itself the name "African" to signify its concern for Black solidarity and autonomy—grew out of the mass appeal of the Baptists and Methodists, and their ministers and lay leaders set the tone for the earliest agitation of northern Black churchmen against slavery and African colonization.

It is well to note, however, that not all of the militant leadership of what we are calling "the Black church freedom movement" came from the two Methodist connections and the independent Black Baptist churches. The influence of Presbyterian, and to a lesser extent, Episcopal and Congregational preachers began to be felt early in the nineteenth century, particularly when the Black Methodists of Philadelphia began to lose interest in the National Negro Convention movement after it moved out of Bishop Allen's control and the pressures of ecclesiastical housekeeping in the burgeoning new denominations began to distract them from secular affairs.

The convention movement, in a sense, was the secular adjunct of the Black churches. It soon became ideologically autonomous, but its important contribution to the growing radicalization of Black abolitionism in the 1840s and 1850s cannot be separated from the influence of Black religion. It was the spirit of uplift and self-expression cultivated in the independent Black churches that originally infused it, and except for a brief interim when a white agenda dominated it, the movement was the secularization of Black religious impulses which surfaced in the religiously inspired slave insurrections, in Walker's *Appeal*, and in Allen's walk out of the Methodist Episcopal Church. The practice of Black people holding national and state conventions to coordinate their opposition to slavery, African colonization and various social ills began in 1830. Howard H. Bell, commenting upon the basic factors in the development of the movement, writes:

> Insisting upon separate organizations so that they might worship as they chose without submitting to the humiliating practice of segregation within white churches,

Negro leaders gradually built their new Zion during the early years of the 19th century. By 1830 there were many a Negro pastor, and layman as well, who was grounded in the principles of self-expression, and who could give a good account of himself in debate. These men were ready and willing to grapple with the problems of the antebellum era.[37]

These men used the convention movement as their sounding board. They sent delegates to the meetings from their congregations, provided meeting space in their churches and, in the beginning, played a leading role in all of its deliberations. The Allenites of Philadelphia and the Zionites of New York competed with one another in calling the first National Negro Convention. Bishop Richard Allen, a shrewd organizer and a man who understood how to use power, won out and the convention met on September 15, 1830, at Mother Bethel Church in Philadelphia. The National Conventions then continued to meet annually until 1835, when there was an interruption of seven years until 1843, when the meetings were resumed in Buffalo, New York. Rev. Samuel E. Cornish, a New York Presbyterian minister, editor with John Russwurm of the first Black newspaper—*Freedom's Journal*—and later of the *Colored American*, was an active participant in the early meetings, as was another Presbyterian preacher, J. W. C. Pennington of Brooklyn. After Bishop Allen died in 1831, Cornish, Theodore Wright, also a New York Presbyterian preacher, and Charles B. Ray, a Methodist minister, sought to prevent the convention movement from falling under the control of a group of men who were strongly influenced by the irrepressible white abolitionist William Lloyd Garrison and other white friends of the movement.[38] These men, including William Whipper, James Forten, Robert Purvis and William Watkins—mainly Philadelphians, were able and wealthy laymen who represented the first stirrings of revolt in the Black community against the domination of the autocratic Black preacher, but they were not an unmixed blessing for the rapid development of a mass-based Black movement that could continue to receive the spiritual nourishment of militant Black religion as opposed to the theoretical humanitarianism of white Christianity. Their northern backgrounds and their class interests pushed them toward a moralistic and reformist posture more congenial to white abolitionism than to Black, and by 1835 they had taken over the Philadelphia wing of the convention movement and organized the American Moral Reform Society.[39] Cornish strenuously opposed this accommodation to white moderation, and in reply to the Society's effort to substitute the term "oppressed Americans" for "colored people," he wrote in his *Colored American:* "Oppressed Americans! *who are they?* Nonsense brethren!! You are COLORED AMERICANS. The indians are RED AMERICANS, and the white people are WHITE AMERICANS and *you are as good as they, and they are no better than you.*"[40]

Although Cornish became more of a moderate as the years passed, a brilliant group of Black preachers (who also were not members of the predominantly Black churches), including Pennington, Wright, Ray, Alexander Crummel, Amos G. Beman, William C. Munroe and Henry Highland Garnet, kept the convention movement a self-consciously Black organization, politically oriented and essentially radical in its perspective on the problem of slavery. If the Black churches were too engaged in mass evangelization and church organization to insist upon a highly trained clergy, the predominantly white churches were too half-hearted about slavery and too biased to harness the talents and energies of their Black preachers. Consequently, these men were unleashed into the arena of social action and community affairs where their militance was out of all proportion to the size of the constituencies they represented. It is, perhaps, not inappropriate to ask whether a similar phenomenon is operative today in the deep involvement of men from some of the predominantly white denominations in the liberation movement among Black churchmen.[41]

When the National Negro Convention resumed its annual meetings in 1843 at the Buffalo convention, it was well-attended by men who wanted to move against the basically conservative stance of those who were still hoping that the white friends of the Negro would bring about the death of slavery more or less painlessly. The Buffalo meeting was convened by the more radical upstate New York Blacks rather than the moderately nonviolent New York City contingent, who belonged to the abolitionist faction led by the philanthropic New York merchant Lewis Tappan.[42] Theodore Wright and Charles B. Ray, the Tappanites from New York City, were not as conservative in their views as the Philadelphia group which decided to boycott the meeting, but neither were they as ready to take drastic action against slavery as were Samuel H. Davis, the Convention president and Henry Highland Garnet, the fiery pastor of a Presbyterian congregation in Troy, New York. Garnet attempted to lead the convention to a new aggressive position against the slave-holders, and his celebrated "Address to the Slaves of the United States," presented for adoption, is one of the boldest invitations to insurrection in the name of religion in the entire history of American slavery. He called upon the slaves to plead their own cause with the slaveholders, to appeal to their enlightened self-interest and sense of justice—as one last effort to avoid the catastrophe that he believed would surely come.

Tell them in language which they cannot misunderstand of the exceeding sinfulness of slavery, and of a future judgment, and of the righteous retributions of an indignant God. Inform them that all you desire is FREEDOM, and that nothing else will suffice. Do this, and forever after cease to toil for the heartless tyrants, who give you no other reward but stripes and abuse. If they then commence work of death, they, and not you, will be responsible for the consequences. You had far better all die—*die immediately*, than live slaves, and entail your wretchedness upon your posterity. If you would be free in this generation, here is your only hope. However much you and all of us may desire it, there is not much hope of redemption without the shedding of blood. If you must bleed, let it all come at once—rather *die freemen than live to be the slaves*. It is impossible, like the children of Israel, to make a grand exodus from the land of bondage. The Pharaohs are on both sides of the blood-red waters.[43]

Garnet recalled the example of the great heroes of the race who chose violence as a last resort rather than submit any longer to slavery—Denmark Vesey, Toussaint L'Ouverture, Nat Turner, Joseph Cinque and Madison Washington. He called them what so many other Black leaders had been afraid or too moralistic to call them—"Noble men!" whose memories would be cherished by future generations of freedom fighters. And at the end, in a powerful peroration which left his hearers with no doubt about his intention, he called upon the slaves to follow in their train.

Let your motto be resistance! *resistance! RESISTANCE!* No oppressed people have ever secured their liberty without resistance. What kind of resistance you had better make you must decide by the circumstances that surround you, and according to the suggestion of expediency, Brethren, adieu! Trust in the living God. Labor for the peace of the human race, and remember that you are FOUR MILLIONS![44]

Rev. Amos Beman of New Haven, later recalling Garnet's speech, said that it shook "stern men . . . as the wild storm sways the oaks of the forest," and that "every eye" was "suffused with tears."[45] But the motion to adopt the address and transmit it to the South as an antislavery pamphlet failed by the narrow margin of one vote. The young Frederick Douglass and the Garrisonian Charles L. Remond of Massachusetts prevailed upon the convention to try "the moral means a little longer." A second vote was attempted by Garnet and his friends several days later, but by that time more of his upstate colleagues had suffered an attack of faint-heartedness, and the Douglass majority was even larger. As time went on, however, many Black clergy reversed themselves on the issue of nonviolence and came to support Garnet's position. Six years after the convention, Garnet published the address himself, together with David Walker's *Appeal,* and five hundred copies were circulated.[46]

Born in protest, tested in adversity, led by eloquent and crusading Black preachers, the Black church was, during most of the nineteenth century, the cutting edge of the freedom movement among both slaves and freemen, and thereby a living witness against the ambivalence and faithlessness of most of white Christianity during that period. Notwithstanding Frederick Douglass' refusal to believe that there was any place for a Black church in the purposes of a God who was no respecter of persons, the independent Black churches had their own peculiar vocations to fulfill. Their preachers were more concerned about the religious and social needs of their people and the freedom to plot the destiny of their own institutions than the offense of building "exclusive or isolated organizations."[47]

Today, however, criticism of the leadership of the church by Black intellectuals and militants is more likely to be that not more of the preachers were like Nat Turner and that the founders of the Black churches were, by and large, much too imitative of the white clergy in their politics and given to moralizing and peacemaking. This was perhaps true of the majority of Black preachers, most of whom were in the South, but such men had little influence upon the highly significant events we have just recounted. Moreover, it is important to remember that, although Richard Allen and other church leaders were often irenic toward whites and did not use what some regard as the vituperative rhetoric of Black separatism, they were unquestionably "race men." The equanimity of their spirits and the graciousness of their language in addresses and sermons which have come down to us should not mislead anyone to assume that they were "gentlemen of the cloth in the grand English manner," incapable of the acrimonious dissent and fiery passions of revolutionaries. It is true that Allen himself and others of the circle of northern churchmen did not believe that all white men were their enemies, nor did they, as a matter of policy, champion violent insurrection among the slaves. But they hated slavery as much as, if not more than, they loved the Church, and the subject of continuous concern among them was how to organize and employ the extremely limited resources of their churches to fight for freedom. Their churches were regarded by Black and white alike as essentially radical on the subject of slavery. In this regard Benjamin Quarles writes:

> The Negro church had no such squeamishness about bearing witness against slavery (as compared to the white churches). The Negro church had its weaknesses— its services tended to be emotional with an abundance of "rousements," and many of its preachers given to substituting sound for sense . . . But from the viewpoint of social reform, the distinguishing mark of the Negro church was its independence from the white control. Its money came from Negroes. Hence it could speak out on such an issue as slavery without fear of losing members or offending someone in the South.[49]

If not frequently enough in their conventions and conferences, which were as rife with church politics as any white judicatory, certainly individual pastors and laymen, in their own communities, were at the forefront of Black abolitionism, and the slaveholding class regarded their intervention as one of the most dangerous threats to the security of the slave system.

The Black historian Charles Wesley reminds us that the name of the first and perhaps greatest among them—Richard Allen—lost some of its luster outside of A.M.E. circles as the pressure for racial assimilation and church integration increased among Negroes in the twentieth century.[50] The drive for a "nonsegregated church and a nonsegregated society," to which laymen like Frederick Douglass and William C. Nell were unreservedly committed, tended to cast an embarrassed shadow of doubt over the wisdom of Allen's "separatism," as seen from the perspective of those Negroes—mainly of the urban middle class—who felt that there was no longer any need for all-Black congregations and denominations. Today in the post-King era, after rising expectations have fallen upon the hard realities of an inveterate racism in the white church as well as in the society, the pride and power of Black institutions, including the churches, are being generally reasserted throughout the nation. Perhaps Allen's work can now be viewed in a somewhat different light. Certainly he never conceived of what he was doing as "reverse racism" or "Black chauvinism." He upheld the unity of the Church as the divine pattern for the oneness of the human family, and he never lost his esteem for the great white humanitarians who inveighed against slavery, nor did he lose respect for Methodism as the tradition most suited to the religious predilections of Black Americans. But Allen was not given to evading practical necessities in the interest of abstract principles. Always willing to stand alone, he faced in his time—even more critically than many today—what some Black churchmen are now facing, the need for Black institutions to be free of white control, no matter how benevolent, and the need to exercise Black power and self-determination in ecclesiastical and civil affairs.

Allen believed that the Black community had to be organized to deal responsibly with its own problems as long as American prejudice and indifference refused to erase the color line. And he also believed that an independent Black church, which made every aspect of life its field of witness, was the most widely accepted and the most effective instrument among Black people with which to pursue the twin goals of spiritual holiness and civil freedom. In the 1970s he will doubtless be reappraised by Blacks for the pioneering and prophetic role he played in Black church history in the United States and his relevance to the antebellum Black church freedom movement. Young Blacks who tend to regard the church and its leaders of the past as historical oddities having little to inspire the present generation, need to catch the spirit of this man as it was caught by the writer of the obituary notice of his death on March 26, 1831—the year of the Nat Turner revolt—recorded in the pages of *The Genius of Universal Emancipation:*

> When the humble African was even dragged from the altar of God by the inhuman whites who disgrace the land, rendered sacred by the glowing recollections which arise at the mention of the name William Penn, Richard Allen stepped forth as their defender and protector, built, at his own expense and upon his own ground, the first African Church in America. He it was that through persecution, through malice and through envy, walked like the Savior upon the troubled waters, in favor of African Religious Independence.[51]

This was the work which began it all and made possible the emergence of secular agencies of protest and agitation in the Black community such as the later national and state conventions. Without Allen and those early pioneers who came out of the white churches in order to claim their manhood and create more effective instruments for confronting the subjugation of the Black masses, even those who chose to remain outside the church, or in the white denominations as a matter of strategy—the Garnets and the Bemans—would probably not have found an audience to conjure with their antislavery radicalism. The foundation for Black power and self-determination had been lain in the independent Black churches. It remains now for us to trace the further development of that motif through the outreach of the churches to the West Indies and Africa, and its ultimate transfiguration into the quasi-religious Black nationalism of the twentieth century.

CHAPTER V

Black Religion and Black Nationalism

If it be here shown beyond reasonable
doubt . . . that the ancient Egyptians, Ethiopians and Libyans . . . were the ancestors of
the present race of Ham, then the Negro of
the 19th century may point to them with
pride; and with all who would find in him a
return to racial celebrity, when in the light of
a Christian civilization, Ethiopia shall stretch
out her hands unto God.

Rev. Rufus L. Perry, ex-slave Baptist pastor
in Brooklyn, N.Y. Author of
*The Cushites; or the Children of Ham
as Seen by the Ancient Historians and Poets.*

ALMOST FROM the beginning of slavery in the New World, a
process of repatriation and colonization back to Africa made
it possible for a few slaves, who by one means or another had
obtained their freedom, to return to their homeland from
South and Central America, and later from the English colonies in North America. This reverse movement made it possible for an early relationship to develop between Blacks in the
New World and those who remained in Africa. During the
Revolutionary War thousands of slaves who escaped to the
British forces or had been liberated by them made their way
to Canada and Nova Scotia, to the West Indies, or to the

coastal towns of the South American mainland. Some of these later recrossed the Atlantic to take up their lives again in West Africa. John Kizzel, an escaped slave from South Carolina who became a preacher and built a church in Sierra Leone, sailed from Nova Scotia at the end of the Revolutionary War with a group of American slaves and developed a prosperous settlement in the British colony. In 1818, Kizzel met Samuel J. Mills and Ebenezer Burgess of the American Colonization Society, whom he conducted to Sherbo Island, where it was decided to erect the first settlement of the ill-fated Society.[1]

The relationship between American Blacks and Africa was, of course, first established by the African slave trade itself. New England rum manufactured from the sugar and molasses of the West Indian plantations was exchanged for slaves in the markets of West Africa. The captives were shipped across the Atlantic and sold for sugar and molasses to begin the process all over again. By the end of the eighteenth and the beginning of the nineteenth century, this triangular commercial exchange was providing a network of contact and communication between Africa and the New World which laid the foundation for the spiritual and intellectual exchange which was to develop later under the sponsorship of Black Christians on both sides of the Atlantic—the vision of Black solidarity projected by men like Garvey and Du Bois.

One of the first persons who sought to take advantage of the connection between Africa and the Americas was Paul Cuffee, a New Bedford shipowner, a member of a small group of Negroes in Massachusetts who made contact with the Free African Society of Philadelphia and founded the first African Methodist Episcopal churches in Massachusetts and Rhode Island. Cuffee was inspired by African Methodism to Christianize Africa. Moreover, it was his intention to colonize West Africa with American Blacks who could not only carry out an evangelistic mission to their heathen brethren, but would also lay the foundation for forms of commerce between Africa and America which would compete with and finally bring an end to the slave trade.[2] In 1815, at his own expense, he took

nine families and thirty-eight persons to Sierra Leone to begin
the realization of his dream of bringing Christian civilization
and Black-owned and -operated commerce to the shores of
the fatherland.[3] Influences flowing from men like Cuffee,
from the missionary aspirations of the new Black churches in
the United States and the West Indies, from political developments and antislavery pamphlets on both sides of the Atlantic, circulated back and forth between Africa and the New
World and, quite early, generated a spirit of incipient Black
consciousness and anticolonialism more than a hundred years
before what came to be known as Pan-Africanism came into
existence.

Black religion and the newly independent Black churches
played an important role in this development. The emergence of Black Nationalism in America and Africa cannot be
understood apart from an appreciation of the zeal of Black
churchmen to Christianize the land of their forefathers and to
establish an administrative and communications connection
between Black churches for the prosecution of Christian missions in both Africa and the Caribbean.[4] From the early effort of John Kizzel to establish a Black Christian settlement
and mission in Sierra Leone, Black churchmen from the
United States and the West Indies turned their eyes to Africa as an object of Christianization to be effected by mass
emigration from the west and the development of a bond of
friendship and collaboration between Africans and Afro-
Americans. This dream, as we shall see, was never shared nor
supported by the majority of American Blacks—especially
those who were rapidly adopting the values and loyalties of
white America in the free states of the North—but it continued to plague the consciousness of the descendants of the
slaves well into the twentieth century and is inseparable
from the rise of Black Nationalism and Pan-Africanism in
the United States, the islands of the Caribbean, and on the
continent of Africa.

Whatever the ulterior motives of the American Colonization
Society and other white-controlled colonization groups, it must
be recognized that these early efforts of white men, many of

them sincerely motivated by Christian missionary zeal, opened up for Black Americans the whole issue of emigration and forged a connecting link between emigration, Christianization and Black Nationalism. Rev. Samuel Hopkins, a former slaveowner of Newport, Rhode Island, first conceived of the idea of Negro emigration to Africa in 1759. Feeling that some "remuneration was due Africa" for the plunder of its people, Hopkins devised a plan to educate some freemen and to send them back to Africa to bring the blessings of Christian religion and civilization to their benighted brothers.[5] The American Colonization Society grew out of this plan and was to play a central role in the founding of Liberia. The A.C.S. was always a controversial organization among both Blacks and whites in the United States, but it cannot be doubted that the Society gave impetus and continuity to the idea that Black Americans had something to contribute to the awakening of Africa, and that Africa and not America was the natural homeland of Black people.

The presence of free Negroes in the United States presented both southern slaveholders and northern politicians with an irritating and anomalous situation. Theoretically, the natural increase of free Blacks threatened both white hegemony in the North and slavocracy in the South. In the North the specter of an inevitable Black franchise and competition for industrial jobs was combined with Anglo-Saxon race prejudice and antipathy for Black people. In the South the whites feared Black inundation and rebellion. There the very existence of a community of free Negroes, such as in Charleston or Richmond, reminded those who were still in bondage that slavery was not a natural and necessary condition for all Black people and, more importantly, the "uppity," querulous Black freeman represented a potential hotbed of conspiracy and insurrection. The problem of what to do with these people was, therefore, conveniently, if fraudulently, solved by the idea of African or West Indian colonization. Both those whites who favored slavery and those who were genuinely opposed to it found common cause in the proposal to remove a source of embarrassment and danger.

In the same year that the African Methodist Episcopal Church was organized in Philadelphia, a group of white people representing several states, with some of the most distinguished men in America among them, gathered in Washington, D.C., to organize the American Colonization Society. In an atmosphere charged with feelings of both guilt and noble aspiration, these white colonizationists plotted what many of them had come to believe was the ultimate solution of the American race problem. But either through stupidity or self-delusion, the manner in which the argument for African emigration was framed aroused more fear and resentment among northern Negroes than the support which had been anticipated. Leon F. Litwack writes concerning that tumultuous period:

> One month after the organization of the Colonization Society, approximately three thousand Negroes crowded into Philadelphia's Bethel Church to give their reply: the colonization scheme violated professed American principles, it sought to stigmatize the free Negro population, and it countenanced the perpetuation of human bondage and encouraged it by seeking to remove the free blacks. Under these circumstances, it deserved to be repudiated by all Negroes, who should, instead, reaffirm their determination never to part voluntarily from their enslaved brethren.[6]

It should be understood that Richard Allen and the Black Methodists who followed his leadership were not so enamored of the situation of Blacks in the North that they were unable to entertain any thoughts of renouncing American citizenship. The Convention of 1830, which was dominated by Allen and other Black churchmen, strongly recommended Black emigration to Upper Canada, and many who were opposed to the American Colonization Society, such as James Forten, a wealthy sailmaker and abolitionist of Philadelphia, were concerned about the future of Africa and privately of the opinion that the day would come when Blacks would have to separate themselves from their oppressors and return to their native land.[7] It was the arrogance of white men, their miscalculation of the self-esteem of free Blacks and their feeling of solidarity with the slaves, rather than an aversion to the idea of emigration and the Christianization of Africa that made Black leaders repudiate the American Colonization Society. It was the talk of Negro "inferiority" and "degradation," the obvious attempt by the white colonizationists to dodge the question of the immorality of slavery, and the too-enthusiastic participation of the slaveholders themselves in what purported to be a benevolent scheme for "the good" of the people they despised by continuing to hold their relatives and friends in chains, that turned the northern Blacks against the colonization proposal and ultimately disabused their abolitionist friends that such an idea could be made compatible with the emancipation effort.

The expulsory laws of Ohio in 1829 and the desirability of securing a place outside the United States for escaped slaves, infused the first Negro Convention with emigrationist sentiment. The Convention rejected the American Colonization Society because its leaders suspected its real motives, but Negro emigration to some part of the world that would be free from the curse of white racism was upheld. What those who attended the historic meeting, held at Mother Bethel A.M.E. Church in Philadelphia, resented was the coercive, highhanded methods of the white colonizationists. While they recognized the need of many Black people to be relocated "in a land where the laws and prejudices of society will have no effect in retarding their advancement to the summit of civil and religious improvement," they refused to be colonized "in any place which is not the object of our choice." In general, they also objected to emigrating to Liberia or to Haiti, "believing them only calculated to distract and divide the whole colored family."[8]

After the white abolitionists of the North were convinced that Black leadership opposed the Colonization Society, they abandoned the Society themselves and, misunderstanding as usual the real point at issue, they greatly escalated their own campaign against colonization and began to exercise considerable influence over Blacks who did not wish to appear to be betraying the grand cause of abolishing slavery by emigrating to Africa or the West Indies. There was, however, considerable ambivalence over the subject throughout the nineteenth century, and if northern Blacks had not been so trusting that the abolitionists could deliver what they promised and so squeamish about offending Garrison and their other white friends, it is likely that a modified form of emigrationism would have caught on in the North as it did in the South. Black churchmen could never quite divorce their desire to carry the gospel to their unfortunate brethren in the West Indies and Africa from a candid recognition of the intolerable conditions of Black life in America and the opportunities for a better life abroad. Despite their public opposition to the idea of running away from the challenges at home, the missionary implications of the offers held out by the American Colonization Society and other state and local colonization groups continued to intrigue them.

Transatlantic travel was expensive and difficult to arrange. No less so was the founding of a church and settlement once the emigrants from America had arrived at their destination. The newly independent Black churches which had become the focal point of Black community activity and organization had little means with which to implant Christian colonies in Africa or anywhere else. It is not surprising, therefore, that the Allenites, for all their criticism of the white-controlled colonization movement, could still justify its utilization as an agency for helping to relocate those among them who wanted to cut the umbilical cord and were constrained to answer the Macedonian call from Africa. With the obvious success of the English repatriation program for liberated and rescued slaves and West Indians, which eventuated in the establishment of Sierra Leone as a Crown Colony in 1808, and with the rising missionary fever in the A.C.S. as white churches and prominent clergymen took a more active role in it, the twin interests of Christian missions and overseas colonization oscillated between polarity and convergence in the minds of many Black church leaders. Although a majority continued to be skeptical of colonization, there was among Black Americans—particularly in the churches—enough interest in what may be called "missionary emigrationism" to keep the American Colonization Society alive and kicking well into the twentieth century.

Four years after the African Methodist Church was organized, one of its ablest ministers, Daniel Coker, went to Africa with the help of the A.C.S. as the first Black Methodist missionary.[9] Although he was not officially commissioned by the A.M.E. Church, the foreign-mission program of the denomination not having been established at the time, "he carried the unanimous consent and good will of his brethren."[10] Coker's destination was the island of Sherbro, a part of Sierra Leone, where the American Colonization Society planned to develop the first Black American settlement. Coker accompanied the first group of slaves to be expatriated by the Society and a group of freemen who, like himself, had the hope of finding greater freedom and opportunity in Africa. Before the ship landed at Campelar, the brilliant and controversial young minister had organized a church among the eighty-nine colonists aboard and was conducting worship services in accordance with the Discipline of the African Methodist Episcopal Church. Like the self-styled missionary John Kizzel, who preceded him to West Africa with another group of ex-slaves, Daniel Coker saw Negro colonization not only as a bid for independence and freedom for America's oppressed Blacks, but as a part of God's plan to bring the Christian faith to the land of his fathers through the ministry of the Black church.

Mills and Burgess, the two emissaries of the A.C.S., had been helped by Kizzel in 1817 to locate a site for the settlement, and in 1820 they accompanied Coker and the little group of pioneers. The choice proved to be an unfortunate one because of frequent inundation of the low-lying terrain. An epidemic soon broke out in the group, nearly wiping it out and taking the lives of the two agents. Coker suddenly found himself heir to the responsibilities of the two men and decided to lead the survivors back to Sierra Leone, where he later settled in Freetown and built a church. The resolute

spirit and commitment of the man may be gleaned from a remarkable letter he sent back to the Society:

> We have met trials; we are but a handful; our pro-
> visions are running low; we are in a strange heathen
> land; we have not heard from America, and know not
> whether provisions or people will be sent out; yet, thank
> the Lord, my confidence is strong in the veracity of his
> promises. Tell my brethren to come; fear not; this land is
> good; it only wants men to possess it.[11]

The attitude of the first Black Americans to colonize Africa
was unquestionably one of condescension and paternalism.
The Africans were regarded as a benighted race of men who
were in need of salvation and the superior virtues of American civilization. As unpalatable to Black Nationalists as such
unwarranted assumption may be today, this was the missionary spirit of the time, and Black and white churchmen shared
it alike. Daniel Coker and others who went to Africa believed
it was nothing less than God's grace that had brought the
Black church into an independent existence on American soil,
and that one of its great purposes was to return Africa's sons
to the land of their fathers to preach the gospel of Christ and
lift the souls of millions who languished in darkness. As
presumptuous as such an attitude may have been, it was,
nonetheless, motivated by an enthusiastic dedication to Christian service, by a profound compassion for Africa's plight, and
a willingness to take up the vocation of suffering for her redemption. In a letter from Campelar to a friend in Baltimore,
Coker eloquently expresses his deep tenderness and humanity
toward his African brethren and the faith he shared with
other Black Christians of the day that "Ethiopia would soon
stretch forth her hands unto God" and become one of the leading nations of the world.

> The millions in this land, are the thousands in Amer-
> ica, and the thousands unborn are deeply interested in
> it. Oh! my dears, what darkness has covered the minds
> of this people. None but those who come and see, can

judge. You would be astonished to see me travelling in the wilderness, guided by a little foot path, until, coming suddenly upon a little town of huts in the thickets; and there, to behold hundreds of men, women and children, naked, sitting on the ground or on mats, living on the natural productions of the earth, and as ignorant of God as the brutes that perish. You would see them coming round me, shaking hands, (but very different from our way of shaking hands) and gazing on me, and spreading a mat, and offering me of such food as they live upon. In a word, they are friendly and kind. Such is their conduct, that any one who loves souls would weep over them, and be willing to suffer and die with them. I can say, that my soul cleaves to Africa . . . I expect to give my life to bleeding, groaning, dark, benighted Africa. I expect to pass through much, if I should live. I should rejoice to see you in this land; it is a good land; it is a rich land, and I do believe it will be a great nation, and a powerful and worthy nation; but those who break the way will suffer much.[12]

Early American Negro missionary effort in Africa included the work of Rev. Lott Carey (1780–1828), a slave preacher of Richmond, Virginia, who took the second shipload of colonists from the United States to Liberia in 1821. Carey founded Baptist churches which were supported by the Baptists of Richmond. In 1815, Carey organized the pioneer African Missionary Society and raised seven hundred dollars for its work. Six years later he sailed for Liberia, arriving before the agent of the American Colonization Society. His gifts were soon recognized and he was made vice-governor and later served as governor during the absence of Governor Ashmun from the colony. The Blacks of Richmond, with whom he kept in close contact, were stirred by the prospects of missionary emigrationism, despite Carey's open criticism of the Colonization Society. Carey became for them the symbol of Afro-American involvement in Africa and the freedom and independence of Black missionary endeavor.

Benjamin Lundy, the Quaker pacifist who met and influenced the young William Lloyd Garrison to join the abolition movement in 1828, like Rev. Samuel Hopkins, had an early interest in missionary emigrationism. It was Lundy who encouraged Bishop Richard Allen to establish a branch of African Methodism in Haiti, where Lundy had started a colony of free Negroes from the United states.[13] In 1824, Haiti became the first official mission field of the A.M.E. Church. At the invitation of Haiti's President Jean Boyer, two thousand emigrants settled in the new Black republic. Many of the people in this group were members of Allen's own Bethel Church in Philadelphia. With the aid of Rev. Scipio Beans of the Baltimore Conference, they built St. Peter's Church at Port-au-Prince and selected Richard Robinson as their first pastor.[14]

By 1830, the Black Methodists had mission congregations at Port-au-Prince, Samana and Santo Domingo. Here again we have an indication of the missionary interest of the independent Black churches and the convergence of the spirit of missions with that of Black emigrationism in the nineteenth century. The spread of Africa Methodism throughout the Caribbean, and the consequences of this development for increasing reciprocal relations between Blacks in the West Indies and American Negroes, is a matter requiring careful research. But there can be little doubt that African Methodism and the work of the Black Baptist churches in America contributed to the spirit of Black pride and independence throughout the area.

In British territories such as Barbados and Jamaica, where the former Georgia slave, Rev. George Liele, founded the first Baptist church in Kingston in 1782, Black congregations became the seedbed of rebellion in the early nineteenth century by developing new forms of leadership among the slaves based upon church government. The leaders of the rebellions in Demerara in 1823 and Jamaica in 1831 were strongly supported by church people. In all likelihood, these Blacks were inspired by the report of African Methodist involvement in the Denmark Vesey revolt of 1822. The Akan slave, Kwame, who led the revolt in Demerara, was the First Deacon of

Bethel Chapel, and many of the participants in the 1823 uprising were members of the Chapel. The slave revolt in Jamaica was known as the Baptist War. Monica Schuler writes: "it is clear that in both Demerara and Jamaica, the slaves had detached the London Missionary Society and Baptist church organizations from missionary control, and used them as organizations of social protest."[15] The news of slave revolts and the role of Black Baptist and Methodist churchmen in instigating them encouraged Blacks on the mainland and in the West Indies to shake off their chains and to be mutually supportive of one another. Christian missions and Black emigrationism thus worked hand in hand to foment unrest and the spirit of independence throughout the Caribbean and in the southern region of the United States.

The planting of churches from the United States was widespread. Before the end of the nineteenth century, in addition to Haiti, A.M.E. missions had been established in Cuba, Jamaica, Antigua, the Virgin Islands, Tobago, Barbados and Trinidad. There were also mission points in the Bahamas and Bermuda. From about 1850, missionaries from the African Methodists labored at Paramaribo, Dutch Guiana, and at Georgetown, British Guiana.[16] When Marcus Garvey traveled throughout the Caribbean and Central America preaching the gospel of Black Nationalism and the "Back to Africa" movement, he found some of his most sympathetic audiences among Black Baptists and African Methodists whose families had emigrated from the United States or whose churches had been founded by Black American denominations which had been cultivating the spirit of independence and self-reliance for many years.

The early missionary movement of the Black denominations toward Africa and the West Indies is not to be regarded as an authentic expression of what we have come to know today as Black Nationalism. Even those efforts which were linked to emigration and sponsored by the American Colonization Society were not primarily political in nature or related to a self-conscious rejection of American values and civilization. It is true, of course, that some of the first Black preachers who took the gospel to foreign parts and encouraged others to follow had visions of a better life than was available to Black people anywhere in the United States. But their overarching concern was not the founding of a Black nation free of slavery, poverty and racism, but the inauguration of a great mission to heathen people who happened to be Black and among whom the African Methodist and Negro Baptist traditions could be expected to take root and flourish even as they were doing in America. After the Civil War a few men like Edward W. Blyden of the Presbyterian Church, Bishop Henry M. Turner of the A.M.E. Church, Bishop Theodore Holly of the Episcopal Church, and Bishop Lucius H. Holsey of the Colored Methodist Episcopals became strong advocates of Black separatism and attempted, with little success, to give impetus to a kind of religious Black Nationalism under American leadership in the Caribbean and Africa. Their efforts bore fruit in the early years of the twentieth century, but whatever success they enjoyed cannot be attributed to the support they received either from their respective denominations or from the Negro public in general.

The fact is that neither colonization nor overseas missions were very effectively maintained or promoted by the Black American churches. To have developed a strong and well-supported missionary program in Africa would have required considerably more funds than the struggling Black churches had available after taking care of the urgent needs at home. The white colonizationists, having committed a strategic error in their approach to the emigration issue, were never in a position financially or in terms of policy to generate much enthusiasm among Black churchmen for Liberian emigration or to demonstrate in Africa the kind of success in nation-building that might have encouraged greater response from the Black denominations. The fiasco of naïveté, broken promises and stranded emigrants destroyed any real possibility for a mammoth encampment of Black America at the doorstep of the colonization societies.[17] The white churches, for their part, had the money and should have had the vision to assist the development and expansion of Black missionary activity overseas as a genuine contribution to Black freedom and independence. But it apparently rarely occurred to white American Christians that what they hoped to do for Africa could have been done, and to better purpose for both Africans and Afro-Americans, by the Black churches of the United States. Torn with theological and sectional strife during most of the nineteenth century and having either segregated their Black constituencies or dismissed them to Black denominations, they studiously avoided giving anything more than paternalistic handouts to "orderly" Black churches at the parish level. For the most part, they ignored what the Black churches, as national denominations, were trying to do both in the United States and overseas.

The tragedy of the Black American missionary effort in the Caribbean and West Africa during the nineteenth century was its neglect by the churches themselves. The predominantly white denominations, which were relatively affluent and could have helped in the spirit of ecumenism and fraternal cooperation, looked the other way. The ambition of the Black denominations to maintain a healthy missionary enterprise outside the United States far exceeded their ability to do so. It was not so much that missionary emigrationism had no appeal to the free Negroes of the United States. By the time of the Civil War almost every Black leader of consequence either favored or was at least open to the idea of colonization in Africa or the West Indies, and Christian missions were regarded not only as the noblest, but the best method for African colonization.[18] It was rather that there was neither sufficient money nor personnel to demonstrate that missionary emigrationism was an appropriate form of Black churchmanship and that it could succeed. The work initiated by Daniel Coker, Lott Carey and others could not be adequately supported with missionaries and emigrants from the United States or provided with enough funds to develop its full potential without greater help than the white churches were prepared to give. The demands upon the nickel and dime collections in the Black churches were overwhelming. The normal requirements for building national denominations and strengthening home missions to care for the steadily mounting tide of Black folks moving northward and into the cities of the South drained off both the manpower and the monetary resources needed to continue the work that was so auspiciously begun by Black American preachers in West Africa.

At the New York Annual Conference of the A.M.E.s in 1853, Bishop Willis Nazrey, a great promoter of African missions, proudly reminded his brethren that their church had as much responsibility in Africa and the West Indies "as any other Christian Church upon the face of the globe." It took the practical-minded Bishop Daniel A. Payne, however, to remind the African Methodists of the formidable difficulties of establishing missions in foreign lands without money. The recognition of Black responsibility, he said, was no guarantee of the ability of Black people to perform it. Such was the sad but realistic acknowledgment of the impossibility of Black American churchmen of the time carrying on a program of foreign missions that even wealthy white denominations were having problems financing.[19]

The fact that most Black ministers and their denominations did little to foster the emigration fervor that developed prior to Emancipation does not mean, however, that religion played no significant role in the rise of Black Nationalism. It was, in fact, a Black theology of missionary emigrationism and racial destiny which evolved from the aggressive thrust of Black folk religion toward liberation and an African homeland. This inchoate, unofficial theology gradually took the initiative from the churches and laid the groundwork for Garvey, Padmore and others of the twentieth century. It was by no means unrelated to the contribution of Hezekiah Grice, the young man who started Allen thinking about colonization, Willis Nazrey and other churchmen who were basically orthodox in their understanding of the faith, but who were infused with great race pride and race consciousness. But the most eloquent expression in the antebellum period of this rudimental Black theology came from a man who was not a clergyman, but a prominent physician and journalist, Martin R. Delany. Although he "had rather be a Heathen *free-man,* than a Christian *slave,*" Delany was nevertheless a prominent churchman and a lay theologian of remarkable insight.

Martin R. Delany was born the son of free Negroes in Charleston, West Virginia, in 1812. His parents fled from persecution to Chambersburg, Pennsylvania, where he was educated until moving to Pittsburgh in 1831. There he began the study of medicine and commenced publication of *The Mystery,* later converted to a journal of the African Methodist Episcopal Church.[20] From 1847 to 1849 he joined Frederick Douglass in publishing the *North Star* in Rochester, and in 1849 he entered the Harvard Medical School. Although he opposed the American Colonization Society, Delany became a proponent of Black emigration and played a leading role in the Negro Convention movement, where he had close association with the prominent churchmen of the day. Delany's outstanding contribution to Black Nationalism was a book published in 1852, *The Condition, Elevation, Emigration, and Destiny of the Colored People of the United States, Politically Considered.* The book was sharply attacked by the white abolitionists for its nationalistic advocacy of colonization, and Delany, realizing that his opponents were also working for immediate emancipation, ordered that the sale be stopped, although he remained a theoretician of Black Nationalism and emigrationism until his death in 1885.[21]

Notwithstanding his nationalistic leanings and his belief that white Protestants were the cruelest oppressors of the Black race, Delany was an outspoken supporter of the missionary outreach of Christianity. He believed that Protestant missions were the most important gift of Europe and America to Africa and that they would eventually bring a "purer and higher civilization" to that continent, but he also believed that the missionaries should be "homogeneous in all the natural characteristics, claims, sentiments, and sympathies—the descendants of Africa."[22] That is to say, Black men. His problem with religion in the Black community was that the Black churches, imitating the pietism of nineteenth-century

Protestant evangelicalism, were giving Negroes the impression that the reason for their miserable condition was their immorality and that what was required for salvation was "being good."

This exaggerated moralism was never, in fact, central to Black folk religion, as several white missionaries to the slaves attested. Delany, for all his erudition and sophistication, was closer to the realism and practical wisdom of folk religion than he was to the churches. To him it was sheer nonsense and bad religion to believe that God would prosper white people, but had placed the Black race in the condition in which they found themselves "for not half the wickedness as that of the whites." He reasoned that the right use of religion required an understanding of its function and limitations as ordained by God himself. Delany thereby extrapolated a theological principle from Black folk religion that was not unknown to that American pragmatist and agnostic Benjamin Franklin— "God helps those who help themselves." Unlettered Black Christians have always believed that those words were found in the Bible and were the essence of the faith. Essentially, they have agreed with Delany that it is foolish for Blacks to try to gain equality and the power to elevate themselves by praying for it. The universe is governed by spiritual, moral and physical laws, each limited to effectiveness within its own sphere of operation. Hence, said Delany, a spiritual blessing is to be prayed for, a moral good sought by exercising one's sense of justice, and a physical end requires the use of might and muscle.[23]

Delany recognized the crucial significance of the Black church in lifting and ennobling Black people, but he faulted the church for teaching an excessive spiritualism which expected spiritual means to equip Blacks to compete with the white man in the moral and physical areas of life. God, said Delany, did not provide mystical solutions for the hard problems of Black power and Black destiny, nor did he expect Black Christians to accept white definitions of Christian reality when those definitions presumed white jurisdiction over the progress and destiny of the race. Thus, more than any person of his period, be anticipated and developed one of the major emphases of Black theology:

> We are no longer slaves, believing any interpretation that our oppressors may give the word of God, for the purpose of deluding us to the more easy subjugation; but freemen, comprising some of the first minds of intelligence and rudimental qualifications, in the country. What then is the remedy, for our degradation and oppression? This appears now to be the only remaining question—the means of successful elevation in this our native land? This depends entirely upon the application of the means of Elevation.[24]

The means of Elevation had to be in strict conformity with the laws governing politics and economics. Delany's rationalistic analysis of the situation led him to the conclusion that self-effort, "attainments," and finally, emigration were the only means relevant to the search for equality and social progress.

More than anyone else, Martin Delany helped to clarify in the 1850s the cultural vocation of the Black church, particularly its responsibility to assist in the redemption of Africa. He was a member of the African Civilization Society, a group founded in 1858 with the express purpose of bringing about "the civilization and christianization of Africa and of the descendants of African ancestors in any portion of the earth, wherever dispersed." In 1861 he was influential in reformulating the purpose of this Society to include the encouragement of selective emigration to Africa of persons "practically qualified and suited to promote the development of Christianity, morality, education, mechanical arts, agriculture, commerce and general improvement."[25]

During his lifetime Delany considered several possibilities for mass emigration of Blacks from the United States. At first he favored colonization in Central America or East Africa, but finally settled upon selective emigration to West Africa after leading an exploration of the Niger Valley in 1859. Henceforth, his life and labors were devoted to that objective.

Throughout his career he retained an explicit theology of racial redemption, which he shared with such distinguished churchmen as Bishop James T. Holly and Alexander Crummell. It was essentially an understanding of God as the liberator of oppressed Black people, who were being called by him out of the land of their captivity to a place which he had appointed for them and their posterity forever. This was a salient contribution of an elite group of Black churchmen of the antebellum period to the development of a theology which explicated the subtle and clandestine meaning of the illiterate preaching and many of the spirituals of the Black folk religious tradition. It never became the official theology of any major Black church, but had its propagators in both the Black and the predominantly white denominations. It was a theology of struggle against the powers of political and social evil which now supplanted and represented the wild and mysterious forces of nature that were once the objects of conjuration by the African witch doctors and the early plantation preachers who succeeded them. Its foundation was in the Biblical revelation of the justice of God, who "has put down the mighty from their seats and exalted them of low degree," and who gathered the scattered children of Israel under Nehemiah and helped them build the wall of Jerusalem "because the people had a mind to work" (Luke 1:52; Neh. 4:6). Martin R. Delany believed in such a God and was his prophet to America. His conviction that God had ordained greatness for the lowly Black race and that Black people could claim that destiny only by their own power and initiative, is sung with lyrical passion in his writings:

> The time has now fully arrived, when the colored race is called upon by all the ties of common humanity, and all the claims of consummate justice, to go forward and take their position, and do battle in the struggle now being made for the redemption of the world. Our cause is a just one; the greatest at present that elicits the attention of the world. For if there is a remedy; that remedy is now at hand. God himself as assuredly as he rules

the destinies of nations, and entereth measures into the "hearts of men," has presented these measures to us. Our race is to be redeemed; it is a great and glorious work, and we are the instrumentalities by which it is to be done. But we must go from among our oppressors; it can never be done by staying among them. God has, as certain as he has ever designed any thing, has designed this great portion of the New World, for us, the colored races; and as certain as we stubborn our heats and stiffen our necks against it, his protecting arm and fostering care will be withdrawn from us.[26]

By the time of the publication of his *Official Report of the Niger Valley Exploring Party* in 1861, Delany had shifted his sights from Nicaragua and New Grenada to West Africa. In Lagos he found a Black Christian community that strengthened his belief in the divine election of Black Americans for a special work in Africa for which an enlightened Black Christian church would be the vanguard. As he wrote as early as 1852:

"Princes shall come out of Egypt; Ethiopia shall soon stretch out her hands unto God." With the fullest reliance upon this blessed promise, I humbly go forward in—I may repeat—the grandest prospect for the regeneration of a people that ever was presented in the history of the world. The disease has long since been known; we have found and shall apply the remedy. I am indebted to Rev. H. H. Garnet, an eminent Black clergyman and scholar, for the construction, that "soon," in the Scriptural passage quoted, "has reference to the period ensuing *from the time of beginning*." With faith in the promise, and hope from this version, surely there is nothing to doubt or fear.[27]

The outbreak of the Civil War interrupted the execution of Delany's grandiose plans for Black emigration and the redemption of Africa. During the war his energies were given to the recruitment of Black soldiers, and he was commissioned a major in the medical corps of the Union Army. After the Civil War he worked for the Freemen's Bureau during the Reconstruction period. Although the war and the period immediately following revived his hopes that justice could be secured for Black people in the United States, those hopes were once again to be dashed to pieces on the hard realities of the post-Reconstruction period, which brought the Compromise of 1877 and the Supreme Court's repeal of the Civil Rights Act of 1775 only two years before his death in 1885.

Another great proponent of missionary emigrationism and the theology of Black liberation was Alexander Crummell, born in New York in 1819, who was a boyhood friend of the great Presbyterian minister Henry Highland Garnet. Refused matriculation at General Theological Seminary, the leading seminary of the Episcopal Church, Crummell subsequently studied for the priesthood in Boston and in 1844 was ordained in Philadelphia. Throughout his life he was a brilliant spokesman of Black pride and solidarity, and in his early years was an outstanding supporter of nationalism and colonization. In 1853 he went to Liberia as a missionary under the influence of supporters of the American Colonization Society even though, like Delany and others, he had been highly critical of the Society. On the way to Africa he resided briefly in England and received a degree from Queen's College, Cambridge, where he developed a penchant for Black scholarship and the elitism which adumbrated Du Bois' later theory of the "Talented Tenth." Crummell advanced the idea of the responsibility and leadership of Black intellectuals as the first president of the American Negro Academy, which he helped to organize shortly before his death in 1898.[28]

After spending twenty years in missionary and educational work in Liberia and Sierra Leone, Crummell returned to the United States, in 1873, somewhat less visionary about the possibilities of mass emigration. He became pastor of the fashionable St. Luke's Episcopal Church in Washington, D.C. and thereby had available a national pulpit for his controversial views regarding the advancement of the race. Like

Booker T. Washington, Crummell had little confidence in political agitation, although he continued to demand civil rights for Negroes. His major call was for Black self-help, industrial education and racial solidarity. He spoke out strongly for what he called "the Social Principle"—the principle of association which "binds men in unity and brotherhood, in races and churches and nations"—and without which no nation or people could hope to achieve greatness.[29]

As a minister of the gospel, Crummell's primary interest in Africa rested upon his belief that the message of Jesus Christ had to be preached in all the world, as the Lord himself commanded. African colonization, however objectionable its promotion by some whites may have been, was for him one of the means by which "God's beneficent providence" chooses to work for the propagation of the gospel among all people, and particularly among the heathen kinsfolk of the American Blacks. It was, moreover, through the Black man's efforts to bring Christianity and civilization to Africa (and also to South America and the West Indies) that he would be able to prove to the world that his "previous condition of servitude" and the color of his skin had no effect upon his capacity for racial progress and nobility. When, as he said, Black men question the responsibility they have for the destiny of Africa, they only reveal their lack of self-respect and racial pride. Liberia was the "land of their fathers," and the shame which many Black Americans felt because of their African origin was unworthy of men who were obliged to realize that America could never be their true home—that "*all* men hold some relation to the land of their fathers."

Alexander Crummell was one of the first Black theologians to question the *agape* doctrine of orthodox Christianity by expounding self-love as a Christian principle which the oppressed Black race must espouse if it is to cast off the chains of oppression and rise to equality with the white nations of the world. Black Americans should not emigrate to Africa, said Crummell, merely for philanthropic reasons, but for reasons of the natural desires and ambitions of men who have regard for themselves and for the acquisition of power to accomplish something worthy of a great people. Thus he wrote in 1860:

> I am referring to that sentiment of self-regard which prompts to noble exertions for support and superiority. I am aiming at that principle of SELF-LOVE which spurs men on to self-advantage and self-aggrandizement— a principle which, in its normal state and in its due degree, to use the words of Butler, "is as just and morally good as any affection whatever." In fine, I address myself to all that class of sentiments in the human heart which creates a thirst for wealth, position, honor and power.[30]

Such counsel from a clergyman was a telling blow to the pietistic religion of the northern missionaries and the subservient Black preachers who taught Negroes to humble themselves under the yoke of the meek and gentle Jesus while white men laid claim to the glory and riches of this world. Christianity for Crummell was a religion for tough-minded, enterprising men who developed their natural energies, skills and *"worldly* talent" to serve their own needs first precisely because they believed that only so could God, who had brought them out of bondage for that purpose, use them to serve the needs of others. Thus, early in his career, Crummell developed ideas pointing toward the "secularity" of the Christian faith and the institutionalization of the Black church as an agency in which secular and religious purposes coalesced. For Crummell the sacred and secular roles of the Church were united in the promotion of economic and social development through self-help and in the prosecution of a civilizing and humanizing mission to the world. This was, in fact, a further extension of the concepts around which the first "African Societies" were founded prior to the organization of the Black Methodist denominations and a theme which runs through the quasi-religious Black Nationalism of the twentieth century.

Crummell's criticism of the Black churches of his period related to their excessive piety and disinclination to take seriously the challenge of missionary emigrationism in Africa.

Throughout his life he had lingering doubts about the ability of Black Americans to shake off the psychological encumbrances of the experience of slavery and rise to the stature of the Christian manhood which for him characterized the essential quality of true religion.

But I say it deliberately, that the difficulties in the way of our brethren doing a goodly work for Africa, are more subjective than objective. *One of these hindrances is a want of missionary zeal.* This is a marked characteristic of *American* black Christians. I say *American,* for from all I hear, it does not characterize our West Indian brethren; and the infant church of Sierra Leone is already, in sixty years from its birth, a mother of missions. *This* is our radical defect. *Our* religion is not diffusive, but rather introversive. It does not flow out, but rather inward. As a people we like religion—we like religious services. Our people like to go to church, to prayer-meetings, to revivals. But we go to get enjoyment. We like to be made happy by sermons, singing, and pious talk. All this is indeed correct so far as it goes; but it is only *one* side of religion. It shows only that phase of piety which may be termed the *"piety of self-satisfaction."* But if we are true disciples, we should not only seek a comforting piety, but we should also exhibit an effective and expansive one. We should let our godliness exhale like the odor of flowers. We should live for the good of our kind, and strive for the salvation of the world.[31]

A younger contemporary of Martin R. Delany and Alexander Crummell was the West Indian propagandist of missionary emigrationism Edward Wilmot Blyden. Blyden was born in St. Thomas in 1832 and came to New York in 1847. Like Crummell he was discriminated against by a white institution of higher education, and the incident undoubtedly influenced his life as an ardent champion of Black Nationalism. In 1850 he went to Liberia as a missionary, and from 1881 to 1885 was president of Liberia College, where he distinguished himself as the leading Christian educator and scholar of West

Africa. Professor George Shepperson calls Blyden the "pioneer theorist of the 'African personality'" and the outstanding example of the "three-way process" which bound together the intellectual contributions of militant Black leaders of the United States, Africa and the West Indies in the incipient pan-Africanism of the late nineteenth and early twentieth centuries.[32]

Blyden was widely traveled and lectured to Black and white audiences at some of the leading colleges and seminaries of the world. Between 1872 and 1888 he visited the United States eleven times, speaking in behalf of Africa and the solidarity of Black people and maintaining contact with the leading Black intellectuals of his day. In the early years of this century he devoted himself to the study of the African past and, together with Carter G. Woodson and W. E. B. Du Bois, laid the foundation for the Negro history movement in the United States.

Perhaps even more than Delany and Crummell, Blyden's writings represent the most systematic development of the seminal Black theology which provided the intellectual substructure of Black Nationalism. He was convinced that Liberia was the place that God had chosen for the stolen race of Black Americans and West Indians and spent many years trying to persuade the leaders of the Black church in the United States to sponsor Liberian emigration. Like many others of his time, he had no special problem with what today would be regarded as a bid for Black American cultural and political imperialism in Africa. His understanding of the place of the Negro in the *heilsgeschichte* of Black religion justified such a position and made it the cornerstone of his theology. By means of their enforced sojourn with the Anglo-Saxon race in the New World, God had bequeathed to the Black American and West Indian a cultural superiority over the native African precisely for the purpose of lifting the veil of darkness from their less fortunate brethren and opening up the continent of Africa to modern political, economic and religious development. The native African, Blyden believed, were so tractable "that it would be a comparatively easy matter for civilized, Christianized Black men to secure all the land to Christian law, liberty and civilization." In this regard Blyden's thought was almost identical with that of Paul Cuffee and others who earlier had perceived the providential relationship between Christian missions and the economic and political development of Africa by Afro-Americans.

Today when organized Christianity is in such disrepute among Black intellectuals because of its complicity in American imperialism and the oppression of nonwhite peoples, it will be difficult for some to understand the esteem in which radical protagonists of Black Nationalism like Blyden, Delany, Crummell, Garnet, Russwurm and many others held the Christian faith. It is, however, important to observe that, for all its defects, Christianity provided what was for these men the only familiar and coherent body of moral and ethical principles available for organizing and disciplining a distressed and chaotic people. As practical men of affairs they would not permit a Black chauvinism to deny them the white man's religion as an instrumentality to serve their own purposes even as it had served so well the economic and political fortunes of the Anglo-Saxon civilization of which they were the most recent and favored benefactors. Blyden, much like Crummell, did not consider himself an orthodox Christian in the tradition of American evangelicalism. Theologically, he felt a greater congeniality with the most nonconforming luminaries of New England Protestantism—the Channings, Theodore Parkers and Emersons—all of whom were more dependable as friends of the Black man than the revival and camp-meeting preachers or the pious clerics of the main-line denominations.

In this, the powerful bishops and the prominent, though poorly educated preachers of the established Black churches did not follow Blyden and his theologically trained friends. As a consequence, the instruction of the Black seminaries and the Christian education offerings of the Black denominations remained hopelessly irrelevant to many of the postwar needs of the persecuted Black community. Blyden, nevertheless, like Martin Delany in Africa, continued to respect the white missionaries and ministers who, with all of the discrepancies of their Christianity, of which he constantly reminded them, were the means by which Black people were introduced to the Kingdom of God. "The lessons they have taught us," he wrote in an exceptional encomium on American Protestantism, "from their uplifting effect upon thousands of the race, we have no doubt, contain the elements of imperishable truth, and make their appeal to some deep and inextinguishable consciousness of the soul."[33] And it may be for this same reason that Black religion in America, throughout its history, has remained essentially Christian and has attracted, until well into the present century, the fidelity of some of the most militant and capable leaders of the race.

Blyden became one of the most distinguished Presbyterian ministers in the world, and his lectures in some of the great churches and theological seminaries in this country marked him as the outstanding Black theologian and theoretician of Black progress in the postwar period. His association with white people did not prevent him from being an unswerving proponent of "Africa for the Africans," and this motto, which he or Delany coined, meant "African Americans" as well as those born on the continent. Despite his appreciation of Christianity, he bitterly criticized the white Christian missions in Africa, particularly for their intolerance of the practice of polygyny, and he encouraged the secession of African Christians from them in order to form their own native churches.[34] His effort to this end in Nigeria helped to create the United Native African Church of Majola Agbebi, the Baptist Yoruba founder of the first independent church in West Africa.

Blyden's interest in the early movement for promoting the study of Black history grew out of his attempt to develop a Biblical and theological interpretation of the origin and destiny of Black people, and it was this interpretation which provided a Christian platform for his program of Black emigration to Africa. In a sermon entitled "The Call of Providence to the Descendants of Africa in America," he took his text from Deuteronomy 1:21:

Behold, the Lord thy God hath set the land before thee:
go up and possess it, as the Lord God of thy fathers
hath said unto thee; fear not, neither be discouraged.

In typical fashion Blyden proceeds to develop in this sermon
what became the central motif of Black religion in the latter
half of the nineteenth century as Black preachers sought to
pierce the mystery of the enslavement and suffering of God's
people at the hands of an unrighteous nation. What was the
meaning of the forcible removal of the millions of Africans
from their native land to these alien shores, and how could
positive religious meaning and good be found in their desperate
situation in America? These were the questions which haunted
men like Blyden. One of the ways he sought to resolve them
was by a doctrine of Providence. According to Blyden, God
speaks to men in two ways: by his word and by his Providence. In the case of the American Negro, God had spoken
providentially in the following ways:

> First, by suffering them to be brought here and placed
> in circumstances where they could receive a training
> fitting them for the work of civilizing and evangelizing
> the land whence they were torn, and by preserving
> them under the severest trials and afflictions. Secondly,
> by allowing them, notwithstanding all the services they
> have rendered to this country, to be treated as strangers
> and aliens, so as to cause them to have anguish of spirit,
> as was the case with the Jews in Egypt, and to make
> them long for some refuge from their social and civil
> deprivations. Thirdly, by bearing a portion of them across
> the tempestuous seas back to Africa, by preserving them
> through the process of acclimation, and by establishing
> them in the land, despite the attempts of misguided
> men to drive them away. Fourthly, by keeping their
> fatherland in reserve for them in their absence.[35]

Behind this understanding of the operation of divine providence with respect to Afro-Americans lay a distinctive interpretation of the origin of Black people in the history of

the races of mankind which Blyden and others made the basis for their attack upon the pretensions of white American theology. Many white Christians, fortified by distinguished churchmen of the South, claimed that the Black skin of the African was the dire consequence of the curse that Noah had invoked upon his youngest son, Ham, when the latter had the indiscretion to look upon the drunken nakedness of his father. Actually, the curse in Genesis 9 was upon Canaan, the son of Ham, who as a result, was to become "a servant of servants" to his brothers—Cush, Mizraim and Phut—and to his uncles, Shem and Japheth. Inasmuch as the curse was spoken to Ham and since the Hebrew word *ham* probably meant *hot* and *black,* and further, in view of the inclusion of the people of Ethiopia and Egypt among the descendants of Ham (Genesis 10:6–14), the accepted interpretation of the whites was that the Negro was of Hamitic origin and that his skin color was God's punishment because of the sin of Ham.

It was by means of this interpretation of the Genesis story of the origin of the races that Black converts to Christianity first learned of the cause of their misery. Even though many Black preachers discounted such a convenient and sacrosanct excuse for Black enslavement, many others were too convinced of the essential reliability of Scripture to dismiss it out of hand. Instead of flatly denying that the Bible was accurate about the Hamitic genealogy of the colored races, Blyden, Garnet and others sought rather to reverse the significance of the Genesis passage by emphasizing the previous fulfillment of Noah's malediction and the fact that the regenerating and elevating power of the gospel superseded the judgment of the Old Testament. In other instances they emphasized the positive, even superlative implications of the Hamitic genealogy.[36] In accordance with the latter interpretation, Blyden wrote in 1862:

> The all-conquering descendants of Japheth have gone
> to every clime, and have planted themselves on almost
> every shore. By means fair and unfair, they have spread

themselves . . . The Messiah—God manifest in the flesh— was of the tribe of Judah. He was born and dwelt in the tents of Shem. The promise to Ethiopia, or Ham, is like that to Shem, of a spiritual kind. It refers not to physical strength, not to large and extensive domains, not to foreign conquests, not to wide-spread dominions, but to the possession of spiritual qualities, to the elevation of the soul heavenward, to spiritual aspirations and divine communications. "Ethiopia shall stretch forth her hands unto God." Blessed, glorious promise! Our trust is not to be in chariots or horses, not in our own skill or power, but our help is to be in the name of the Lord. And surely, in reviewing our history as a people, whether we consider our preservation in the lands of our exile, or the preservation of our fatherland from invasion, we are compelled to exclaim: "Hitherto hath the Lord helped us!" Let us, then, fear not the influences of climate. Let us go forth (to Africa) stretching out our hand to God, and if it be as hot as Nebuchadnezzar's furnace, there will be one in the midst like unto the Son of God, counter- acting its deleterious influences.[37]

By searching the Scriptures and the works of historians of antiquity, Black preachers eloquently repudiated the argu- ment that God had forsaken Black people and looked toward Africa, which would experience a revival of ancient glories in the name of Jesus Christ. Martin Delany, for example, called upon the writings of the historians Herodotus and Diodorus Siculus to prove that the world was indebted to Egypt and Ethiopia for the gifts of an enlightened and progressive civilization.[38] There was no denying the fact that, according to the Biblical record, Egypt and Ethiopia were among the earliest and greatest of the ancient civiliza- tions. In Genesis 10:6–20, Mizraim and Cush, the sons of Ham, were said to be the progenitors of the people of Egypt and Ethiopia respectively. By 1860, however, white scholars—particularly the group which came to be known as the "American school" of anthropology—were loath to surrender ancient Egypt and Ethiopia to Black people and began to undermine the implications of what seemed so obvious in the Bible and ancient history about the origin of the Africans.[39] White Biblical scholars joined the counterattack by insisting that the Hamites were a white race. But the abolitionists persisted in the other point of view. "The ancient Egyptians," declared Frederick Douglass, "were not white people, but were undoubtedly, just about as dark in complexion as many in this country who are considered Negroes." William Wells Brown, the Black antislavery lecturer and friend of Douglass, contended in 1862: "I claim that the Blacks are the legitimate descendants of the Egyptians." Other spokesmen pointed to the fact that the Egyptians called their country *Kemet*, or "the black land." Similarly, they recalled Solomon's beautiful Black Egyptian wife, immortalized in the Songs of Solomon 1:5–6, and the clear implication of Jeremiah 13:23: "Can the Ethiopian change his skin, or the leopard his spots?"[40]

Thus the Black abolitionist preachers of the nineteenth century, undaunted by the ethnology of the anthropologist Louis Agassiz of Harvard and the testimony of many religious books and pamphlets on Negro inferiority, stubbornly relied upon what has been an ineradicable characteristic of Black religion in America—an interpretation of Scripture based upon the perceptions and experience of the race. They identified themselves with the Canaanites, who built great cities across the Jordan and resisted the invading Israelites for centuries; with the Carthaginians, who produced Hamilcar and Hannibal and were related to the descendants of the Canaanites; with Nimrod, the great Cushite hunter and warrior whose might founded and conquered cities from Babel to Nineveh; but pre-eminently, they identified Black people with Egypt and Ethiopia, the two surpassing African monarchies which had been the incubators of so much of Western culture and civilization. The great prophecy of Psalms 68:31 became the earnest of the ultimate fulfillment of the Black man's spiritual yearning. It is impossible to say how many sermons from this text were preached from Black pulpits during the nineteenth century, but we know that Richard Allen, Lott Carey, Henry Highland Garnet, Alexander Crummell, Edward W. Blyden, James T. Holly and Bishop Henry M. Turner were all eloquent expositors of Psalm 68:31 and made it the cornerstone for missionary emigrationism in the Black church both in the United States and in Africa. In his own commentary on this crucial text, Bishop Hood wrote in 1895:

> But the promise is that princes shall come out of Egypt, and that Ethiopia shall soon stretch forth her hands unto God. Whatever shall become of the two younger sons of Ham, this promise assures us that the two elder sons shall cast aside idolatry and return unto the Lord. That this prophecy is now in the course of fulfillment the Negro Church stands forth as unquestionable evidence. It is the streak of morning light which betokens the coming day. It is the morning star which precedes the rising sun. It is the harbinger of the rising glory of the sons of Ham. It is the first fruit of the countless millions of that race who shall be found in the army with banners in the millennial glory of the Christian Church.[41]

Thus did the Black church in the United States come to symbolize, at the turn of the century, the ark of safety for the regenerate children of Ham—the "old ship of Zion" which would ride out the storms and perils of oppression and deliver the children of Africa to the Ararat of racial redemption. The mysterious purpose of God in making the African Black and subjecting him to the subjugation and persecution of the white race was, after all, unfathomable. Some, like Bishop Hood, reasoned that it was because of the idolatry which had to be stamped out under the feet of Christ by the present generation. Others, like Delany and Blyden, wondered if God had not meant to toughen the Black man for some great task in behalf of all humanity. Still others, like T. Thomas Fortune, the militant editor of the *New York Age*, held that the theory that God had brought Blacks to America in chains in order to evangelize Africa at a later time was "so much religious nonsense boiled down to a sycophantic platitude."

But the problem of the divine intention, which nagged Black preachers for generations, was never solved to the satisfaction of anyone. Actually, it was transcended by a metaphorical comparison of Black Americans with the liberated children of Israel, an identification with the crucial significance of Africa in the history of the Judeo-Christian religion, and by the belief that God had promised something better for those who trusted in him—that the despoiled and despised people of Africa who had been stolen from their Fatherland had also to be delivered from darkness by the light that shone in the face of Jesus Christ. Black theology, as it developed in this period, was neither superficial nor parochial. It taught that the descendants of the slaves were destined to be delivered not only from the bondage to sin, but from prejudice and oppression to become the agents by which the millions of Black brothers and sisters who remained in Africa would also be liberated.

The secular emigrationists who later articulated their aspirations in political rather than theological terminology, can never be dissociated from this basically religious interpretation of the nature and destiny of the Black race. They shared it even when, like Garvey, they were most critical of the Black church for failing to give the leadership needed to break the Black community away from its obsequious adjustment to white oppression. The Black nationalism which followed the disillusionment over Reconstruction and appealed to the Southern Blacks who poured into the cities after the First World War was rooted in an ethos of Blackness which, in large measure, had been created by the Black destiny motif in Black religion. That motif had, to some extent, been betrayed, but it had never been totally eliminated from the Black church. In fact, it was fostered and nurtured by the Church throughout the nineteenth century, and in the present time it continues to be the deep undercurrent of revolutionary Black Christianity.

It was Henry McNeal Turner, the vociferous and controversial bishop of the African Methodist Episcopal Church, who was the most radical and consistent exponent of this point of view in the closing years of the last century. More than any other single individual, Bishop Turner not only made a Black theology of liberation central to his preaching and writing, but also helped to implant the spirit of revolutionary religion in the independent churches of Africa which took up the struggle against colonialism and racism. Turner was born free in South Carolina in 1834. He worked for a time as a laborer on a cotton plantation, and later as a porter in a law office where the young clerks, recognizing his intelligence, taught him to read and write. In 1854 he was ordained by the Methodist Church and traveled throughout the South. In 1858 he happened upon an African Methodist Episcopal church in New Orleans and decided to take training in Baltimore to become an A.M.E. pastor.

During his stay in Baltimore before the Civil War, Turner became convinced that white America would never give justice to the Negro and that emigration was the only sure answer to the race problem. In 1862 he heard an address by Alexander Crummell, and from that day the mission of the Black church in Africa and African repatriation of the American Negro became the great *cause célèbre* of his life. His intense interest in Africa did not, however, preclude his enthusiastic involvement in the war, first as an agitator for the use of Black troops, and later as a chaplain in the Union Army. After the war he went into Reconstruction politics as a Republican party organizer in Georgia. Turner built the mass base in Georgia, which he needed as a springboard for his ambitions within the A.M.E. Church. Like many other Black preachers, he astutely mixed his religion and his politics to the advantage of both himself and the Black community. By 1876 he had attained the powerful position of manager of the A.M.E. book concern, and his sermons and essays received national notoriety. He was, without question, the leading champion of the southern wing of the denomination and enjoyed a tremendous following among the disillusioned and restless Black Methodists of the region, many of whom became caught up in the African emigration movement. In 1880, with this support, Turner was elected a bishop of the

A.M.E. Church over the opposition of conservative northern churchmen, who resented his brazenly unpatriotic attitude toward the United States and sharply disagreed with his missionary emigrationism.[42]

Henry M. Turner was, perhaps, the first to raise seriously the issue of reparations for the years of Negro slavery, which he regarded as necessary for financing mass emigration to Africa. In an article entitled, "The Negro Has Not Sense Enough," which appeared in his *Voice of Missions* in 1900, he wrote:

> We have worked, enriched the country and helped give it a standing among the powers of the earth, and when we are denied our civil and political rights, the fool Negro who has no more sense than a jackass, yet he wants to be a leader, ridicules the idea of asking for a hundred million of dollars to go home, for Africa is our home, and is the one place that offers us manhood and freedom, though we are the subjects of nations that have claimed a part of Africa by conquest. A hundred million of dollars can be obtained if we, as a race, would ask for it. The way we figure it out, this country owes us forty billions of dollars, and we are afraid to ask for a hundred million.[43]

Turner had little respect or affection for America, although (or because) he served as a token Negro in several positions for the United States Government. "In this country," he wrote, "white represents God, and black the devil, but little thought is given to the Black man's future." He did not believe that every Black person would or should emigrate to Africa. What he pleaded for was "a highway made across the Atlantic" upon which regular social and economic intercourse between Black America and Africa could be carried on and self-reliant and energetic Black men could be permanently settled in Africa if they chose to do so.[44] He believed that the Black man needed a place where he could demonstrate his ability to build and govern a nation—a theater in which Black young men and women could express the gifts of the manhood and womanhood denied to them in the land of their birth. As few as a half-million Christian Blacks, he said, could build a new nation in Africa. But he was stringently discriminatory about the kind of people who would be up to the task. Only young people of courage, pride, ambition and resourcefulness would be of any use to themselves or to Africa.[45]

Although he was consummately a politician, Turner was also a theologian of Black liberation. It was God, he said, who permitted the Black man to be brought to America in order to be equipped for a great missionary task in Africa. In this opinion he followed the position that had been popularized by Crummell and Blyden and espoused by his South Carolina contemporary, A.M.E. Bishop R. H. Cain. But in the pages of the *Christian Recorder* and the *Voice of Missions,* powerful mouthpieces for the dissemination of his ideas throughout African Methodism, Turner made it clear that the American white man had been disobedient to God's command by not receiving the Negro as a brother, sharing with him the riches of America and helping him to return to his fatherland with the education and financial resources necessary for the mission of the church—the building of a Black nation free from imperialistic exploitation by the European nations which were then dividing up the continent among themselves. He expressed his most radical theological views in the *Voice of Missions* between 1893 and 1900, when mounting opposition from within the church removed him as its editor, and in an independent publication called, significantly enough, *The Voice of the People,* which he edited between 1901 and 1907.

Turner's theology was the culmination of almost a hundred years of Black theological reflection about the origin, destiny and responsibility of Black people to demand their God-given rights in the United States and, at the same time, to bring freedom and the Christian faith to their African brethren. By 1898 he believed that Black religion was essentially a protest movement against the disobedient white church, which had reduced Blacks to obsequious believers in their own spiritual inferiority and the right of the white man to dictate the terms of religious faith. When an "Observor" in a letter to the

Voice of Missions offered the opinion that Turner must be "becoming demented" to teach that "God is a Negro," Bishop Turner replied that:

> We have as much right biblically and otherwise to believe that God is a Negro, as you buckra or white people have to believe that God is a fine looking, symmetrical and ornamented white man. For the bulk of you and all the fool Negroes of the country believe that God is white-skinned, blue-eyed, straight-haired, projecting nosed, compressed lipped and finely robed *white* gentleman, sitting **upon** a throne somewhere in the heavens. Every race of people since time began who have attempted to describe their God by words, or by paintings, or by carvings, or by any other form or figure, have conveyed the idea that the God who made them and shaped their destinies was symbolized in themselves, and why should not the Negro believe that he resembles God as much so as other people? . . . Yet we are no stickler as to God's color anyway, but if He has any we would prefer to believe that it is nearer symbolized in the blue sky above us and the blue water of the seas and oceans; but we certainly protest against God being white *at all;* abstract as this theme must forever remain while we are in the flesh. This is one of the reasons we favor African emigration, or Negro naturalization, wherever we can find a domain, for, as long as we remain among the whites the Negro will believe that the devil is black and that he (the Negro) favors the devil, and that God is white and that he (the Negro) bears no resemblance to Him, and the effect of such a sentiment is contemptuous and degrading, and one-half of the Negro race will be trying to get white and the other half will spend their days in trying to be white men's scullions in order to please the whites.[46]

Bishop Turner's first visit to Africa took place in 1891 under the authorization of the Council of Bishops of the A.M.E. Church. Accompanied by Rev. J. R. Geda, the Bishop received an enthusiastic reception in Freetown, Sierra Leone, where he organized the first annual Conference on the African continent, with a lay membership of 405 tribesmen. Enraptured by this highly successful first encounter with the land and people who had for many years been the object of his yearning, he went on triumphantly to Liberia, where, following a brief visit with the leading officials in Monrovia, he sailed up the St. Paul River for Muhlenberg and there convened the Liberian Annual Conference on November 23, 1891.[47] Turner's letters back to the *Christian Recorder*, later printed together as a pamphlet, were full of glowing reports of the stability and prosperity of the places he visited, the accomplishments of the Black immigrants from America, and the myriad opportunities in West Africa for those who would follow them. "I get mad and sick," he wrote, "when I look at the possibilities God has placed within our reach, and to think that we are such block-heads we cannot see and use them." With the economic and social problems Liberia was experiencing as the influence and resources of the American Colonization Society declined toward the end of the century, and with adverse publicity about the Negro emigrants being bandied about by his opponents, Turner's visit to Africa was a strategic contribution to the revival of missionary emigrationism within the A.M.E. Church, and his exaggerated descriptions of what he found were calculated to make the most of it.

Bishop Turner, even more determined to open up Africa and to cement ties between African Christians and the A.M.E. Church, returned to the continent in March 1898 on an episcopal visit which was to have far-reaching implications for African-Afro-American fraternalism and the development of African nationalism through the independent church movement. This time his travels took him to South Africa, where, amid great celebration, he held conferences, organized churches, and ordained native ministers, charging them to dedicate their lives to a Black church that stood for God, freedom and independence from the control of white people.[48]

The stage for this development had been set prior to 1893,

when a group of singers, brought to the United States from South Africa, included a Basuto girl, Charlotte Manye, whose uncle was Rev. Mangena M. Mokone, a Wesleyan Methodist minister who became disaffected with segregation in the South African mission and withdrew in 1892 to form the Ethiopian Church in Pretoria. When the singing group became stranded between engagements in the United States, Rev. Reverdy C. Ransom, an A.M.E. minister in Ohio who was later to become a prominent bishop, arranged to have them go to Wilberforce University, where Miss Manye graduated with honors before returning to her home. Through her letters to her uncle in Pretoria, Charlotte Manye drew the attention of Makone to the existence of a church "owned and operated" by Black Americans—the African Methodist Episcopal Church. The Africans requested further information from Bishop Turner, and after studying the Discipline, the Hymnal and other books concerning the A.M.E. Church, decided to unite with the denomination in the United States. Union was consummated by Turner at the Allen Temple Church in Atlanta on June 19, 1896. Rev. James M. Dwane, one of the Ethiopian Church's emissaries to the General Conference, was appointed General Superintendent in South Africa. Although Dwane later withdrew from the A.M.E. Church over the failure of the denomination to provide funds for a school and dissatisfaction with the title of General Superintendent, he never gave up his belief in the unity of the Black church and became a powerful leader of the separatist movement throughout Southern and East Africa as well as in the Sudan, Egypt and Ethiopia.[49]

The Ethiopian Church was preceded by the separatist Tembu National Church, which was founded by Rev. Nehemiah Tile in 1884. Tile was accused by the white Wesleyans of "taking part in political matters and stirring up feelings of hositility against magistrates in Tembuland (South Africa). The Ethiopians followed in this rebellious tradition and took their name from the interpretation of Psalm 68:31 as referring to the African race. Originally it was a schismatic movement within the white-led mission churches and sought to bring together Black Christians across tribal and national lines into one independent African Church. It had, from the beginning, an implicit political appeal based upon a growing national consciousness among the segregated and discriminated African churchmen—especially in the industrialized areas of South Africa. Its anti-white bias soon aroused the opposition of the colonial governments as well as the embarrassment of white missionaries, who began losing hundreds of their converts to the new movement. James M. Dwane, who by 1896 had successfully challenged Mokone's leadership to become, in effect, the bishop of the Ethiopians, told the American Black Methodists in Atlanta that "the Africans would never allow the white man to ride roughshod over their country. Africans were rapidly imbibing civilized habits and would soon be able to run great civilized governments. Then they would say to the European nations, 'Hands off!' "[50]

Nothing could have pleased Bishop Turner more, and he devoted his visit in 1898 and subsequent contacts with Africa to the welding together of this potentially powerful native movement and his own nationalistic aspirations for the A.M.E. Church. The Ethiopians, on their part, made remarkable gains under the impact of the combined influence of Dwane and Turner. In 1896 the membership was reported to be 2800. On June 17, 1898, Turner reported a membership of 10,800, and after he reached home word was received that it had grown by another 1200. The total figure received by the Board was 12,000 members in a church extending widely in Cape Colony, the Orange Free State and the Transvaal.

Turner's efforts in behalf of Africa were generally supported by the A.M.E. Church in the 1890s. Already in 1892, the bishops of the church, responding to the growing feeling among Negroes of kinship with the Africans, had declared:

Africa is the largest and most important of the fields that lie before us. First, because of the number of persons involved in the work; second, on account of the relationship that exists between our race and the inhabitants of the Dark Continent; third, because our church is better adapted to the redemption of Africa than any other organization among the darker races for the moral and religious training of the people . . .

Thereupon followed nineteen specific items to be undertaken by the A.M.E. Church with respect to mission. Item sixteen called for the formation of an organization that would bring unity among the Black people of North, Central and South America, and would promote their common moral and spiritual uplift. The statement continued:

> And then pursuing our onward march for the Dark Continent, we will speak to more than 200 million of men and women, bone of our bone, and flesh of our flesh, and say to them, "Arise and shine, for the light of civilization is waiting for thee."[51]

The affiliation of the Ethiopian Church with the A.M.E. Church was the first significant achievement of this policy. The key role of Dwane was recognized by Turner, who created for him the office of Vicar-Bishop. Although the House of Bishops supported this move, Dwane ran into difficulty with Bishop W. J. Gaines, who raised objection to his holding the title when he was introduced to the several annual conferences he itinerated in 1898. Dwane's disappointment over the objections raised about his position and the failure of the A.M.E. Church to send the $10,000 he believed had been promised for Queenstown College, led him to schism. In 1899 he succeeded in leading about thirty of the Ethiopian ministers out of the A.M.E. Church and organized the Order of Ethiopia, which he placed under the jurisdiction of the Anglicans. Rev. Julius Gordon, Rector of the Queenstown Church, explained the doctrine of apostolic succession to Dwane and told him that the A.M.E. Church could not possibly pass on valid episcopal orders. Ironically, he never became an Anglican bishop, and even his appointment as Provincial was subsequently withdrawn.

The emergence of revolutionary church movements in Africa as a result of the inspiration of Black Christians in America was out of all proportion to colonialist expectations. One group which appeared in Natal in the 1890s was the African Christian Union, which listed some of its officers as residing in America. In a twenty-one-point Manifesto the A.C.U. announced as one of its intentions "To solicit funds [from Europeans] to restore Africans [in America] to their fatherland . . . and to pursue steadily and unswervingly the policy of AFRICA FOR THE AFRICANS, and look for and hasten by prayer and united effort, the forming of the AFRICAN CHRISTIAN NATION by God's power and in his own time and way."[52]

Shepperson and Price point out that similar developments were taking place in various Black communities in the United States. They report, for example, that in Richmond, Virginia, in addition to the Negro Baptists, there were "a host of infinitely less orthodox sects, with their prophets and messiahs, which flourished in the atmosphere of open-air, river baptisms, with their associations of John and the Jordan."[53] Actually, many members of the National Baptist Convention (organized in 1895), such as Rev. Lewis G. Jordan and Rev. Charles S. Morris, were themselves very much at home in this chiliastic atmosphere. They were ardent educators of young Black revolutionaries, and the Black church schools of the time, especially those in the South, "taught doctrines and inculcated attitudes which some call politely 'racial radicalism,' and others, more bluntly, 'sedition.' In this they anticipated the later trend of independent native schools in Africa."[54]

The influence of American Blacks on nationalism among African Christians at the turn of the century is best illustrated by the career of Rev. John Chilembwe of Nyasaland, who returned to Africa with Charles S. Morris, after studying in the United States, to lead his people in the Nyasaland Rebellion of 1915. Chilembwe at first came under the influence of a remarkable Australian missionary, Joseph Booth, who visited Negro Baptist churches in the United States for three months in 1895. During this period he evidently completed a book, *Africa for the Africans*, which was published in 1897 by the

Morgan College Press in Baltimore. It was during this period also that Booth made contact with a pre-Garveyite group in Washington, D.C. and wrote his daughter on April 9, 1897: "There are many signs that a great work will spring from this side of the ocean also. I am lecturing on 'Africa for the Africans.' "⁵⁵

Young Chilembwe, whom Booth had met at Chiradzulu (British Central Africa) and had introduced to his ideas, accompanied him on this eventful visit to the United States. Both men readily perceived the commonality between the oppression Blacks were suffering in Africa and the situation of Black people in America. Moreover, they were well briefed by the Black preachers they met and talked with in both the North and the South. In Richmond, Booth and Chilembwe were even attacked by a mob of young toughs for walking together in the streets and because they lived together for a time in the Negro section of the city.

Chilembwe later attended the Virginia Theological Seminary and College at Lynchburg, Virginia. There he met and was inspired by many leading Black Baptist preachers like Dr. Lewis G. Jordan, Secretary of the National Baptist Convention, which financed Chilembwe's work in Nyasaland for fifteen years, and Dr. Gregory W. Hayes. Radical religious ideas were rampant at the school in those years, and Chilembwe transported them back to Africa, where he subsequently organized an independent Baptist denomination which became increasingly hostile to the incursion of Europeans into the Nyasaland Protectorate. On Saturday evening, January 23, 1915, reminiscent of Nat Turner's insurrection, Chilembwe led a revolt in which three Europeans were killed and two wounded. The uprising was overwhelmed in ten days by the settlers, and Chilembwe was killed as he tried to escape across the border into Portuguese territory.

The religious resistance to white rule started building up in South Africa, the Belgian Congo, Nyasaland, French Equatorial Africa, Kenya and West Africa in the 1880s and continued through the first half of the twentieth century. The dramatic defeat of the Italians by the Abyssinians at Aduwa in

1896, which greatly emboldened the Ethiopianists, segregation and discrimination in the mission churches, the increasing pressure of the white settlers on African tribal lands and traditional ways of life, and the influence of the Black churches of the United States—all conspired to unleash a torrent of anti-white agitation and schismatic activity among the African Christians.

In South Africa, Ethiopian preachers were involved in the Zulu uprisings of 1906. In the Cameroons serious anti-European agitation was led by a rebellious Baptist preacher named Lotin Same. In the Congo, following the First World War, African separatists called for political emancipation and raised the leaders, Simon Kimbangu and Andre Matswa, to the level of Black gods. In 1909, John Msikinya, a dismissed African Methodist preacher, visited the United States and returned to South Africa as Bishop of The Church of God and the Saints of Christ, an American Negro denomination. Msikinya died in 1918, and his second-in-command, Enoch Mgyima, split the church and organized a new sect called the Israelites, which rejected the New Testament, celebrated the Jewish Sabbath, and saw themselves as followers of the patriarchs of Israel who had been delivered by God from foreign oppression. In May 1921, the Government sent police and militia to destroy their sacred village, Bullhoek, near Queenstown in the Ciskei, and a massacre occurred when the Israelites attacked with swords and spears. One hundred and sixty-three Israelites were killed and one hundred twenty-nine wounded. The incident was widely publicized and worldwide attention was focused on the racism in South Africa and the repressive policies of the Smuts government.[56]

In the Transkei another prophet, named Wellington Butelezi, who said he came from America, organized a cargo cult and told his followers that all Americans were Black people and that they would soon be coming to liberate their brother Africans and put an end to white rule. He promised that the Americans would arrive in airplanes, and when they came "the Europeans would be driven into the sea and the Bantu would not have to pay poll taxes anymore."[57] In Kenya, between June 1921 and April 1922, Harry Thuku, leader of the Young Kikuyu Association, organized to protest against the reduction of native wages, rising taxation and the seizure of ancestral lands by the white settlers. Although Thuku was not an ordained minister, he had strong religious motivation and, making the missionaries the target of his attack, gathered many lapsed Christians into the movement. His followers were reminded:

> . . . how that our God brought the Children of Israel out of the house of bondage of King Pharaoh . . . and to Him let us pray again, for He is our God. And also let us have faith since in the eyes of God there is no distinction of white or Black. All are sons of Adam, and alike before Him, Jehovah our Living God . . . Thou Lord Jehovah, our God, it is Thou who hast set apart to be our Master and Guide Harry Thuku; may he be chief of us all.[58]

According to a study by Joseph S. Coleman, the work of Blyden and other Black American clergymen in Nigeria is reflected in the political disorder which broke out among the sectarian groups they had visited after 1899. In the Delta region, for example, a movement began about 1914, led by a Nigerian who called himself the Second Elijah. It was essentially an ascetic Christian movement, but became openly anti-European when its leader was convicted of sedition. Another movement which sought to combine Christianity with the traditional Yoruba religion was called "Orunlaism." Its prophet, not unlike the leaders of American Negro cults in the ghettos after the First World War, called upon his people to:

> Scrap the imported religions . . . [There can be no] political emancipation without spiritual emancipation . . . Paint God as an African . . . the angels as Africans . . . the Devil, by all means, in any color than an African . . . and thou shalt be saved.[59]

The predominantly white churches of the United States and Europe—particularly the Anglican Church in the Cape

Colony—were not entirely without some salutary effect on the growth of African political consciousness. Their influence was mainly through the mission schools. In South Africa the missionaries at first fought against the enslavement of the aboriginal population, but gradually yielded to the application of the color bar in the churches under the pressure of the white colonists. More than any other denomination, the practice of the Anglican Church did make some contribution toward African freedom and opposition to the prevailing color prejudice. Both John Tengo Jabavu and Rev. Walter Rubusana, the two outstanding Black political leaders in South Africa, were educated in white mission schools and received guarded approbation from liberal white churchmen. Rubusana, ordained by the London Missionary Society in 1884, received a degree from a Black college in the United States and went back to South Africa infected with Black nationalist sentiments for which the moderate Jabavu had no sympathy.

Thus a socioreligious atmosphere favorable to revolutionary change, or the *Zeitgeist* of sub-Sahara Africa, can be attributed to a combination of factors, among which must be included the teaching of Christianity by white missionaries, some of whom—like the radical Baptist Joseph Booth and the American-based Watchtower Bible and Tract Society—introduced highly inflammatory elements into African religiosity which were freighted with Western ideas of political freedom and economic justice in the vesture of radical evangelicalism and apocalypticism.[60] As yet almost no research has been done on the effect of American missions on the development of independent churches and nationalism in Africa, but there is scattered evidence that the Americans were more sensitive to the injustices of the colonial regimes than were some of the European missionaries. The American mission schools and churches were, of course, less directly related to the colonial authorities, with whom missionaries from Europe were involved by national ties. Moreover, in some instances the American missions included highly competent Black personnel from the United States.

In 1909, ten American denominations and mission boards

united in an attempt to get the United States Government to use its diplomatic channels to support Rev. William M. Morrison, white, and Rev. William Henry Sheppard, a Black missionary, in a libel trial brought against them by the Belgian Government's *Compagnie du Kasai* in the Congo. Sheppard and Morrison, representatives of the Board of World Missions of the Presbyterian Church in the United States, for several years had supported the cause of social justice in the Belgian Congo and had incurred the wrath of Leopold's economic and colonial authorities by protesting the brutalization of the rubber workers in the Kasai region.[61] To these crusading missionaries must go much of the credit for the amelioration of conditions in the Kasai. Their trial and vindication were widely discussed in the United States and helped to make more Americans aware of the requirements of preaching the gospel in Africa. William H. Sheppard was in great demand as a speaker in Black churches, and many American Blacks first learned of Africa and the struggle for freedom there from his lectures and sermons.

The major evidence of the American contribution to the African independent churches and the rise of Black nationalism points, of course, to the influence of the Black Baptist, Methodist and Pentecostal churches, which introduced to the converts of white-controlled missions in Southern, Central and West Africa, the free spirit, prophetism and passion for liberation which were fundamental characteristics of Black religiosity in the United States and the Caribbean. Towering above all was the figure of Bishop Henry M. Turner, who inspired Mokone and Dwane and implanted the African Methodist Episcopal Church, with its rich heritage from the days of Richard Allen and Daniel Coker, among thousands of questing African tribesmen from Monrovia to Cape Town. Turner was more political than either Crummell or Blyden and, with perhaps the exception of Marcus Garvey, had a more profound and lasting influence on Africa than any other Black man from America. Shepperson and Price, in their authoritative work on John Chilembwe, appreciatively summarize the place of Turner and other Black American preachers in the movement of revolutionary Black religion in Africa:

Turner was a man full of the concept of the "manifest destiny" of coloured Americans to redeem their unhappy brethren in Africa. After the mid-1890's, American Negroes of like persuasion were to have a growing influence in South Africa and the regions to which it was allied. They added a new nuance to the concept of Ethiopianism, and for many whites in South and Central Africa their schools and colleges in the United States became nests of agitators, American or African Negro, who brought growing elements of political consciousness of a rebellious nature to the African separatist churches, from which, through the influence of the Negro minister, they spread out amongst the masses of the native people who only wanted inspiration and organization to raise them anew against their white masters.[62]

The nationalistic aspect of Black religion in America, Africa and the Caribbean has been greatly neglected. E. U. Essien-Udom is one of the few historians and political scientists who have recognized the significant role of the Black church in the development of Black Nationalism and the demand for racial justice.[63] For many years the eminent and influential Black sociologist E. Franklin Frazier commanded the respect of white Americans as the leading authority on Black religion, but Frazier had little appreciation of the contribution of the Black church to social progress. In recent years, however, a few writers have begun to sense the inadequacies of his analysis. Horace Cayton, for example, attributes this flaw in Frazier to the fact that he did not live through the civil rights movement and have an opportunity to reassess his earlier judgment on the basis of subsequent events. Thus, Cayton writes:

Frazier did not live to witness the fervor of the continuing Negro rebellion and the position of leadership which the church and churchmen are taking in it. Perhaps, if he had, his final judgment on the importance and resilience of the Negro church might have been tempered.[64]

Essien-Udom, however, whose manuscript for *Black Nationalism* was completed before the civil rights movement reached its zenith in 1963–64, perceived the enmeshment of the Black church in the web of historical factors leading to the emergence of militant Black nationalism in the United States, although he seems not to be aware of its influence in Africa and the West Indies. He asserts that the church gave the Black man pride in success, grass-roots participation in a national movement, independence from white control and a center for social life in the Black community.[65] This is all well and good, but it does not go far enough. The contribution of the Black church to Black nationalism in the United States, Africa and the Caribbean is considerably more profound than simply providing the pride, sense of independence and the organizational and social skills requisite for the development of nationalistic movements in the twentieth century. The Black church, as the primary institutional expression of Black religion, and a vocal minority of Black ministers from predominantly white churches, erected the politico-theological foundation for Black nationalism which provided some of the major building blocks for the structure of Black nationalism and pan-Africanism as it developed from the early Du Bois to Malcolm X.

The thrust of missionary emigrationism, the search for roots for the Black race in the pre-Mosaic history of Israel, the challenge to the ethical interpretation of love and redemptive suffering in white Christianity, the prefigurement of Black liberation in the story of the Exodus, the willingness to speculate about the color of God and the vocation of Christ as Liberator, and the development of Ethiopianism—all of these tendencies in the Black church inspired and gave spiritual momentum to the evolution of Black nationalism, a rising sense of racial identity and messianism wherever Black people writhed under the heel of white oppression. Before the end of the nineteenth century the theology of Black nationalism had been secularized by an ideology of political and cultural separatism which reached its most explicit articulation in the resolutions of the Pan-African Congresses and the secular philosophy of Marcus Garvey. But well before that occurred, Black preachers and laymen had drawn cultural and political implications for African colonization and Black self-determination in the United States—not from egalitarian ideologies flowing from Moscow, Paris or Washington—but from the Bible and Black theology as interpreted by men who believed the gospel and found in it the most penetrating and moving justification for racial solidarity and elevation.

At the center of this theology of liberation was the mission of the descendants of Africa to return, if not *en masse,* in selective cadres of courageous and trained missionaries, filled with the spirit of God, zealous with the determination to free Africa from white oppression, and "proclaiming the gospel of light and peace to those millions of poor souls identified with ourselves in color, who in this gospel day are still sitting in the valley of the shadow of death."[66]

Read in the light of the policy of Christian missions among most denominations today, the books, sermons and editorials on the need for Afro-American solidarity with Africa sound presumptuous and deprecatory of the religions and cultures of Africa. We cannot, however, doubt the sincerity of these men, many of them ex-slaves, in bringing to the land of their fathers whatever material assistance and enlightenment their poor churches could afford at a time when they themselves were struggling for survival under the abuse of white racism. Whatever error they committed in their estimate either of the state of civilization in Africa or the ability of Christianity to correct its deficiencies, must be absolved by the grace of the God they trusted to guide them and our appreciation of what the church meant to them in terms of self-respect, a sense of meaningful participation in the affairs of the world, and an institutional base for Black enterprise and culture. It was their intention to share these gifts with all men, in obedience to the commandment of Christ to "go and make disciples of all nations . . . baptizing . . . and teaching," and especially with those to whom they were bound by common ancestry and the experience of white subjugation. In so doing, they believed that God was using the Black churches of America in a special way to help fulfill the promised glory of the Ethiopian people, of whom they were a privileged and chosen remnant singing their song in a strange land.

CHAPTER VI

The Deradicalization of the Black Church

There are indications that a new church is arising among Negroes, a militant church, one that is concerning itself with the problems of the masses . . . Yet it cannot be said that today even this church is an influential factor in the lives of the whole Negro working population. Extremely significant in Negro life, however, has been the inordinate rise of religious cults and sects.

Ira De A. Reid, 1940

WHEN BISHOP HENRY M. TURNER died in 1915, there were no clergymen of his stature who could, by temperament or ideology, assume the leadership role he had played in a persistent but unsuccessful attempt to radicalize the Black church. Among the Methodists the possible exceptions might have been the Pan-Africanist Bishop Alexander Walters of the A.M.E.Z. Church and the young A.M.E. minister Reverdy C. Ransom of Boston and New York, who was not to become a bishop until 1924. Both of these men were militants and had greater political influence in their denominations than Bishop Turner, but neither was as tough-minded, unconciliatory and pessimistic about the United States as was Turner.

Turner entered his seventieth year, in 1904, somewhat less strident than he had been earlier, and four years later he was removed from his pivotal position as editor of the *Voice of Missions*. By 1910 he still represented a certain charismatic and radical influence among the unsophisticated masses of Black churchmen, but his age and the weariness of the years had taken their toll. What was now called for was his reincarnation in some younger member of the episcopacy if the historic Black churches were to shape the future of Black people in the critical period of the First World War. None came forward. Even though the first decade of the twentieth century saw a rising tide of opposition to the leadership of Booker T. Washington, those who openly attacked the great educator, with a few exceptions, were not clergymen. The thin line of anti-Bookerite churchmen were members of the new bourgeoisie of Atlanta, Washington and Boston, who regarded civil rights agitation as a means of entering the mainstream of American society rather than a tactic for confronting the basic assumptions of the American system. The most creditable successor to Turner was the brilliant Atlanta University professor W. E. B. Du Bois—a religious man in the broadest sense, but one who did not regard himself as a churchman.[1]

Turner had never really taken up cudgels against Washington with the vehemence of Du Bois or the determination of J. Milton Waldron and Sutton E. Griggs, two anti-Bookerite Baptist preachers, or the great orator of the Niagara Movement, Reverdy Ransom.[2] This is not to say that he approved of Washington's Cotton States Exposition position of compromise and accommodation. Turner's prestige among the burgeoning Black church population of Georgia helped to create a climate unfavorable to Washington which was turned to good effect by Du Bois and others. Moreover, when a group of Boston radicals shouted down Washinton at a meeting in 1903, Turner supported their protest although he could not agree with their strategy, which he judged to be essentially hopeful about the possibility of obtaining justice in America for Black people. As for Washington's address, he wrote on that occasion:

Washington's policy is not worth a cent. It accomplishes no racial good except as it helps a thousand students at Tuskegee . . . [Although] we agree with our Boston friends in spitting on everything that would appear to underrate the value of the Negro in every particular, they are doing no more good than Washington . . . Nothing less than a nation owned and controlled by the Negro will amount to a hill of beans.[3]

But Turner did not seek a position in the front lines of those who skirmished with Washington. When Frederick Douglass died early in 1895, Turner, if he had desired to do so, could have challenged Washington for national leadership. With his excellent connections among the Black Methodists of the South and his willingness to say publicly what many undistinguished Blacks felt privately, he might have toppled Washington's pedestal. But Turner was, after all, not a stranger to certain important aspects of Washington's thought—the emphasis upon Black people raising themselves up by their own bootstraps, the concentration upon agricultural and mechanical arts as the prerequisite to economic independence, and the rejection of Douglass' belief that social intercourse with whites was the first step toward equality. In these respects Turner and Washington understood one another well, and both were understood and appreciated by Marcus Garvey, the man who was perhaps the true inheritor of Turner's mantle of Black nationalistic leadership.

Booker T. Washington, however, had little else in common with the bishop. Like Douglass, he was an implacable foe of emigrationism. He remained a loyal Republican. He was, first of all, a gentleman who impressed whites with his good manners and conciliatory demeanor, both of which he used artfully to manipulate white people of means in behalf of his favorite projects. Bishop Turner, on the other hand, never ceased his mauling of the southern whites and the servile, fawning Negroes whose criticism of his position he labeled as "the billingsgate of this young fungus class, and some of these old fossils." Although he began as a Republican, he came to distrust them and was one of a small group of Black leaders who turned to the Democrats with the election of Grover Cleveland. He had no confidence in America and believed it to be the highest folly to expect white people ever to give the Blacks their due. His experience with Reconstruction politics in Georgia more than convinced him that the whites were determined to return Negroes to their former state and that the only salvation was to return to Africa.

At the close of the century, when white hostility was greater than at any other period in American history, Turner's tower of strength was his willingness to take a public offensive, to refuse to bow before the canons of respectability at a time when white men were all too willing to require that Negroes "grin and bear it" while they turned the screws of oppression with the greatest dignity and pious pretense. Turner simply refused to play the game and struck out mercilessly against white hypocrisy and deception. In fact, he was not at all beyond violence and in a *Voice of Missions* editorial had urged that "Negroes Get Guns" to defend themselves against the lynch mobs.[4] Rather than counsel Negroes to make themselves acceptable to whites and work for eventual assimilation, Turner confronted America with the demand for reparational relief and release. When it became obvious to him that the Government would not undertake the financial burden of the Black colonization of Africa, he turned to the Black community itself and involved himself in numerous ill-fated emigration schemes. He was so single-mindedly intent upon getting Blacks out of the United States that he had neither the time nor interest to mount a campaign against Washington's well-fortified position as the leader of the race. Suffering a stroke at the turn of the century, he practically turned his back on the internal leadership struggle and devoted himself to emigration, even though he suffered the embarrassment of having both Blyden and Crummell attack him publicly.[5]

Turner's influence was also diminished by his alleged connection with Robert Charles, a New Orleans agent of the International Migration Society, who avidly imbibed Turner's radical propaganda and harangued Blacks to arm themselves. When, in the summer of 1900, Charles was slain by the police after killing six white men, the authorities uncovered stacks of the *Voice of Missions*. The New Orleans *Times-Democrat* reported that "it was from these booklets that Charles originally derived his fiendish animosity against the white race in general."[6] Negro leaders viewed the incident as nothing less than the expected by-product of Turner's excesses, and his authority within the church dwindled until his death in 1915.

The Charles affair, however, did not silence him. He shifted to *The Voice of the People* and promoted an emigration convention in Nashville in 1901. There he and William H. Heard, an A.M.E. pastor in Atlanta, organized the Colored National Emigration Association, which for several years attempted to purchase a ship to take colonists to Liberia. After several disappointments and a storm of opposition from "responsible Negro leaders," Turner apparently abandoned the Association and began publishing announcements of commercial fares to Africa. Unfortunately, he had been accused by Heard and others of misuse of the funds of the organization which he served as treasurer. By 1906 he had lost interest in the Association and became deeply involved in local politics.[7] He did, nevertheless, continue his interest in emigration. When he died in his eighty-first year he stood alone, as he always had, as the most original and independent Black churchman of his time, a man who had combined the acuity of a Black theologian with the passion of an indefatigable activist. Although in the Niagara Movement and the newly organized National Association for the Advancement of Colored People there were other radical churchmen —like Bishop Ransom and Francis J. Grimke, the Washington Presbyterian—none of them had the grass-roots following or the uncompromising audacity of Turner. In commemoration of his death, W. E. B. Du Bois, whose spirit became more and more reminiscent of Turner's as the years sped by, wrote of him:

> The late Henry McNeil Turner who recently died at the ripe age of 82 was a man of tremendous force and in-

domitable courage. As army chaplain, pastor and bishop
he was always a man of strength. He lacked, however,
the education and the stern moral balance of Bishop
Payne. In a sense Turner was the last of his clan: mighty
men, physically and mentally, men who started at the
bottom and hammered their way to the top by sheer brute
strength; they were the spiritual progency of ancient
African chieftains and they built the African Church in
America.[8]

Turner's prophetic leadership was sorely missed during the
turbulent years which preceded and followed the First World
War. Brawley called the period just prior to the war, "The
Vale of Tears," but the years from 1918 to the Great Depression were no less trying for a church under the strain of
white hostility, the impact of massive social and economic
change and the torrential rush of southern migrants into the
cities. The background of the crisis was the unprecedented
mob violence and terrorism perpetrated against Negro citizens between 1890 and 1914. Between 1885 and 1915, 3500
Blacks were the known victims of lynch mobs, with 235 lynch-
ings in the year 1892 alone.[9]

In addition to physical intimidation and murder, the so-
called "Redeemers" of the white South, relieved of the presence of federal troops in 1877 and encouraged by northern
apathy, began to use chicanery and economic reprisals against
defenseless Negro landowners and tenant farmers. The situation in the North was not much better. White workers
resented the rising demand of Negroes for equal rights and
violently resisted the threat which jobless Blacks posed for the
lily-white trade unions.

After 1900, a formidable structure of Jim Crow laws grew
up in the South and erected barriers of racial segregation and
discrimination on trains, streetcars, steamboats and in almost
every other area of interracial contact. States and local communities passed discriminatory legislation prohibiting the races
from working together in the same room, using the same en-
trances, doors, stairways, drinking water and toilets. Blacks

were excluded from public institutions such as theaters, auditoriums, and parks, and from residential neighborhoods. In Baltimore, Atlanta and other cities, all-white and all-Negro blocks were so designated. In 1909, Mobile passed a curfew law exclusively for Blacks that required them to be off the streets by 10 P.M., and the journalist Ray Stannard Baker found Jim Crow Bibles for Black witnesses in the Atlanta courts.[10]

Negroes had enjoyed an abortive participation in politics in the South during Reconstruction, and many of their preachers had held office while pastoring churches or had abandoned the pulpit altogether to take up politics. But with the defection of the northern Republicans in the election of Rutherford Hayes in 1877, the complete disenfranchisement of the freedmen was rapidly consummated by southern legislatures. By the election of 1912, most southern states had purged their political systems of Black voters and office-holders, and many, like Bishop Turner, Rev. T. McCants Steward of Brooklyn, and the radical New York journalist T. T. Fortune, became deeply disillusioned with the conservatism of the party of Lincoln.

In the realm of ideas the popular literature of the period was undergirded by the philosophy of Social Darwinism and the pseudo-scientific interpretations of race by Count de Gobineau and Houston Chamberlain in Europe, who presented theories of the innate inequality of the races, the superiority of Nordic blood in the Anglo-Saxon nations, and the dire necessity of maintaining its purity. American racists seized upon these ideas to justify the southern conspiracy to wipe out the results of the Civil War and return the Negro to subservience. Charles Carroll's *The Negro a Beast* appeared in 1900, and in quick succession other works provided the literary and intellectual basis for segregation—William P. Calhoun's *The Caucasian and the Negro* (1902); William B. Smith's *The Color Line* (1905); Robert Shufeldt's *The Negro: A Menace to American Civilization* (1907); and Madison Grant's *The Passing of the Great Race*, published in 1916 and used to stem the tide of immigration in the Quota Act of 1921.

The enormous popularity of this literature even reached the White House, where President Warren G. Harding quoted Lothrop Stoddard's *The Rising Tide of Color Against White World Supremacy* in support of Booker T. Washington's doctrine of social separation. The novelist Thomas Dixon spewed his anti-Negro invective in *The Leopard's Spots* in 1902 and *The Klansman* in 1905. Bishop Turner regretted only "that there will be a host of Negroes that will have to spend eternity in hell with Tom Dixon."[11]

The resistance of Black leadership to the direction which the nation was moving was consistent but moderate. Washington's gradualism, while opposed by a few men who were not dependent upon his influence for personal advancement, was adopted by most Black preachers not only because they lacked the courage to fight back, but because it was entirely consonant with the ethics of the white Christianity which increasingly influenced them. The picture of the nonviolent, self-effacing, patiently suffering white Christ which was held up by the conservative evangelicals and ethical revivalists became for Black preachers the dominant image of what it is like to be Christian. That image provided irrefutable confirmation, supported by Scripture, of the wisdom and expediency of Washington's position.[12]

Many Blacks, however, were not entirely beguiled by this religious program of pacification and retaliated against marauding whites who invaded their neighborhoods to enforce the codes of white supremacy. Serious riots broke out in Philadelphia and Chester, Pennsylvania, and in East St. Louis, Illinois, in 1917, in which scores of Blacks lost their lives. Black soldiers returning from France in 1919 refused to accept the indignities and proscriptions. Many of them were involved in over twenty race riots in the "Red Summer" of 1919. The basic cause of these riots, which found Negroes responding with retaliatory violence, was the great influx of Blacks into the cities and the resulting panic of lower-class whites, who were terrified and embittered by the new competition for jobs and political power.[13]

While many found it necessary to abandon the Christian

pacifism and gradualism their churches espoused, most Negroes drew back from the hard-line, self-defense position of men like Robert Charles and Bishop Turner. They enlisted in the church's program for community betterment, self-help and mild agitation against the most destructive aspects of white racism. But as a whole, Black Christians "minded the preachers" and eschewed the radical strategies of massive resistance and confrontation. In commenting upon this characteristic of the Black community in the period under discussion, one scholar writes:

> The afflicted exercised unusual restraint and self-discipline, engaging in thoroughly polite, deferential opposition. In the second decade of this century, hardly more than a generation removed from the demise of Reconstruction, Negroes were in considerable part an ex-slave population . . . It is a commonly accepted principle of social science that a submerged group must reach a certain plateau before it can even begin to rebel, and most Negroes of the Wilson era were still struggling toward that level.[14]

But that something more than the economic condition of the Negro was operative in the passivity of the postwar years is suggested by the fact that the Niagara Movement, the NAACP and the churches exhibiting this "polite, deferential opposition" were not composed of the ragtag, down-and-out Negroes who were so economically submerged that they could not mount a more forceful program. These organizations were certainly not to be compared with the mutilated rubber workers of the Belgian Congo who followed Simon Kimbangu, or the impoverished industrial laborers of South Africa who joined the Ethiopian Church movement. Quite the contrary. The leaders and many of the constituents of these organizations were the new Black bourgeoisie, or at least "lower class strivers" who were rapidly gaining the relative economic security which permitted them to participate in programs of social uplift.

At the turn of the century many Negroes, especially the

light-skinned mulattoes who had been educated, were artisans and skilled laborers—mechanics, seamstresses, teamsters, expert domestics—men and women who, although they were discriminated against in countless ways, were able to earn a living and raise families with some semblance of security. It was from this rising lower-middle class, which had begun to move northward and westward during Reconstruction and came in ever-growing numbers after the First World War, that the churches, fraternal orders and the new civil rights organizations received the bulk of their members. There were, of course, millions of wretchedly poor Negroes—particularly in those areas of the South which suffered most from the ravages of nature and cyclical depressions, and they were to come later to the urban ghettos seeking a better way of life. But many of them found that those who had preceded them and now occupied positions of prestige and power in the older institutions of the community looked down upon them with as much scorn as pity and quietly relegated them to a subordinate status.[15] Schoolteachers, college educators, government employees and most of the northern-based bishops of the three major Methodist bodies were generally members of this relatively privileged class, which in some respects rivaled the white middle class in culture, exclusiveness and sophistication.

The Black church was closely related to the organization of the Niagara Movement, the National Urban League, the NAACP, and other groups for the uplift of the Black community. But the conclusion must be drawn that the fact that these organizations were essentially moderate in their social-action strategies had little to do with the poverty and low morale of their members. The reason for the restraint which Nancy J. Weiss finds in their approach to social change may be found in this symbiotic relationship to a church which exercised a morally elevating but politically conservative influence on the groups with which its members were intimately associated. As Gary Marx has shown, the factors of social class and church membership overlap in their relationship to militance.[16] It is difficult to know which has priority,

but from what is known about the white church's distrust of
radicalism and its *status quo* maintenance function, it is
clear that orthodox Christianity played an important role in
restraining Negro Christians at a time when their churches
were most imitative of the standard American variety.

By the end of the First World War, the independent Black
churches of the United States were becoming respectable
institutions. Having rejected the Black nationalism of Turner,
they turned more and more toward white Christianity to find
a prototype of authentic spirituality. The dominant influence
of clergymen in the social betterment and civil rights groups
helped to keep these organizations on an accommodationist
path. The NAACP met in many churches immediately after
the benediction, and it is not an exaggeration to say that the
Black church was "the NAACP on its knees." *Crisis,* the
official organ of the Association, made a regular feature of
church news, and Du Bois, who became its first editor in 1910,
regarded the Council of Bishops of the A.M.E. Church as the
most prestigious and influential group of men in the Black
community. Du Bois was, however, critical of the church for
not fulfilling its high calling to edify and lead the race. Thus,
he could write in the pages of *Crisis* in 1918:

> Everybody knows that the Negro church has a large
> number of disreputable scoundrels in its ministry. Against
> these venal immoral men—the indirect heritage of the
> slave regime—the forces of honesty and uplift in the
> church are fighting and making gradual headway. But
> they have not won.[17]

The period of the Great Migration following the war had a
decisive impact of the Black churches. It brought them face
to face with a larger number of newcomers to the city than
they had ever seen before and strained both their capacity to
assimilate the southern rural style of worship and the resources available to expand their ministries. A propertyless,
disoriented *lumpen proletariat* crowded into the northern
ghettos. Many of them were young men and women who had
experienced the degradation and harshness of racism in the

South and had no great admiration or desire to "be like white folks." They sought a better way of life, and some had already been intrigued by the possibility of emigrating to Africa or some other place.   ,

Between 1890 and 1910, the proportion of urban Negroes in the United States rose from 20 to 27 percent. Between 1900 and 1910, increases in Black population were notable. Birmingham increased by 215 percent, Atlanta by 45 percent, New York by 51 percent, while Philadelphia and Chicago reported gains of more than 30 percent. Even before the First World War, therefore, Blacks were pouring into other cities, North and South. The census of 1910 recorded over 90,000 each in New York and Washington and more than 80,000 each in New Orleans, Baltimore and Philadelphia.[18] The Black city church was practically inundated by this deluge of migrants.[19]

The influx began in 1915 and continued in waves through the Second World War. In 1915, disasterous floods in Alabama and Mississippi upset the precarious economy of Black farmers. Cotton agriculture suffered from the boll weevil, and northern factories advertised through the pages of the *Chicago Defender* and dispatched agents to the South to recruit immigrants with promises of train fare and unprecedented earnings. The estimates are that in the three years between 1915 and 1918 from 500,000 to 700,000 Negroes migrated to the North while 360,000 entered the armed services. It was, undoubtedly, the most dramatic population shift in American history. Unlike the earlier "Migration of the Talented Tenth" these war-period migrants were largely poor and uneducated and had to be assisted in making a rapid adjustment to urban life. They became the mass base of the churches of the North, many of which were composed almost entirely of people from one rural area in Virginia or North Carolina, as preachers followed their flocks and migrants wrote home to entice their families and neighbors to join them in the "Promised Land." The Baptist and Methodist churches received the bulk of the newcomers, if only to swell the membership rolls and help pay off the debts of the buildings white congregations had abandoned in the flood. The Presbyterian, Episcopal, Congregational and Roman Catholic churches were less besieged, and as they received increasing numbers of the upwardly mobile constituents of the mass churches who were uncomfortable with the newcomers, they became even less inviting and more selective.[20]

While a small minority of migrants, especially those of lighter color, were joining Negro churches of the predominantly white denominations, a much larger stream flowed into the marginal Pentecostal and Holiness churches and the various cults which developed during the period of the war and continued to grow rapidly through the Depression of the thirties. A third group remained outside of the churches altogether and formed the beginning of a growing segment of the Black urban population which was almost totally unchurched. The migrants who entered the major Black denominations, many of them enterprising and resourceful young people, moved rapidly toward middle-class status—particularly those in the Methodist Episcopal churches whose ministers tended to be better educated than the Baptist clergy. The leadership of many of these Black churches was, in many instances, the product of Negro colleges in the South that had emphasized the Washingtonian doctrine of industry, frugality, good manners and moderation. Despite the spirited preaching and emotionalism, the prevailing norms of these postwar Black churches were those of the white Methodist and Baptist churches of the North—conservative, revivalistic evangelical Protestantism.

Joseph Washington, Jr., has examined the folk religion of the southern migrants and how it was repressed and transformed by the Black churches of the North after the First World War.[21] His central thesis, modified in his later works, is that the folk religion of the Negro, suffused with the yearning for social justice and bearing the role of protest and relief, was betrayed by moralistic and dictatorial Black preachers who had little appreciation for the authentic theology of historic Protestantism.

According to Washington, the Black preacher, isolated from

the mainstream of American religious life by racism in the white church, permitted the Black church to become little more than a social club involved in meaningless organizational busyness and ecclesiastical politics. The irrelevance of the Black church, said Washington, is due to the curbing of the militancy of the folk tradition in the face of the resumption of rigid segregation in the South and discrimination in the North following Reconstruction. He writes:

> In that era of decline in the quest for freedom, the Negro minister remained the spokesman for the people with this difference—faced by unsurmountable obstacles, he succumbed to the cajolery and bribery of the white power structure and became its foil. Instead of freedom he preached moralities and emphasized rewards in the life beyond . . . From this point on, the black contribution lay dormant while the white contribution was active and dominant.[22]

Despite the excesses of Washington's first book, his contribution to a correct view of Black religion in America is considerable. Particularly helpful is his analysis of the nature of the Black folk religion and what happened when it merged with the accommodating religiosity of Black preachers who were poorly educated theologically and who sought to gain favor with those who were segregating them and their people from the main currents of American religious and political life. The blame cannot, however, be placed entirely upon the clergy. The push and pull of the secularized white urban society, permeating the ghetto, drew the newcomers irresistibly toward the norms and styles of life which Frazier described in his *Black Bourgeoisie*. The Black preacher who may have been deeply troubled about the direction of Bookerism and who was faced with the necessity of orienting his people to the requirements of urban life, could not successfully hold back the deradicalization process without breaking with orthodox Christianity. Moreover, the powerful white-liberal influence within the NAACP and other groups with which the churches were closely allied, also drew the Black community in the direction of co-optation by the American middle class. The ministers had little choice but to go along if they were to remain within the orbit of acceptable social and political action.

There was, however a segment of the Black community that did not feel itself to be under these restraints. It was ripe for a leadership which could transmute the radical impulses of Black folk religion into a way of life that would flaunt the value system of the majority tradition and erect structures of Black nationalism to counteract the frustrations of second-class citizenship and grinding poverty.

That leadership came first of all from Marcus Garvey. Garvey was born August 17, 1887, in Jamaica. His mother and father were members of the Wesleyan Methodist Church, and Garvey, deeply impressed by his mother's faith, never lost respect for the church. Later in life he insisted upon his children being baptized in the high-church tradition. As a young man he was tutored by Rev. W. H. Sloely and Rev. P. A. Conahan.[23] In Kingston he attended church services regularly and learned elocution and platform decorum from the preachers he heard. At the age of eighteen he worked as manager of a printing company and, in his spare time, trained young people in public speaking.

Garvey, feeling the pull of organizational work, gave up his job as a printer and after 1910 devoted himself full time to politics and the publication of his own paper, *The Watchman*. For a period he left Jamaica and worked at various positions in Costa Rica, Panama and Ecuador, where he observed the oppressive conditions under which Negroes and Indians lived and began to shape his views about Black self-development and economics. From South America Garvey traveled to England in 1912 and there came to know many African sailors and students. He worked for a time on the *African Times and Orient Review* with Duse Mohammed Ali, a brilliant Egyptian scholar and publicist. It was during these years in London that he was introduced to Pan-Africanism and learned of the atrocities and political conditions in colonial Africa. His wide reading brought him eventually to Booker T.

Washington's *Up From Slavery* and he determined to come to the United States, where he hoped to meet the great founder of Tuskegee Institute and discuss with him the founding of a trade school for Jamaican young men who would go to Africa as "Technical Missionaries."

On July 15, 1914, Garvey left England and returned to Jamaica. There he organized the Universal Negro Improvement Association and African Communities League, "with the program of uniting all the Negro peoples of the world into one great body to establish a country and Government absolutely their own."[24] Despite opposition from those who feared what its success might mean for the white minority on the island, Garvey was able to get the Association established in Kingston "with the assistance of a Catholic Bishop, the Governor, Sir John Pringle, the Rev. William Graham, a Scottish clergyman, and several other white friends."[25]

After corresponding with Washington, Garvey received an invitation to lecture in the United States. By the time he arrived on March 23, 1916, Washington had died, but Garvey traveled throughout the nation lecturing and studying the condition of Black Americans. In New York City he organized a division of the U.N.I.A. Again he met opposition—this time from Harlem politicians who sought to take over the Association—and from various factions of West Indians both within and outside the organization, which grew spectacularly to more than two thousand members. He began publication of the *Negro World,* and the impact of his writings and speeches upon the masses of Blacks caught up in the poverty and despair of the cities was almost instantaneous. His statistics have been difficult to confirm, but by June 1919, he claimed that the U.N.I.A. had reached a membership of over two million Blacks. There is little question that he led the largest and most successful mass movement of Black people in the history of the United States.

The U.N.I.A. was an organization of many facets—political, religious, social, recreational, cultural and economic—serving a wide range of the needs of people who were disillusioned with the traditional churches, bitter about their ostracism from the rising Negro middle class, and looking for a new Black savior who could give their lives meaning and direction. The "Liberty Halls" where the Garveyites met were the new churches of the ghetto. Their programs included Sunday-morning worship, afternoon Sunday schools, public meetings and forums, dances and concerts. People in need came to the Hall to find a job, a rooming house, and the unemployed were welcomed by Black Cross Nurses who organized soup kitchens and provided temporary housing.[26] The U.N.I.A. was in the best tradition of the Black church in America.

Garvey fought off his enemies with the ferocity of a tiger, but he constantly pleaded his own innocence and virtue. He was, he said, a friend of Black and white. He meant America no harm. He eschewed communists and "radicals." He used the language of morality and religion and devoted his labors sacrificially to the uplift of Black people, asserting that his work would free Black people and peacefully remove them from the United States, thus saving America from miscegenation and a destructive race war. The U.N.I.A. was the multiform spiritual movement by which this great exodus, under the unchallenged leadership of Marcus Mosiah Garvey, was to be performed. The preamble to its Constitution read as follows:

The Universal Negro Improvement Association and African Communities League is a social, friendly, humanitarian, charitable, educational institutional, constructive, and expansive society, and is founded by persons, desiring to the utmost to work for the general uplift of the Negro peoples of the world. And the members pledge themselves to do all in their power to conserve the rights of their noble race and to respect the rights of all mankind, believing always in the Brotherhood of Man and the Fatherhood of God. The motto of the organization is: One God! One Aim! One Destiny! Therefore, let justice be done to all mankind, realizing that if the strong oppress the weak confusion and discontent will ever mark the path of men, but with love, faith and charity toward all the reign of peace and plenty will be heralded into the world and the generation of men shall be called Blessed.[27]

Garvey's program combined a tough-minded and accusatory attack upon the Black man's enemies with an ethical, constructive, quasi-religious call to unity and humanitarian service. No leader before him had so incisively criticized America and demonstrated the hopelessness of Black people ever obtaining their rights in this country, while at the same time claiming, "We are not preaching a propaganda of hate against anybody. We love the white man; we love all humanity, because we feel that we cannot live without the other."[28]

Garvey argued from Black strength rather than Black weakness:

> We ask for nothing more than the rights of 400,000,000 Negroes. We are not seeking, as I said before, to destroy or disrupt the society or the government of other races, but we are determined that 400,000,000 of us shall unite ourselves to free our motherland from the grasp of the invader . . . we are determined to unite 400,000,000 Negroes for their own industrial, political, social and religious emancipation.[29]

And yet within the strength from which he argued there was an inherent weakness which he exploited skillfully. "The Negro," he said, "is dying out . . . we are the most careless and indifferent people in the world. We are shiftless and irresponsible." On the one hand, he scored the unmanliness and abject groveling of Negroes under the heel of white oppression; on the other, he amazed and angered many Blacks by seeking the support of the Ku Klux Klan for the U.N.I.A.'s "Back to Africa" program. He excoriated Negroes for being "Uncle Toms," and at the same time praised them for their loyalty and sacrificial service to the nations of the world which had so misunderstood and flagrantly misused them.

It was this subtle ambiguity intrinsic to Garvey's message

—his love-separatism, his paramilitary pacifism, his conservative radicalism—which grasped the complexity of the Black psychology and situation in the United States, the West Indies and Africa. It made room for men and women of every level of perceptiveness, temperament and political aspiration and confounded his detractors among the Marxist intellectuals of Harlem and the NAACP, both of whom he castigated and held up to ridicule. He wove an intricate yet transparent pattern of relationship between civil rights and political responsibility without conceding his primary motive of disengaging Blacks from all nations in which they were scattered and gathering them for the reclamation of their ancestral home.

Despite his repudiation of Negro politics, in The Declaration of the Rights of the Negro Peoples of the World, adopted at a New York convention in 1920, the emphasis is upon protest against segregation in places of public accommodation, discrimination in employment, education, "political privileges" and the administration of justice. The Declaration demanded that wherever Negroes form a community among themselves they should have the right "to elect their own representatives to represent them in legislatures, courts of law, or such institutions as may exercise control over that particular community." It proclaimed that all men should live at peace, but affirmed unequivocally the right of self-defense and recognized that war is inevitable and justified whenever races or nations provoke the ire of others by the continual infringement of their rights.

Black preachers were continually disturbed with Garvey's religion, and yet many thought that his position was sound and made sense for Black people. At his Fourth International Convention of Negroes in 1924, the religious question came to the fore.

When this subject came up, and was thoroughly aired by both Clergy and Laity, the pious and the worldlian, it was decided that, as there are Moslems and other Non-Christians who are Garveyites, it was not wise to declare Christianity the state Religion of the Organization; but by establishing the Temple of God in each heart, and letting our every word and action be motivated from that Source, we could reach a state of inner Serenity so as to enable us to establish on earth the Fatherhood of God and the Brotherhood of Man—a belief which is the basis of recognized religions. Christians who were not members of a Church, could join the African Orthodox Church; but all Church members should bear this in mind: that God is everywhere, not just in Churches on Sundays; that attendance at Church was for Christian fellowship, and rededication to righteous living.[30]

Many individual preachers—particularly those who belonged to Baptist churches or smaller sects—were Garveyites. While Garvey was critical of preachers as "so-called leaders of the race" who wrongly persuaded Negroes to postpone the blessings of this life for a future Paradise, he did not mount a direct attack upon religion or upon the Black religious establishment.[31] Indeed, he thought of himself as a deeply religious man. "I would rather stand alone," he wrote, "and be framed for the prison a thousand times than deny the [Black] religion of my mother—mark you, not the [white] religion— the religion that taught me to be honest and fair to all my fellowmen."[32] He preached that inasmuch as God was made in the image of man, Black people ought to visualize a Black God.[33] His approach to Christianity was highly pragmatic. "No hungry man," he said, "can be a good Christian. No dirty, naked man can be a good Christian for he is bound to have bad wicked thoughts, therefore, it should be the duty of religion to find physical as well as spiritual food for the body of man."[34] His theology centered upon the belief which he found in the Black folk tradition that "God helps those who help themselves." God works generally through human agencies.

In His directed, inspired prophecy He promised that Ethiopia's day would come, not by the world changing toward us, but by our stretching out our hands to Him. It doesn't mean the mere physical test, but the universal and independent effort to surround ourselves with the full glory of man.[35]

To institutionalize his radical ideas about Black religion, Garvey called upon Rev. George Alexander McGuire, an Episcopal priest, to become Chaplain-General of the U.N.I.A. in 1920. McGuire was born on the island of Antigua in the West Indies in 1866. After training for the ministry in the Moravian Church, he came first to New York and then to Philadelphia, to be tutored for Episcopal orders by Rev. Henry Phillips of the Church of the Crucifixion. After four years there he served a pastorate in Cincinnati, an administrative post in Arkansas and returned to receive a medical degree at the Jefferson Medical College. He later returned to Antigua, where for six years he served as rector of the Church of St. Paul, but hearing of Garvey's work, he determined to join him in the United States.[36]

McGuire first gathered a group of dissident Episcopalians around him and founded the Independent Episcopal Church, but was unable to receive authorization from either the Protestant Episcopal or the Roman Catholic churches. His work with Garvey led him to seek authority for bringing into existence the African Orthodox Church, and after corresponding with the Most Rev. F. E. J. Lloyd, Archbishop and Primate of the American Catholic Church, on September 2, 1921, he presided over the organizing convention of the African Orthodox Church at the Church of the Good Shepherd in New York City. On September 28, McGuire was consecrated Bishop of the new church by the Exarch and Metropolitan of the American Catholic Church, the Most Reverend Joseph René Vilatte, and enthroned in the Cathedral Chapel of the Good Shepherd Church.

It is interesting to observe that despite the strong emphasis of Garvey and McGuire on Black religion and independence, the Anglo-Catholic orientation of both men required the A.O.C. to be authorized and apostolic succession duly passed on to its first bishop by a white communion. Garvey himself had been brought up in the Roman Catholic faith and carried letters of introduction from the Jamaican church when he first came to New York.[37] The A.O.C. was strongly West Indian and high church. It maintained fraternal relations with the Russian Orthodox Church, and when the General Synod of the Independent Episcopal Church met to become the African Orthodox Church, an unsuccessful move was made to omit "African" from its name and substitute "Holy."[38] The A.O.C. admitted persons of all races, but according to its Constitution—"particularly [sought] to reach out and enfold the millions of African descent in both hemispheres."

In 1942 the church reported 30,000 members in the United States and overseas, 239 priests, 5 bishops, the Endich Theological Seminary in New York, and the George A. McGuire Seminary (McGuire died in 1934) in Miami. It had weathered a storm of opposition from Negro clergy who objected to McGuire's demand that Negroes worship a Black Christ by urging them to "erase the white gods from your hearts . . . we must go back to the native church, to our own true God."[39]

At the session of the Fourth International Convention mentioned earlier, McGuire advised Negroes to name the day when all members of the race would tear down and burn any pictures of the white Madonna and Child and replace it with a Black Madonna and Child. Both Garvey and McGuire were attacked repeatedly by Negro leaders for these "heretical views," but A. Philip Randolph wryly suggested that the preachers opposed the A.O.C. "out of fear of losing their flocks, since their congregations had been conditioned to white religion and the white Christian God."[40]

The influence of Garveyism among the separatist churches of the West Indies and Africa is significant and deserves considerably more study by scholars. The Kitawala movement which grew out of the teachings of the American-based Jehovah's Witnesses and spread throughout southern and central Africa was infused by Garvey's evangelism. In South Africa the Pan-African Congress and other political groups which were in contact with American Blacks adopted aspects of Garveyism. Professor James Thaele, the Basuto president of the Western Cape Branch of the African National Congress and a graduate of Lincoln University, Pennsylvania, was a strong advocate of Garveyism, although, unlike Garvey, he supported communism in 1929.[41]

In Jamaica the Rastafari movement recognized Garvey as one of its principal prophets and had close connections with the Harlem-based Garveyite Ethiopian World Federation. The Rastafari regard Emperor Haile Selassie of Ethiopia as God. Since the early 1930s they have looked forward to a return to Africa—mainly to Ethiopia. In November of 1930, when Haile Selassie (Ras Tafari) was crowned emperor, some Jamaicans read the text of Revelations 5:2–5 as the fulfillment of a prophecy attributed to Garvey: "Look to Africa, when a black king shall be crowned, for the day of deliverance is near." It was also said that Garvey believed that his people would be redeemed and return to Africa in the 1960s, and according to some, in 1960.[42]

The Rastafari movement, like the Nation of Islam (Black Muslims) in the United States, represents an advanced development of the relationship between Garveyism, Black religion and political radicalism. The Smith, Augier and Nettleford study shows that, in addition to their belief in Garvey's prophecy, Joseph N. Hibbert and H. Archibald Dunkley, early Jamaican preachers, were Ethiopianist Christians. Hibbert formed a body called the Ethiopian Coptic Faith. This group may have been more representative of South African Ethiopianism than of the historic Coptic Church, although he instructed his followers from extracts of the *Ethiopic Bible of St. Sosimas*. The early Ras Tafari Missions were related to both Hibbert, who preached from the Ethiopian canon, and Dunkley, who taught from the King James Version of the Bible.

Between 1935 and 1940, Leonard P. Howell, the most successful Jamaican preacher at that time, drew the movement toward the so-called Niyabingi Order of Ethiopia and the Congo. After the Italians invaded Ethiopia in 1935, resulting in a storm of protest and anger raging through Black communities everywhere, the *Jamaica Times* reported that the

Niyabingi Order, of which Haile Selassie was the head, was dedicated to the overthrow of white domination by racial war. "This violent note," write Smith *et al*, "had already been struck by Howell, and Niyabingi was defined in Jamaica as, 'Death to black and white oppressors.' Some of those people who worshiped the Emperor and were locally known as 'Ras Tafaris' or 'Rastamen' came to describe themselves as 'Niyamen.'"[43]

The period between 1890 and the Second World War was one of luxuriant growth and development for many forms of Black religion in the United States and Africa that challenged the bourgeois character of the main-line Black denominations and the racist posture of the white churches. Knowledge of the major Black Baptist and Methodist bodies suffers from the general neglect of Black church history. But even less is known about Black Holiness and Pentecostal churches and their distinctive contributions to the development of Black religion in the United States and overseas. A few recent studies have shown that these latter communions grew rapidly from the end of Reconstruction through the Depression and made a lasting impression in the Black community.[44] There is, moreover, evidence that the most direct influence of the Black church upon white Christianity may have come through the Black Pentecostal and Holiness churches which emerged during this period.

Black Pentecostalism originated in Los Angeles with W. J. Seymour, a Black preacher who had attended a Holiness Bible School in Houston in 1905 and had been convinced that God wanted to repeat the miraculous experiences of the Day of Pentecost. In 1906 Seymour was invited by Rev. Neeley Terry, a Black woman preacher of the Nazarenes in Los Angeles, to preach in her pulpit. He arrived in the city with his two assistants, J. A. Warren and Lucy P. Farrow (who later went to Liberia as a missionary), and preached from Acts 2:4 that the baptism of the Holy Spirit would have to be confirmed by the gift of speaking in tongues.[45] Terry's congregation rejected this "heretical" doctrine, and Seymour was locked out of the church. He began to meet in private homes, and on April 9, 1906, an unusual display of religious phenomena broke out as a result of one of his prayer meetings on Bonnie Brae Street and continued for several days and nights. He then rented an old Methodist church at 312 Azusa Street, which is now considered by Pentecostal writers as the cradle of Pentecostalism. From the Azusa Street revival the Apostolic Faith movement swept through the country, and today Pentecostalism number between twenty-five and thirty-five million people throughout the world.[46] The British Anglican A. A. Boddy, who for many years was the leader of British Pentecostalism, writes of the far-flung influence of Seymour's revival:

> It was something very extraordinary, that white pastors from the South were eagerly prepared to go to Los Angeles to the Negroes, to have fellowship with them and to receive through their prayers and intercessions the blessings of the Spirit. And it was still more wonderful that these white pastors went back to the South and reported to the members of their congregations that they had been together with Negroes, that they had prayed in the Spirit and received the same blessings as they.[47]

In Seymour's Pentecostalism "the color line was washed away in the blood" of Christ, but not all Pentecostalists depreciated racial identity. The Church of the Living God (Christian Workers for Fellowship), founded by William Christian in Wrightsville, Arkansas, in 1889, claims 276 congregations and 72,000 members. The catechism of this church contains the following:

> Was Jesus a member of the black race?
> Yes. Matthew 1.
>
> How do you know?
> Because He was in the line of Abraham and David the king.
>
> Is this assertion sufficient proof that Christ came of the black generation?
> Yes.

Why?
Because David said he became like a bottle in the smoke.
Ps. 119:83.

What color was Job?
He was black. Job. 30:30.

What color was Jeremiah?
He said he was black. Jer. 8:21.

Who was Moses' wife?
An Ethiopian (or black) woman. Num. 12:1.

Should we make difference in people because they are black?
No. Jer. 13:23.

Why?
Because it is as natural to be black as the leopard to be spotted. Jer. 13:23.

Triumph the Church and Kingdom of God in Christ, founded by "Father" E. D. Smith in 1897, differentiated between the militant church of whites and the peace-loving church of Blacks. Smith led the church until 1920, when he moved to Addis Ababa and never returned. It nevertheless continued to grow from 2 congregations and 36 members in 1936 to 420 congregations and a membership of 45,000 in 1967.

Hollenweger calls these Black Pentecostal and Holiness churches "the step-children of church history." His study of 31 Black Pentecostal churches (including 10 for which he was unable to find membership statistics or date of origin) reveals that 21 churches have a total membership of 4,411,000. Only five of these were organized prior to 1900; fifteen were organized between 1900 and 1936; one was organized in 1947. The four largest communions in this study are: the House of Prayer for All People, with 3,000,000 members; C. H. Mason's the Church of God in Christ, which in 1926 had 30,263 members, and in 1970 about 1,000,000; the Apostolic Overcoming Holy Church of God, with 75,000; and Christian's Church of the Living God, with 72,000 members. Even if some of these statistics require further research, it is evident that this remarkable movement, begun by C. H. Mason and W. J. Seymour at the turn of the century, has been one of the most powerful expressions of Black religion in the world and is today outstripping the historic Black denominations both in physical bodies and spiritual dynamic. Many of these groups were splits from those denominations and represent the judgment of Black folk religion upon a church which, as Hollenweger says, "has too long taken sides with the mighty ones, too long . . . told Black history in white, too long . . . destroyed the spontaneity and musicality of the Black people."

In Africa today there are at least five thousand separatist church bodies, many of them foreign transplants of Black American religious movements since the beginning of the present century. Almost all of these African churches began as movements within white mission churches.[48] David Barrett's evidence suggests that between ten and twenty thousand distinct groupings of renewal or dissidence, successful or frustrated, have arisen within the African churches during the missionary era. This situation is remarkably similar to the one in the ghetto areas of the United States and the West Indies. The major difference between the African and the American scenes is that the vast majority of the thousands of house churches, "tabernacles" and storefront churches which appear and disappear regularly in the heart of the Black ghettos of this country are more nearly homogeneous in their theologies, forms of worship and organizational structure. In Africa the traditional religions compete with Christianity for ascendancy and merge with it in many exotic variations.

During the colonial period the unsettling heterodoxy of the African separatist churches posed a threat to the political status quo, and many of them developed as anti-white, revolutionary movements which looked for the destruction of the old white-dominated world and the birth of a new world of Black power. The store-front sects and cults of America have been largely apolitical, or at least quiescent because, despite racial grievances, Black people are more generally assimilated culturally in the ethos of American life. There are indications that a similar development of political withdrawal and conservatism is taking place among the African separatist churches now that independence has been won and accommodation with Black governments is more readily accepted by religious leaders. There are, however, exceptions such as the Jehovah's Witnesses in Zambia.

Similarities between independent churches and cults in Black America and those which developed in many parts of sub-Sahara Africa have not yet been adequately investigated. Consequently, there is almost no knowledge of whether or not, or the extent to which, independent religious movements on both sides of the Atlantic are carriers of themes and motifs which are basic to Black religion as such. Joint theological studies between the All Africa Conference of Churches and the National Committee of Black Churchmen have been proposed for this purpose. Enough is already known, however, about the "collective representations" (Durkheim) of the religious life of poor and oppressed peoples in various parts of the world to make reasonable conjectures. It remains to be determined what patterns of faith and action have been shaped by the peculiar institutionalization of white racism in the Western Hemisphere and in Africa.

The socialization studies of churches like the Mt. Sinai Holy Church of America, Inc., of Bishop Ida Robinson, the United House of Prayer for All People, and Father Divine's Peace Mission show basic similarities with various prophetic movements in South and Central Africa as described by Sunkler, Oosthuizen and others.[49] The classification system Raymond J. Jones has used in his studies of American Negro cults applies almost equally well for the separatist and independent churches of Africa. His list includes:

    I Faith-Healing Cults
   II Holiness Cults
  III Islamic Cults
   IV Pentecostal
    V Spiritualistic Cults
   VI Others

Bishop Ida Robinson's Mt. Sinai Holy Church of America, Inc., was founded in Philadelphia in 1924 and typifies many churches of the ghetto that practice faith healing, foot washing and extensive female participation. A similar movement headed by a prophet rather than a prophetess is the United House of Prayer for All People, which was founded by Bishop Marcerlino Manoel de Graca, "Daddy Grace," who came out of the South to develop a cult which raised him to the status of deity for many of his believers—a phenomenon not uncommon among African cults. Both Robinson's and Grace's groups appear to have grown out of Pentecostal revivalism. They are basically Christian in their theology and provided the Negro migrants to the city with a shouting, dancing religion when many Black Baptist and Methodist churches were moving toward a more subdued emotionalism.

Prior to the Nation of Islam, the best-known Black American cult was Father Divine's Peace Mission. About 1932, one George Baker, who is said to have come from one of the sea islands off the coast of South Carolina where African survivals persisted into the present century, opened a mission in Harlem. He had for a brief period preached in Sayville, Long Island, where he operated a lodging house and employment agency.[50] Beginning his work as Major J. Devine, he attracted immediate attention among poor Negroes by distributing alms and by being regarded as one who had used mysterious powers to bring about the death of a white judge who had prosecuted him for disturbing the peace. He became known as God to his followers, and sermons and addresses in his weekly newspaper *The New Day* fortified that belief by reiterating the familiar tenet of American spiritualism that God is everywhere, everything and everyone.

There was, however, little that was otherworldly about Father Divine's ministry. His disciples were estimated from a few thousand to several million Black and white people—many of whom he fed, clothed and housed at minimal or no expense to themselves. The Mission practiced a form of ascetic love communism in which all things were held in common, and an extremely rigid morality demanded cleanliness, abstinence from liquor and sex, nonprofanity and good citizenship. Politically the movement had more significance for ghetto dwellers than either Bishop Robinson's or Daddy Grace's churches. Father Divine's followers supported civil rights and the social welfare of Black people and were urged to help implement "a plan for a 'righteous government' in which there will be equality for all mankind, with the abolition of such evils as lynching and Jim Crow practices."[51]

Two other movements of the pre-World War I period which continued through the Depression were the Church of God (Black Jews—not to be confused with the Church of God of Elder Solomon Lightfoot Michaux) and the Moorish Science Temple of America. Both were self-consciously Black in cultural and political orientation and illustrate the way the liberation motif in Black folk religion—when neglected in the historic churches—reappears in a quasi-secular guise in "Islamic" or African movements in America. Prophet F. S. Cherry, the leader of the Black Jews, came like so many of these early cult leaders from the South, which he often referred to, with divine license to use profanity, as "a hell of a place." Cherry regarded the white Jew as a "fraud and interloper" and taught his followers, reminiscent of the Black preachers of the nineteenth century, that they were the true Jews of the Bible. Both the Christian Bible and the Talmud were required reading.

Cherry taught that Jesus was Black and during his services would often shout: "Jesus Christ was a black man and I'm offering fifteen hundred dollars cash to anyone who can produce an authentic likeness of Jesus Christ and show I'm wrong!" He would then wave a picture of the white Christ and ask, "Who the hell is this? Nobody knows! They say it's Jesus! That's a damned lie! Jesus was black!"[52]

The Church of God, while forbidding secular dancing and other sins of the flesh, made discretionary concessions to the creeping secularization of the Negro masses by looking in disfavor upon speaking in tongues, tolerating mild profanity and actually encouraging moderate drinking. In this movement, as in other groups like Sufi Abdul Hamid's Universal Temple of Tranquility in New York or the Moorish Science Temple in Chicago, we see the flowering of the Blackenization and alienation themes developed by Bishop Turner and the radicals of the late nineteenth century.

These themes were taken up in another, much more sophisticated way by the West Indian lawyer H. Sylvester-Williams of Trinidad, who called the first Pan-African Conference in London in 1900. Here they became, with Sylvester-Williams and the American W. E. B. Du Bois, political rather than religious in their main thrust, but no less related to the mystique of Blackness and the messianic destiny of the Black race. Moreover, the Pan-African Congresses which met under the leadership of such Black nationalists as Bishop Alexander Walters of the A.M.E.Z. Church, Blaise Diagne of Senegal, Sir Casely Hayford of the Gold Coast, and George Padmore of the West Indies, was the intellectual counterpart of the folk tradition's blunt indifference to white values and Americanization and its interest in Black pride and liberation. While it is true that Pan-Africanism languished in British and American middle-class reformism until the Manchester meeting in October 1945, it was that year that the leadership departed from the moderate and ameliorative appeals for participation in the colonial regimes. Instead, a revolutionary demand was made for the outright, absolute independence of African people and their solidarity with people of color not only in America, but in Vietnam, Indonesia and India.[53]

The religious dimension and significance of the struggle for Black power and independence were marked by the presence of many Black clergymen at the Fifth Congress in Manchester, England. A petition of mutual support and "cooperation among the various African peoples and their descendants in America" was signed by D. W. Jemison, president of the National Baptist Convention, W. H. Jernagin, president of the National Sunday School BTU Congress, and by Bishop W. J. Walling, of the Second Episcopal District of the A.M.E.Z. Church.

While the Black Jews in the United States and various cults in the West Indies carried on this emphasis of solidarity with overseas Blacks on the lower-class level, the historic Black churches did not follow Du Bois and Padmore into the slippery paths of radical Pan-Negroism and Pan-Africanism. The promotion of Africa and the rejection of Anglo-American capitalism and racism were primarily middle class and secular —fostered by the Harlem intellectuals around the *Messenger* and the Black Peoples Alliance in the United Kingdom. Since the Second World War it has been more oriented to the masses in the United States by various abortive Black nationalist groups in Harlem, Malcolm X's Organization of Afro-American Unity, and the more recent Republic of New Africa in Detroit.

The nearest religous approach to Pan-Negroism that expressed itself consistently in an organized form during the period between the wars were the various Moorish American or Islamic cults which grew up around the concept that salvation for the Negroes lay in the rediscovery of their origin outside of America and a non-Christian God. These groups repudiated the name "Negro," "colored people," and even "black people." They referred to themselves simply as Asiatics or Moors and introduced into the historic stream of Black theology an entirely new, non-Western tradition which was to become an abiding and tenacious element in the development of Black religion in America.

The most significant of these groups was the Moorish Science Temple of America formed about 1913 by Timothy Drew, a North Carolinian who was born in 1886. Drew, who came to be known as Noble Drew Ali, the Prophet, established the first Moorish Science Temple, in Newark, New Jersey. The movement proliferated rapidly to Detroit, New York, Philadelphia, Chicago, and numerous southern cities. During his lifetime, membership may have risen to as high as twenty or thirty thousand people.[54]

Drew's private study of oriental religion and philosophy gave him the key for dealing with the plight of Black people in America. Lincoln comments that Drew believed:

> If Negroes could somehow establish an identity with the Oriental peoples, whose religious philosophies either

knew nothing of the "curse of Canaan" or else found it irrelevant, they might become less susceptible to the everyday hazards of being "everyday-Negroes" in America.[55]

Accordingly, members of the Moorish Science Temples would accost whites with hostility on the streets of Newark or Detroit, show them their "Nationality and Identification Card" on which was imprinted the star and crescent, clasped hands, and the mystical number 7, and demand to be recognized with respect and immunity from the humiliations to which "Negroes" were subjected. They were to be regarded as Moslems, "under the Divine Laws of the Holy Koran of Mecca, Love, Truth, Peace, Freedom and Justice," and followers not only of Mohammed, but also of Confucius, Buddha and Jesus of Nazareth. The new religion drew adherents not only from the poor and ignorant who found themselves cast adrift in the unfamiliar urban setting, but also from the growing number of restless, inquiring young men and women who were searching for a better way of life, greater knowledge and understanding of the world in which they lived, and a more satisfactory way of dealing with the tragic reality of color prejudice in a supposedly humane and democratic society. For many of these people traditional Christianity was wearing thin with repetitive sermons and irrelevant moralism honored more in the breach than the observance. The new faith, with its lapel buttons, red fezzes and identification cards, opened up a whole new and fascinating perspective upon themselves and the race "in Babylon"; new books to read, a new "science" to conjure with, and a new style of life in the midst of the drab existence of the great industrial centers of the nation.

The Moorish Science Temples fell upon evil days when Noble Drew Ali permitted some of the parasitic elements of ghetto life to invade the movement and make money from the sale of herbs, magical charms, and other paraphernalia of the occult which many Blacks associated with religious devotion. His mysterious death was attributed to his unsuccessful attempt to purge the movement of racketeers, and the cult split into many smaller groups which scattered abroad the seeds of Black disaffection with the Christian Church. Many of these groups continued the practice of changing the names of believers or attaching "el" or "bey" to them as a sign of Asiatic identity. Other practices such as dietary observance, abstention from cosmetics and conventional attire, worship on days other than the Christian Sunday, asceticism and the study of esoteric literature, began to take root in the fecund and sensational religious life of the ghetto.

As the economic and psychological pressures of the Depression and the brutality of racism drove Negroes deeper within themselves for spiritual resources with which to survive, movements like Father Divine's Peace Mission, Garvey's Universal Negro Improvement Association, the Black Jews, and various expressions of Drew Ali's Moorish Americans began to challenge the Black churches and press them into an even greater defensiveness.

The social gospel had invaded a sector of the white church between the wars and found favor among educated Black preachers who believed that the first responsibility of the church was a ministry of social service to the changing Negro community. A few large urban churches such as R. C. Ransom's Institutional A.M.E. Church in Chicago, H. H. Proctor's Congregational Church in Atlanta, and A. C. Powell, Sr.'s Abyssinian Baptist Church in New York became, in effect, social-welfare agencies which sought to meet the needs of the burgeoning city populations. By 1919 the Olivet Baptist Church in Chicago had a membership of 8743 under Dr. L. K. Williams and conducted 42 departments and auxiliaries with 512 officers and 24 paid staff.[56] The 14,000-member Abyssinian Baptist Church in Harlem, probably the largest Black congregation in the world, became internationally known for its involvement in labor relations, politics, housing, child care and recreation.

These so-called "institutional churches" adapted to the pulse of the city as the people came and the urbanization processes accelerated in both the North and South. But other forces were at work in the city which offset the ability of the older Black church to maintain its influential role of leader and pacemaker among the masses.

In the first place, the number of churches which had an adequately trained leadership and the financial resources to become effective community institutions were more limited than is generally assumed. Several studies have shown that while there were several large, community-conscious congregations in almost every city where Negroes were concentrated in great numbers, most Black churches were small, inefficient and plagued by an inferiority complex in the struggle to compete with the sects and cults. The problem of paying the minister's salary, meeting annual denominational claims and assessments and mortgage payments kept these congregations in a continual struggle for survival.[57] The popular myth that all Black preachers drove Cadillacs during the Depression and that Black churches always have money and political power is just that. The Black church is characteristically poor, pays its clergy less than any professional in the community, and is all but overwhelmed by the anomie and disorganization which accompanied the rapid secularization of Black life in the city.

With a basically rural orientation, most Black churches retreated into enclaves of moralistic, revivalistic Christianity which tried to fend off the encroaching secular gloom and the social pathology of the ghetto. As far as challenging the white society or seeking to mobilize Blacks against poverty and oppression, most Black congregations were too otherworldly, apathetic, or involved in the business of "being church" to deal with such problems. The socially involved, "institutional" church was the exception rather than the rule.

A second fact about the dysfunctionality of the Negro church between the wars is related closely to the first observation. The extreme proliferation of churches weakened the total impact of Black religion in the urban community by reducing the economic and political viability of individual congregations and shattering the institutional integrity of the historic denominations. Rivalry between denominations and congregations, and among elite preachers who sought the most desirable pulpits and preferments, such as national offices and bishoprics, diverted energies and resources from self-help and community concerns to ecclesiastical politics and institutional housekeeping.

The Black community, by the end of the decade of the 1930s, was literally glutted with churches of every variety and description. In Cincinnati, where Blacks comprised 10.6 percent of the total population, Negro churches accounted for 32 percent of all churches. In Detroit and Philadelphia, where the population proportion was 7.7 and 11.3 percent respectively, Negro churches comprised 24 percent of the total number of churches.[58] The increase in the number of Holiness and Pentecostal denominations and independent congregations of the Baptist variety swelled the number of individual worshiping groups and scattered the "tabernacles" and storefront churches alongside the older edifices purchased from fleeing white congregations, throughout the Negro districts. St. Clair Drake and Horace R. Cayton describe the situation in Chicago during this period.

> If you wander about a bit of Black Metropolis you will notice that one of the most striking features of the area is the prevalence of churches, numbering some 500 . . . On many of the business streets in the more run-down areas there are scores of "storefront" churches. To the uninitiated, this plethora of churches is no less baffling than the bewildering variety and the colorful extravagance of the names. Nowhere else in Midwest Metropolis could one find, within a stone's throw of one another, a Hebrew Baptist Church, a Baptized Believers' Holiness Church, a Universal Union Independent, a Church of Love and Faith, Spiritual, a Holy Mt. Zion Methodist Episcopal Independent, and a United Pentecostal Holiness Church. Or a cluster such as St. John's Christian Spiritual, Park Mission African Methodist Episcopal, Philadelphia Baptist, Little Rock Baptist, and the Aryan Full Gospel Mission, Spiritualist.[59]

This scene could be duplicated in New York, Washington, Birmingham, Miami, Detroit, Los Angeles, and a score of cities across the country, and to a somewhat lesser degree, but with equal diversity, in the urban areas of Africa and the islands of the Caribbean. The fact is that religion flourished in Black communities everywhere during much of this century, and Black people, as a general rule, clustered in small congregations in response to highly stylized, individualistic religious leadership. They searched for the associative and expressive opportunities denied to them by the segregated institutions of the dominant society. In the United States the deterioration of the quality of religious life, the stratification of church publics, and the growing irrelevance of religion to the real problems of Black people were inevitable. The Cayton-Warner study during the Depression years confirms the assumption that the masses were becoming increasingly disillusioned with the church even while millions participated in it. The popular criticisms of the church among urban Blacks were:

(1) Church is a "racket," (2) Too many churches, (3) Churches are too emotional, (4) There's no real religion among the members, (5) Churches are a waste of time and money, (6) Ministers don't practice what they preach, (7) Ministers don't preach against "sin," (8) Church places too much emphasis upon money, (9) Negroes are too religious.[60]

A third factor related to the displacement of the Black church from the center of the radical critique and reform of American society was the rising competition for the socialization, ideological unification and social-action functions which secular organizations in the Black community began to present to the churches in the period between the wars. The growth of "social clubs" as small privatized groups offering escape from the loneliness and anonymity of city life and a substitute for public recreational activities from which Negroes were barred undermined the Black church as a social melting pot and induction center for entry into the urban milieu. During the 1920s fraternal orders like the Elks, Masons and Odd Fellows, as well as the Greek letter fraternities of the new Black college-educated class, undertook certain in-group functions that had once been the almost exclusive domain of the church. These groups provided mutual aid in times of crisis such as unemployment or death, education and cultural development, political education and orientation to city politics, and an outlet for emotional expression in wearing colorful uniforms, parading on holidays and finding personal gratification in many forms of organized social activity.

Fraternal societies and social clubs were frequently related to the churches and transmitted basic religious values. But they were also largely free from the control of preachers and increasingly conscious of a responsibility to fill the gap in services caused by the apathy, incompetence and moralism of the churches. This was even more true for organizations like the National Association for the Advancement of Colored People, the National Urban League, and the Black trade unions which carried on the tradition of agitating for rights and privileges which were more and more being demanded by the upwardly mobile working class.

Scheiner has indicated that one competition of the church that had wise appeal was public recreation. He writes:

> For the lower classes, who did not participate in organized social activity to the extent of other classes, public amusements were of particular value. A major portion of the recreational and cultural life that centered for many years around the church shifted to the public arena. As the urban black community spread over a wider area and included more people, it offered a market for theaters, cabarets, sports events, and other forms of public amusements.[61]

Thus the church, which throughout most of the nineteenth century was able to integrate much of the activity of the Black masses around the core of its own ideology of uplift and racial advancement, now found itself relegated to the periphery of the closed circle, which was the segregated Black community. From that eccentric and unfamiliar position it began to provide a "place to hide" for the older adults of the lower-middle class who were now surrendering the center to the street people, the lower-class Black folk, as "the strivers" became more conservative in life style and more desirous of the emoluments of white society. At the same time the Negro intelligentsia, whom Robert A. Bone has called "the second generation of educated Negroes . . . the wayward sons of the rising middle class," identified psychologically with the masses and rebelled openly against the authority and leadership prerogatives of the church. Langston Hughes, Claude McKay and Countee Cullen were three representatives of the "New Negroes" of the Harlem Renaissance who could proclaim in the pages of the *Messenger:*

I am an Iconoclast
I break the limbs of idols
And smash the traditions of men.

Although the *literati* of the Renaissance recognized the historic importance of the church and even honored what they considered the primitive religious instinct of Blacks as reflected in the jazzy Harlem revival meetings, they moved from an unabashedly secular base into an arena in which the ordinary Black church seldom ventured—the arena of interracial social and cultural contact. Notwithstanding the New Negroes' emphasis upon Black roots and the culture of the Black folk, their association with white socialites and Marxists pushed them toward a form of social criticism, in Richard Wright and others, which was not only foreign to the Black church perspective, but tended to further its isolation within the *sanctum sanctorum* of old-fashioned ethical revivalism.[62] It was, for the Black intellectuals, the NAACP activists and the new lower-class hipster of 125th Street in Harlem or South Park in Chicago, simply out of style. Its perception of urban reality was illusory and maudlin. Its program for racial progress was fettered by gradualism, manners and morals, and the prerequisite of "accepting Jesus." Its preachers were regarded, often unfairly, as racketeers and con men who could shout about heaven on Sunday morning and play around with "the sisters" other days of the week when the Black brother was catching hell with back-breaking, dirty labor for scarcely enough money to keep his family alive.

Attacked by both the "nigger" on the block, who had abandoned the too-removed, too-unjust God of white Christianity, and by the educated class of New Negroes, who imagined themselves superior to preachers and too sophisticated for religion, many Black ministers retreated to what they knew best—preaching and raising money. With a few outstanding exceptions, their churches turned inward to the spiritual needs of a deprived and oppressed people who found emotional release from the victimization of the white world in the ritual and organizational effervescence of Black church life. As one man commented upon this situation to researchers:

> I used to be active in the church; I thought we could work out our salvation that way. But I found out better. These Negro preachers are not bothered about the Race —about all they think of is themselves.[63]

The deradicalization of the Black church, like its counterpart in the white community, was almost complete by the middle of this century. Although many perceptive observers recognized the unique role it continued to play and its freedom from some of the sins of the white church, it could nevertheless be said—with a note of disappointment and nostalgia —that "in relations with the white community (the Negro church) has been for the most part a defensive and accommodating institution."[64]

Ruby F. Johnston, in her sympathetic study of Negro religion in the mid-fifties, found that traditional religion had significantly declined among Negroes in favor of a faith characterized by empirical concerns with practical life, but her analysis concludes with the judgment that the movement of the Black church toward the middle-class norms and values of the dominant group alienated it from the Black folk with whom it began and therefore from the basic problem of the Black community. She writes:

In the empirical type of church . . . affinity is seen in the formation of associations of persons of education and money. Internal division in the structure of the church promotes relegation of traditional Christians or economically insecure groups to an obscure position. Thus men seek new religions.[65]

In the next chapter we turn to the "new religion" of the Black community which emerged, between the late fifties and the mid-sixties, from the brokenness and insipidity of the Negro church. It may be, however, that this "new religion" of Black Power was nothing more than a revival of old themes in the distinctive religious tradition of the folk—particularly the theme of Black liberation. Indeed, it was the "oldtime-newtime" religion of Martin Luther King, Jr., that disturbed the placid surface of life in the ghetto and released from the masses of Black people those deep-lying spiritual powers which were exemplified in Malcolm X, James Forman, and the radical Black churchmen who seek to renew the church as an instrument of Black liberation today. The dry bones were to be knit together once again and Black people were to "hear the word of the Lord" from a young seminary-trained Black warrior who could hobnob with the great without losing the ability to call forth "soul" from the Black folk.

CHAPTER VII

The Dechristianization of Black Radicalism

Go to church on Sunday,
Sleep and nod,
Trying to duck the wrath of God,
Preachers filling us with pride
Telling us what he thinks is right.
He must be some kind of stupid nut,
Trying to make it real,
But compared to what?

Gene McDaniels

I don't know whether there's an old man up there with a beard. I don't know if I'm going to be thrown before his throne and sentenced to hellfire and brimstone and damnation throughout eternity. But I know one thing, that I can't relate to that either. Because if he casts me down into the hellfire, I'm going to look around for you. I'm going to look around for the members of the Black Panther Party, and say, brothers, let's get this shit together and deal with the devil.

Eldridge Cleaver

To BEGIN this discussion it is necessary to differentiate between radicalism as it developed in the Black community in America from the beginning of slavery, and radicalism as it developed in Europe after the publication of the *Communist Manifesto* in 1848 and in the United States in the movement of Populism, which arose among lower-class whites following Reconstruction and continued to find expression in the Democratic party and the labor movement. Radicalism in the two latter senses was animated by an intense class consciousness and hatred for existing society. It projected farreaching and sometimes utopian schemes for the transformation of established political and economic institutions. In communism and syndicalism it proposed a revolutionary transfer of power by means of force and violence. Black radicalism, on the other hand, historically has been less political, less obsessed with ideology on the grand scale, and less committed to violence as a revolutionary strategy. From time to time it has flirted with socialist ideas, but without submission to doctrinaire Marxism, and it has dallied with revolution without the anarchistic violence that has characterized the most extreme form of revolutionary communism or the New Left radicalism of the post-civil rights period.

Black radicalism, from the Negro abolitionists to the Student Non-Violent Coordinating Committee and, with some qualification, the Black Panther Party, has been basically a homegrown, race-conscious challenge of the roots of prejudice and discrimination in American life. In its most extravagant separatist form, as with Turner and Garvey, it despaired of any possibility of Black freedom in the United States and called for a return to the African homeland. In its more moderate integrationist form, as with Douglass, and later with James Weldon Johnson and Walter White of the NAACP, it was an attack on institutionalized racism without calling into question the underlying structures of the society.

Both forms of Black radicalism have, of course, been penetrated by Marxism as the Communist and Socialist parties sought to make Black industrial workers the mass base of a revolutionary proletariat following the Fourth World Congress of the Communist International in 1922. But for many reasons which cannot be examined here, communism has not been able to fuse with the peculiar radicalism of Black people in the United States, and among Black intellectuals, trade unionists and social activists generally, the doctrine of dialectical materialism has either been rejected or made to serve the special interests of the Black community.[1]

Although Marcus Garvey sometimes used the term to discredit his opponents, he once defined radicalism as "a label that is always applied to people who are endeavoring to get freedom."[2] For the most part, Black Americans have understood themselves to be radicals in this special sense and have never permitted themselves to be more than temporarily distracted from the main objective of Black liberation. The experience of Black people with the native American radicalism of the Populists at the turn of the century convinced many of their leaders that in the final analysis, in the minds of the white working class, political equality had little to do with shared power and social equality, and as Black people were used to draw lines between white people for purposes related to the alteration of white power, they would also be used to bring whites together again for its preservation.

Black radicalism, therefore, has been and continues to be a form of protest indigenous to the Black community in its struggle for first-class citizenship. Accordingly, it has been consistent, in terms of objectives and style, with the whole history and culture of the Black community. For most of its existence it has been an adjunct of Black Christianity because it was precisely through the Biblical story, the Negro Spiritual and the event of Christian worship that Black people knew the experience of being bound together in the persecuted family of a righteous God who destined them to break someday the bonds of oppression. That this religious experience has been primarily Christian is an accident of history. It might well have been Judaic or Islamic. It happened that the nations of the Christian West were the ones to enslave the African and separate him from his ancient religion. Indeed, the Christian religion was used by the white man as an instrument of control, and its pronouncements of the Brotherhood of Man and the Fatherhood of God were perverted to justify the paternalistic dominance of colored peoples as the Manifest Destiny of the superior white race. As Richard Wright wrote in his introduction to *Black Metropolis:* "The apex of white racial ideology was reached when it was assumed that white domination was a God-given right."

Notwithstanding this perversion, the "invisible institution" of Black religion and the independent Black church discovered at the core of the Christian faith, something which had been obscured by white Christians: a radical predisposition for liberation and justice which stood in stark contrast to the benign conservatism of the white church and its sanctification of the Euro-American hegemony. It was this discovery, aided by conspiratorial white Christians like Lovejoy and John Brown in the United States and Booth in Africa, that opened up the possibility of an African–Afro-American radicalism which broke out first in Black churches and religious movements and gradually worked its way into the most permeable institutions of the Black secular community.

Bishop Henry M. Turner was, of course, the principal exponent of that *genre* of Black radicalism closest to a Christian view of the meaning and destiny of Blackness. In a way, he was a voice crying in the wilderness of Negro servility and resignation to the hypocrisy of the white Christian conscience. Although rebuffed by the bourgeois leadership of his day and unable to persuade the majority of Black Christians to follow him, he nevertheless represented the irrepressible tradition of resistance which began with the preacher-led slave revolts. He preserved in the hearts and minds of Black folk an important connection between Black Christianity and a fundamental incompatibility with the dominant values of a white racist society. Turner, therefore, pointed the way toward a unique, Blackenized form of Christianity which went far beyond anything that had developed out of the Black church thus far—a Black religion that was essentially radical both in its analysis of the Black condition and in its programatic solution to racism and oppression.

After Turner the mainstream of Black radicalism in America split in three directions. The Christian stream, which he represented, continued as a marginal excrescence of the Black church and as a quasi-religious Black nationalism in Garveyism and the syncretistic cults of the ghetto. Another stream threw off religious influences altogether and continued as a belligerent and thoroughly secularized Black racism, devoid of any self-conscious ideological or redemptive significance. It was characterized by the cynicism and hatred of the white man which could be found among the sporting crowd and criminal elements of Harlem and other ghettos. Many young men and women from this stream found their way into Black nationalist groups and into the Islamic cults which nourished their personal resentment and nonconformity. A third stream arose in Du Bois and the Niagara Movement—later in the NAACP. It included not only members of the Black middle class who wanted only to remove the barriers to full participation in American society, but also the social radicals and Marxist-oriented Black intellectuals who gathered around A. Philip Randolph's *Messenger* and the National Negro Congress of the late thirties. Some of the latter group overlapped with the second and first streams, but they were the radicals of the Harlem Renaissance—an essentially middle-class movement whose identification with the masses was primarily intellectual.

This third development, while not entirely dissociated from the churches, moved in a secular direction and found its motivity not in the apocalyptic vision of a Black Christian civilization which would restore the ancient glories of Africa, but in the vision of a democratic or socialist society, unabashedly interracial, moving toward the realization of the American Dream for all people. Its primary institutional expression was the NAACP—an organization in which the radical racialism of Du Bois was constantly moderated in favor of the egalitarianism of a few wealthy white integrationists, and finally proscribed altogether. On one flank it fought off the Black and white Marxists who sought first to destroy it and then to make it captive of a program to revolutionize American society. On the other, it battled against Garveyism—the main undercurrent of the first stream of Black radicalism—and against what it considered to be the unrealistic pan-Negroism of the ghetto nationalist movements.

The NAACP's integrationist, revisionist position became the dominant social outlook of the Negro middle class. But of far greater significance for the future were the other two streams of Black radicalism, which have through the years maintained a closer relationship with the Black folk and continues as quasi-religious ideologies of cultural nationalism and Black separatism—a repudiation not only of pro-Marxist and anti-Marxist integrationism, but also of Christianity as it developed in the historic Black churches after Turner.

The dechristianization of the first two streams of Black radicalism began with the frustration and disillusionment of the masses of Negroes whose hopes were shattered by the crass realities and hypocrisies of existence in the great white world of the northern cities. Their alienation is described by the poets and writers of the Harlem Renaissance like Langston Hughes, Claude McKay and Richard Wright who, although they were of a relatively privileged class of educated Negroes, understood what was happening to the folk under the impact of urbanization and the grinding poverty of the great industrial centers of the North.

James Baldwin describes the metamorphosis of some of these migrants to the city in his powerful novel *Go Tell It on the Mountain* when he makes Elizabeth, in her revery, reflect upon her lover Richard and his Harlem friends[3]:

> Not one of them ever went to Church—one might scarcely have imagined that they knew that churches existed—they all hourly, daily, in their speech, in their lives, and in their hearts, cursed God. They all seemed to be saying, as Richard, when she once timidly mentioned the love of Jesus, said: "You can tell that puking bastard to kiss my big black ass."

Rather than recoil in horror, the masses of Blacks in the great ghettos of the northern cities would have laughed at

Richard's irreverence. They were becoming, in the years following the First World War, the most secularized segment of American society. Bereft of the moral cement and social pressures of the religious ethos of the southern rural community, deeply disillusioned by the betrayal of whites and embittered by the antagonism of the Black middle class, many Black newcomers to the city turned their backs on the Christian Church. These people found psychological security in the close-knit fellowship of the corner beer garden where Black music wailed and the good times rolled and one could learn the lore of the big city from cut-buddies and coons. No group of immigrants to the American city were more systematically exploited and dehumanized, and no group fought back more desperately and joyfully to survive.

The "deferred dream" of freedom and equality and the dehumanization of Black life in the teeming ghettos of the North released the catch by which millions of Black people were coupled to the norms and values of the Evangelical Protestant ethic. When Blacks discovered that not only was the American Dream a pious fiction where they were concerned, but that the Black church—with a few notable exceptions—was generally indifferent to their plight, a spiritual vacuum opened up in their lives like a great crevasse after an earthquake, and a shock wave of disenchantment and unbelief swept the moorings of faith into the abyss. Thus in her poem "The Sundays of Satin-Legs Smith" the celebrated Black poet Gwendolyn Brooks writes[4]:

> The past of his ancestors lean against
> Him. Crowd him. Fog out his identity.
> Hundreds of hungers mingle with his own,
> Hundreds of voices advise so dexterously
> He quite considers his reactions his,
> Judges he walks most powerfully alone,
> That everything is—simply what it is.

There is probably no place in the world where the Christian Church has been under a more sustained and determined attack from those who once were within it than in the Black ghettos of the United States. The attack has been intensifying since the end of the First World War. It was joined in the twenties and thirties by the Black intellegentsia who identified religion with ignorance and superstition and looked upon Black preachers as the "lickspittle of their white masters."[5] Although Garvey avoided a direct confrontation with the Black church, the Black nationalist leaders who regard Garveyism as the wellsprings of their radicalism have not been sparing in their open criticism of the Black clergy and their followers. In Harlem during the mid-sixties a street gang calling itself the "Five percenters" demanded 5 percent of the monthly salary of ministers in the neighborhood because "blood-sucking preachers and their churches" drain off the wealth of the Black community and make no relevant contribution to "the struggle."[6] In other cities Black churches which had been unresponsive to community needs have been defaced and vandalized. It is likely that more churches would have been destroyed during the ghetto rebellions from 1964 to 1968 had it not been for the new image of the ministry that was projected by men like Martin Luther King, Jr., and Albert Cleage, and the participation of some of the younger clergy in the northern liberation movements.

The direct attack on the churches which was instigated by the *Black Manifesto* in April 1969 was, in a sense, the culmination of a growing hostility to religious institutions among young Black radicals. The fact that the *Manifesto* addressed itself primarily to "the white churches and synagogues of America" resulted from a last-minute tactical decision to avoid a divisive struggle with Black preachers and to enlist a certain faction within the Black church in support of the Black Economic Development Conference.[7] But there is no doubt that the Black church was the secondary target of the Forman attack and was being called upon, like the predominantly white churches, to make redress for its defection from the cause of Black liberation.

In recent years the Nation of Islam has been the most consistent critic of the Black Christian church. While millions of Black people continue to attend church, many of them are secret admirers of Elijah Muhammad's denunication of the sins of Christianity and, in public meetings with Muslims, will give a sober "Amen" to a biting attack on "chicken-eating nigger preachers." Muslims have picketed churches in the ghetto and passed out literature to churchgoers. C. Eric Lincoln reports that such action is not uncommon in many cities and that Negro churches have been known to seek police protection from Muslim hostility. Paraphrasing the Muslim attitude toward Black ministers, he writes:

> The black Christian preacher is the white man's most effective tool for keeping the so-called Negroes pacified and controlled, for he tells convincing lies against nature as well as against God . . . the black preacher has taught his people to stand still and turn the other cheek. He urges them to fight on foreign battlefields to save the white man from his enemies; but once home again, they must patiently present themselves to be murdered by those they have saved . . . Thus, in an unholy and unnatural way, the "Negro clergy class is the white man's right hand over the so-called Negroes," and the Black preacher is the greatest hindrance to their progress and equality.[8]

This is not an isolated phenomenon among the Black Muslims. For many years an offensive strategy against Negro preachers and their churches has been one of the characteristics of various Black cults and nationalist movements. As the largest and most powerful institution in the Black community the Negro church has presented a formidable obstacle to the takeover and radicalization of the Black community and has enjoyed certain emoluments from the white-power structure for doing so. Mass leaders from Marcus Garvey to Huey P. Newton recognized that the sacrosanct position of the Christian Church in American society and the Black man's long association with Christianity made it difficult to get him to submit to another form of belief even after he had become thoroughly secularized and withdrawn from the organized church. It is, however, possible to undermine the authority of the church in the Black community by discrediting its leadership and proving that its teaching is the echo of the white slavemaster who uses Black preachers to emasculate the race.

The central message of the cults which emerged in the 1930s from the charisma of Noble Drew Ali and Wallace D. Fard was that Christianity was the white man's religion and that no Black man can be a Christian without betraying the cause of Black manhood and liberation. The Bible, therefore, is "a poisoned book" of a "slave religion." Its basic purpose is to teach Black people that a white man named Jesus was God and that they are supposed to love their oppressors and "turn the other cheek" to the white man's brutality in order to get to a fictitious heaven after a life of hell on earth. In the pages of *Mr. Muhammad Speaks,* the Muslim tabloid, the honored leader of the Nation of Islam reaches thousands of Black people with a continuous critique of the false teachings of the Christian religion:

> You fear and love [white Christians] though you are even disgraced, beaten and killed by them, from your ministers of their slavery religion . . . down to the lowly ignorant man in the mud. You have made yourselves the most foolish people on earth by loving and following after the ways of the Slavemasters, whom Allah has revealed to me to be none other than real devils, and that their so-called Christianity is not His religion of Jesus or any other prophet of Allah [God].[9]

Islam, the religion of "peace, justice and equality," is commended to Blacks as the faith by which the race can achieve brotherhood—for all Black people are Muslims, whether they know it or not, and only their true religion can give them the knowledge and power to stand up to the white man. The Muslims continue to invite Negro Christians to attend their meetings, and so powerful was their threat to Black churches in Harlem in 1963 that Adam Clayton Powell, minister of the great Abyssinian Baptist Church, began to link himself with them.[10] There is no evidence that there has been a widespread exodus from the churches into the Nation of Islam, as the Muslim preachers predicted, but since the Muslims, Black churchgoers have measured what their preachers say about the Black condition in America by what they recognized as the painful truth from the late Malcolm X and other Muslim ministers. And many younger Blacks who once followed Martin Luther King, Jr., as at least nominal Christians, have joined the Nation of Islam, or have changed to Arabic or African names, considering themselves Muslims without formally uniting with a mosque. Only the split between Malcolm X and the Honorable Elijah Muhammad in 1964 and the assassination of Malcolm on February 21, 1965, prevented the Muslim movement from making serious inroads in the ranks of organized Black Christianity.

If the period from the end of the First World War to mid-century saw a growing disillusionment with the Black church because of the conservatism of traditional Christianity, it must be said that it was the young Baptist minister Martin Luther King, Jr., who reversed that trend and gave new vitality and relevance to Black Christianity in America. Black radicalism in the late 1960s found its most ostensible expression in the highly secularized Black Panther party and continues to be suspicious of Black churches and churchmen, but King's contribution to the Black revolution gave the lie, once and for all, to the allegation that Black preachers were nothing but Uncle Toms and that Black Christianity was hopelessly out of step with the temper of the times. Despite the fact that he was never able to muster the full resources of the Black church and received only token support from many of the most prestigious Black ministers, King nevertheless projected upon the nation a new image of the Black church and a new awareness of the radical possibilities inherent in Black religion. "The peculiar genius of Martin Luther King," writes Lerone Bennett, "is that he was able to translate religious fervor into social action, thereby creating political leadership under the rubric of his religious ministry . . . under . . . conditions of extreme danger and liability."[11]

Martin Luther King, Jr., came from a long line of Georgia

Baptist preachers and was one with them in every respect except education. When he came to the Dexter Avenue Baptist Church of Montgomery, Alabama, in 1954, he had earned degrees from Morehouse College in Atlanta and Crozer Theological Seminary—a predominantly white seminary in Chester, Pennsylvania—where he graduated at the head of his class. A year later he received the Doctor of Philosophy degree from Boston University. As the son of one of Atlanta's leading ministers, a member of one of the most prominent Negro families in the South, a graduate of a distinguished Black mens' college with degrees from white graduate schools in the North, King had everything he would need for a successful if prosaic career as a privileged, pampered minister of a fashionable, middle-class Baptist congregation in the capital of the Black South. It might have been reasonably predicted that he would remain in Montgomery for only a few years, move up to the leading Baptist congregations of Birmingham or Atlanta, and after a few years of revival preaching and baccalaureates for friends and cronies and building up a reputation in the Baptist conventions, that he would finally settle down in one of the great pulpits in New York, Los Angeles or Chicago with five-thousand-dollar Anniversary Sundays, winter vacations in the Bahamas, and summers traveling in Europe.

King had, as Joseph Washington remarks, "that Baptist hum which makes what is said only as important as how it is said."[12] He could moan and shout in the finest Negro Baptist style and "get down" with the lowliest folk on a given Sunday, or he could soar to the heights of erudition with complex ideas, vocabulary and cultured tones that would please the best educated in the congregation. He knew the right people in Black society in the South, married the right girl (Coretta Scott of Marion, Alabama, graduate of Antioch College and a voice student at the famed New England Conservatory of Music), and had the right credentials in terms of background and breeding to have gone as far in Negro society and church circles as he desired. All that would have been required was that he avoid getting into difficulty with women, the Internal Revenue Service, and rednecks. When Mrs. Rosa Parks refused to give up her seat on a city bus on December 1, 1955, and the Blacks of Montgomery rose up with a weary acceptance of the inevitable, King could have scarcely avoided that ultimate peril—a confrontation with Mr. Charley. James Baldwin, who understood this situation well because of his own religious background, wrote:

> Until Montgomery, the Negro church, which has always been the place where protest and condemnation could be most vividly articulated, also operated as a kind of sanctuary. The minister who spoke could not hope to effect any objective change in the lives of his hearers, and the people did not expect him to. All they came to find, and all that he could give them, was the sustenance for another day's journey. Now, King could certainly give his congregation that, but he could also give them something more than that, and he had . . . once he had accepted the place they had prepared for him, their struggle became absolutely indistinguishable from his own, and took over and controlled his life.[13]

The Montgomery bus boycott began by agreement among a handful of the city's middle-class Blacks and their preachers. The first meeting, which took place in King's church, was opened with devotions by Rev. H. H. Hubbard, president of the Baptist Ministerial Alliance, and was dominated by clergy.[14] But it was the ordinary Black people of Montgomery, the laborers and domestic workers, "many of them well past middle age, trudging patiently to their jobs and home again, sometimes as much as twelve miles," who gave it success.[15] It was the Black folk, first in Montgomery and then in more than sixty communities throughout the South, who rose up together in an almost compulsive response to the call of Black preachers—as if following the script of an old, half-forgotten scenario which had been played long ago, but had fallen into disuse—and defied the laws and traditions of the South to demand redress of their ancient grievances. From the winter of 1955 to the winter of the following year, despite insults, physical assault, bombings and shootings, they walked for freedom, and as they walked, millions of their brothers and sisters took new courage and began what was certainly the most remarkable mass movement of nonviolence since the Gandhian protests in India during the 1930s.

King had been greatly influenced by the great Indian barrister's concept of *Satyagraha,* or truth-force, during his period at Crozer Seminary, after hearing a sermon by Dr. Mordecai Johnson, the president of Howard University, at Fellowship House in Philadelphia.[16] The bedrock of his philosophy of nonviolent resistance, however, was the Sermon on the Mount. He came to believe that Christian love, which would not return evil for evil but would "turn the other cheek" to the oppressor, was not only valid for individual relationships, but could be "a potent instrument for social and collective transformation." His study of Reinhold Niebuhr, the American theologian, taught him of the radical evil in society, and in his doctoral studies at Boston he examined the German philosopher Hegel's analysis of dialectical process and the possibility of growth and reconciliation through struggle and conflict.

These ideas, honed and polished by Bayard Rustin of the Fellowship of Reconciliation, who joined King during the Montgomery crisis, provided the scaffolding for the strategy and tactics of his nonviolet direct action as a weapon for social justice. The substructure was the Christian doctrine of a love which relentlessly pursues its object through suffering and death, to ultimately triumph over enmity by an appeal to the highest and best in human beings. These were the resources of mind and spirit that King appropriated and reserved during his student days against the moment of truth which he had neither foreseen nor precipitated. In *Stride Toward Freedom,* he recalls:

> When I went to Montgomery as a pastor, I had not the slightest idea that I would later become involved in a crisis in which non-violent resistance would be applica-

ble. I neither started the protest nor suggested it. I simply responded to the call of the people for a spokesman. When the protest began, my mind, consciously or unconsciously, was driven back to the Sermon on the Mount, with its sublime teachings on love, and to the Gandhian method of non-violent resistance.[17]

King's effectiveness in the early days of the civil rights movement cannot be attributed solely to the cogency of the idea of nonviolence as a mode of practical action. The real power of his southern campaign lay in his ability to combine dexterously a simplistic but highly sophisticated philosophy and tactic with the folk religion and revival technique of the Black Baptist preacher. He was able to elicit from the thousands who flocked to hear him throughout the South the old-fashioned religiosity of the Black folk converted into a passion for justice. The passion for justice was already there. Suppressed by years of subjugation and domesticated by the prudence of a mute Black church, it was nevertheless deeply embedded in the religion of the masses. King made the familiar religious language and the old Biblical images burst into new life. Lerone Bennett caught the spirit of what happened when King brought from his creative mind and training gifts new and old for the Negro peasants of the South:

> The opening to Gandhi was facilitated by two factors: King's propensity—largely because of his philosophical training and his original choice of himself as a symbolic being—for large ideas and concepts; and the further fact that the movement was already based on the solid rock of the Negro religious tradition. What King did now— and it was a high achievement—was to turn the Negro's rooted faith in the church to social and political account by melding the image of Gandhi and the image of the Negro preacher and by overlaying all with Negro songs and symbols that bypassed cerebral centers and exploded in the well of the Negro psyche.[18]

The people instinctively understood what he was saying. They recognized in his sonorous words and symbolic actions something akin to what they had always believed Christianity was about, what they had heard the preacher saying, somewhat vaguely, every Sunday, but had, at some point, ceased to believe he took seriously. What the South experienced between 1955 and 1960 was a revival of Black religion—a revival that broke out not with sawdust trails and mourners' benches, but with picket lines, boycotts and marches through the downtown sections of scores of southern towns and cities. Martin King, Ralph Abernathy, Fred Shuttleworth, C. K. Steele, Matthew McCollum, J. Metz Rollins and a hundred other Black preachers, most of them undistinguished and unsung, were there only as the instruments—sometimes the reluctant instruments—upon which the theme of freedom, rising like a great crescendo from the depths of Black religion, were played out. The Southern Christian Leadership Conference (SCLC), which King helped to organize and headed in 1957, was dominated by Baptist preachers—with a second echelon of middle-class Black professionals and a few ministers from other denominations—but its program rested upon the courage, the discipline and determination of the poor Blacks of Albany, Danville, Tallahassee, Birmingham, Montgomery and a score of other cities, some of them church people, many of them not, who forced the movement into the streets and made their preachers march at the head of the line singing "We Shall Overcome."

The Montgomery bus boycott not only brought a Supreme Court decision against segregation in public transportation, it stirred up a whirlwind of protest activity in Black communities throughout the South and in many other parts of the nation. In the South, Black preachers, theological students, seminary dropouts and church lay leaders figured prominently in much of what took place as SCLC affiliates were spawned in town after town. Black college students, many of them led by seminarians like John Lewis and Charles Sherrod, or sons of ministers like Joseph Charles Jones, Jr.,[19] pressed the clergy and the adult generation to assume a more militant posture. During 1960 the student sit-ins broke out in Greensboro, Durham and Winston-Salem, North Carolina, also in South

Carolina, Georgia, Florida, Tennessee and Texas. By the end of the year, public accommodation facilities had been desegregated by sit-ins in 126 cities. By January 1962, the number of cities had risen to 200.[20]

Out of this student movement, which received its initial inspiration from King, came to the Student Non-Violent Coordinating Committee. Formed in 1960, SNCC became—with SCLC and the older Congress of Racial Equality—the third national civil rights organization to emerge to the left of the NAACP and the National Urban League.[21] SNCC came to represent a hard core of militant Black and white students and former students who plunged into civil rights field work for subsistence pay—concentrating largely, after 1960, on voter registration projects in Mississippi. Many of its early leaders were middle-class Negro students from northern as well as southern colleges who quickly drew around them the poor, unemployed Black youth of the rural areas who drifted in and out of the program, but gave it the flavor of a new populist movement, challenging the traditional leadership of the communities in which they worked.

In its pioneering days SNCC was closely aligned with King and fiercely loyal to him as their symbol of new Black militancy. From the beginning, however, there were young people in the movement who mistrusted the Christian orientation of Black preachers. Fired with a social gospel, but one almost devoid of Biblical and theological tradition, the students had little confidence in what could be expected from the Black churches—many of which refused to grant them sanctuary or to cooperate with their free-wheeling program of living off the land in communal groups, agitation and confrontation. These young Black warriors sang and prayed when logistics demanded, but they relied much more upon organizing and politicizing the masses and upon a direct and often derisive confrontation with southern white power. Many Negro preachers in the South were impressed with their courage and vaguely identified them with King's church-centered movement, but they were not prepared to follow into the jaws of death or to regard as Christian a movement in which disrespect for local customs, profanity and sexual laxity between Black and white seemed so openly practiced. On their part, the SNCC workers were increasingly aware that traditional Christian values did not have the same binding power in their movement as they had in the Southern Christian Leadership Conference. Hence, they became more and more hostile to the church and to preacher-leaders. One student, during the height of the 1960 protests, voiced what was undoubtedly the sentiment of SNCC leaders like James Forman and Robert Moses: "We have been singing and praying for three hundred years. Now is the time we should do something for ourselves."[22]

Despite his close identification with the organized church, King himself became increasingly conscious of the fact that he could not depend upon the majority of Negro preachers and their congregations. The great national Black denominations made polite gestures in his direction, but never mounted a strong offensive program that would have thrown their full resources into the struggle. Individual congregations raised money for SCLC, a few preachers joined the marches, and others offered facilities for mass meetings, food and clothing collection points, SNCC "freedom schools" and other purposes, but it must be acknowledged that the Black church in its national institutional form, almost as much as the white church, was more of a spectator than a participant in the events which marked the progress of the civil rights movement under SCLC, SNCC and CORE.

King was too loyal a churchman to voice a public complaint about the failure of the Black church to support him, but he did on occasion point out that "too many Negro churches . . . are so absorbed in a future good 'over yonder' that they condition their members to adjust to the present evils 'over here.'"[23] His general criticism of organized religion's defection from the cause of racial justice obviously included the Black church.[24] The difficulty of getting massive and sustained support from the churches, both Black and white, had to do somewhat with the clannishness of the small clique of Baptist preachers at the head of SCLC, the jealousies and rivalries of leadership, and the unstructured manner in which SCLC and SNCC worked, which made it awkward for bureaucratic organizations like the national denominations to plug into them. But the fact remains that King was considered too radical by Black as well as white clergymen, and many Black churches carried on business as usual Sunday after Sunday while the SCLC and SNCC workers suffered for the lack of bail and program funds and were being harassed, beaten and jailed throughout the South. In 1963–64 the situation changed significantly when the National Council of Churches and several denominations made an unprecedented effort to bring the churches into the center of the struggle. Some denominations began to shift to more militant tactics and give open support to the movement in the South. The religious community as a whole played an important role in the March on Washington and in the effort leading to the passage of the Civil Rights Act of 1964.[25] But as the Stated Clerk of the United Presbyterian Church, Eugene Carson Blake, said at the Lincoln Memorial, "The churches come late." Perhaps it was too late.

During the early 1960s the teachings of the Black Muslims, ACT, RAM, William Epton's Harlem Progressive Labor Movement, and various local-based "united front" groups began to infiltrate the civil rights movement. RAM (Revolutionary Action Movement) was organized in the winter of 1963 by supporters of Robert F. Williams, the deposed NAACP leader of Monroe, North Carolina, who advocated organized violence. At about the same time, the idea of an all-Black political party surfaced among left-wing northerners like William Worthy, a journalist, and Conrad Lynn, a civil rights attorney. The Freedom Now party, as the new organization was called, brought together a mixed group of Black intellectuals, revolutionaries, Black nationalists, Marxists and civil rights integrationists, and centered mainly in Harlem and Detroit.[26] The ideas which flowed from this group of northern radicals seeped into the SNCC leadership ranks and gave further momentum to its recession from the ideological center of the King-Wilkins-Young coalition. Finally, in 1963, the New York Congressman and pastor Adam Clayton Powell, Jr., began to attack the NAACP and, somewhat less vociferously, King himself for what Powell considered their co-optation by white liberals. At a Chicago rally in May 1965, Powell spoke of Black Power, and on May 29, 1966, in a baccalaureate address at Howard University he declared:

> Human rights are God-given. Civil rights are man-made
> . . . Our life must be purposed to implement human
> rights . . . To demand these God-given rights is to seek
> black power—the power to build black institutions of
> splendid achievement.[27]

The Howard address set the Black radical circles of the North humming with excitement. When, on the James Meredith march between Memphis and Jackson, Mississippi, in June 1966, Stokely Carmichael of SNCC raised the cry of "Black Power," the ground had already been prepared for an eruption of Black nationalism within the freedom movement. It was nourished by new revolutionary groups developing in the northern cities, and actualized by a series of devastating ghetto rebellions which broke out across the country in the summer of 1964 and continued in succeeding years through 1968. King and the ministerial leadership of SCLC fought back, but without either great enthusiasm or effect. In *Where Do We Go From Here: Chaos or Community?* King describes the debate between himself, Stokely Carmichael, who replaced the former seminarian John Lewis as national head of SNCC, and Floyd McKissick, who took over from former clergyman James Farmer as the national director of CORE, over the split that was opening up between the three groups over the Black Power issue:

> Sensing this . . . I asked Stokely and Floyd to join me
> in a frank discussion of the problem . . . For five long
> hours I pleaded with the group to abandon the Black
> Power slogan . . . Stokely replied by saying that the
> question of violence versus nonviolence was irrelevant.
> The real question was the need for black people to

consolidate their political and economic resources to achieve power . . . Floyd insisted that the slogan itself was important. "How can you arouse people to unite around a program without a slogan as a rallying cry? Didn't the labor movement have slogans? Haven't we had slogans all along in the freedom movement? What we need is a new slogan with "black" in it.[28]

The reaction within the middle class, interracial coalition that was the civil rights movement was predictable. Dismay over the turn toward Black nationalism spread a blanket of gloom over liberal whites in the National Council of Churches and the few predominantly white denominations which had stepped up their involvement in the struggle. Black church leaders such as Dr. J. H. Jackson, president of the National Baptist Convention, Inc., a denomination of more than five million Black Baptists, deplored the nationalist trend just as he had deplored King's militant leadership prior to 1966.[29] Individual pastors who all along had stayed aloof from SCLC and SNCC, preferring the NAACP style of reformist activity through the courts, were more than ever convinced that there were radical, anti-Christian elements with whom the Black church was incompatible, working within the freedom movement.

The northern city rebellions had already unnerved the white denominations and the liberal Jewish community. There were signs, by the winter of 1966–67, that a serious retrenchment in the racial-justice programs was developing and that funds for the civil rights groups were beginning to diminish. King's slashing attack against United States policy in Vietnam in 1964 had already alienated some of his support. The violent resistance of whites in Cicero, Illinois, during his ill-fated attempt to develop a foothold for SCLC in the North by demonstrating against the housing situation in metropolitan Chicago, unmasked once and for all the naked reality of white power in the conspiracy of northern business, labor and big-city machine politics. The almost indifference of the highly urbanized masses of the northern black ghettos to King's Negro Baptist brand of civil rights evangelism was equally apparent. Thus, he began, in 1967, to shift away from his earlier rejection of Black consciousness. That year he made preparations in Washington for the Poor Peoples' Campaign with "Black Is Beautiful" and Che Guevara posters going up on the walls of the SCLC headquarters and wondered if the Black nationalist groups would join him for the last-ditch assault on the Johnson administration.[30]

Following the Newark rebellion in July 1967, the first National Black Power Conference, which originated with Adam Clayton Powell in 1966, was held in the riot-scarred city with a thoughtful examination of the Black condition and soulful celebration. The conference was called and headed by Chuck Stone, Powell's legislative assistant, Dr. Nathan Wright, the Episcopal urban church executive from Newark, Omar A. Ahmed and Isaiah Robinson of New York, and Maulana Ron Karenga of Los Angeles—all of whom were outside of the SCLC orbit and rising stars in the Black Power movement. The conference was a notable success, but King was not present, nor were Wilkins, Rustin or Young. It was becoming increasingly clear that the NAACP-Christian, nonviolent hegemony over the Black revolution had entered upon and was out of phase with a development in the revolution that was primarily northern-based, cultural as well as political, self-righteously secular and radically alienated from American values and the traditional quest for Negro civil rights. By late 1967, SNCC had consolidated an alliance with revolutionary movements outside of the United States and was deep into relationships with the independence movement in Puerto Rico and with Fidel Castro. Carmichael was the new Messiah of a resurgent Black radicalism, although he was soon upstaged by his SNCC associate H. Rap Brown, who was even more committed to breaking out of the civil rights bag. The Black Christian radicalism which had made Martin Luther King, Jr., the high priest of the religion of civil rights in the American context was giving way to a somewhat less santified, less precise and less American ideology of Black Power. When someone at a meeting in Chicago asked Carmichael to move North "and help us get rid of Martin Luther King":

> Stokely broke into a smile. The mood of the meeting had shifted, and from that moment on there was no more criticism of Stokely. It became clear that the earlier criticism was something of a ritual. The full love which they all felt for him began to flow through the room, and you could feel it in the air. "We can't be everywhere at once," Stokely answered. "And we don't want to get into a fight with King. We have enough on our hands fighting the Man. Daley would like nothing better than for SNCC to get into a fight with King. That way he could get rid of us both. If you want to get rid of King— or anybody else—it's up to you to get together right here in Chicago. There are enough black people in Chicago to take over—if you get together and get rid of the Uncle Toms."[31]

Martin King, for all of his boisterous detractors, ushered in the idea of Black Power by making Black Americans conscious of their power to change the world. He could not sustain the dominance of Black Christian tradition, and before his assassination on the terrace of the Lorraine Hotel in Memphis on April 4, 1968, he was obliged to share the leadership of the masses with the aggressive secularity of Stokely Carmichael and H. Rap Brown. But more significant for Black Power and the dechristianization of Black radicalism was another son of a Baptist preacher, Malcolm X.

Malcolm Little—later to become Malcolm X—was born in Omaha, Nebraska, one of eleven children of a Black preacher who was an ardent disciple of Marcus Garvey. Malcolm grew up in the ghetto of Lansing, Michigan, where his father met a violent death by whites as a result of his independent spirit and outspoken Black consciousness. From Michigan the family moved to Harlem where Malcolm learned to "become one of the most depraved parasitical hustlers among New York's eight million people—four million of whom work, and the other four million of whom live off them."[32] After a brief career in various criminal pursuits, from con games and dope peddling to armed robbery, he was convicted of burglary in Boston and in February 1946, at the age of twenty-one, was sentenced to ten years in the Massachusetts State Prison at Charlestown. It was in prison that Malcolm, through correspondence with his family and later with Elijah Muhammad, learned of a religion which changed the course of his life.

In the *Autobiography* Malcolm recounts his remarkable ascent from the ignorance of a Harlem hoodlum to the knowledge of a self-made scholar. He read everything he could get his hands on, and by the time he was released by the Parole Board in 1952 had educated himself beyond the limits of anything he could have received at the best New England universities. Later he could tell an audience in London, England:

> . . . my alma mater was books, a good library. Every time I catch a plane, I have with me a book that I want to read—and that's a lot of books these days. If I weren't out here every day battling the white man, I could spend the rest of my life reading . . . I don't think anybody ever got more out of going to prison than I did. In fact, prison enabled me to study far more intensively than I would have if my life had gone differently and I had attended some college.[33]

Malcolm's extraordinary gifts were quickly recognized by Elijah Muhammad. After a period of recruiting for the Black Muslims in the bars and poolrooms of Detroit, to which he returned following release, he was named Assistant Minister to Temple Number One of that city in the summer of 1953. His favorite topic for sermons was "Christianity and the horrors of slavery," and with his knowledge of the history of Western civilization, he was able to link the two in a way that was to become the standard line of the Muslim polemic against Christianity—an attack that was practically irrefutable.

My brothers and sisters, our white slavemaster's Christian religion has taught us black people here in the wilderness of North America that we will sprout wings when we die and fly up into the sky where God will have for us a special place called heaven. This is white man's Christian religion used to *brainwash* us black people! We have *accepted* it! We have *believed* it! We have *practiced* it! And while we are doing all of that, for himself, this blue-eyed devil has *twisted* his Christianity, to keep his *foot* on our backs . . . to keep our eyes fixed on the pie in the sky and heaven in the hereafter . . . while *he* enjoys *his* heaven right *here* . . . on *this earth* . . . in *this* life.[34]

Malcolm's most devastating indictment of American society was his analysis of the religious hypocrisy of the white man and function of Christianity in the enslavement and subordination of Black people. He never wearied of holding Christianity up to the test of its own failure to make good its promises of peace, freedom and brotherly love for all the world. To him the abysmal failure of the church was self-evident. No intelligent Black man could be persuaded that a faith which had spawned the hatred and oppression of nonwhite peoples had anything of value to give mankind. The spectacle, said Malcolm, of white deacons barring church doors to young civil rights activists in the South who had come to pray for racial justice was more than enough proof that the white man's religion is blasphemously racist and that "very close at hand is the *end* of Christianity."

What was the response of the Black church to this barrage of truth? C. Eric Lincoln indicates that because of the freedom of the Black pulpit and the openness of Black theology, Muslim ministers, at first, were welcome and could speak frankly against Christianity in many Black churches across the nation.[35] Beyond the traditional "leniency" of the Black church, however, was the persuasiveness of the Muslim critique. When it was expeditiously modified to refer to *white* Christianity, it commanded the assent of many lower-class

Black Christians and presented the Black minister with an articulate competitor for the loyalty of his people. It was obvious to many ghetto pastors that they would be at a greater disadvantage not to allow Muslims to address their congregations than to submit and cheerfully acknowledge the truth of what they had to say.

In the 1960s when the Muslims were receiving dramatic notices in the press and "fishing" increasing numbers of Black Christians, it became more difficult for their ministers to gain access to Negro pulpits. Malcolm, in a genial, almost humorous vein, stripped Black preachers and churches of the last shred of dignity by pointing out, as Garvey had before him, their responsibility for "the Negro's deplorable economic condition" and how preachers conspired with the white power structure to keep their people impoverished. A reporter of the *Amsterdam News* heard him at a Los Angeles meeting and specified the angle of attack:

> He said $90,000,000 is spent annually in Los Angeles in upkeeping Negro preachers and churches, while [only] $60,000,000 is spent for houses and furniture combined . . . Malcolm X then pleaded with the Negro preachers to return to their churches and put their members' money to work "for the members" . . . building factories and supermarkets instead of [more] churches.[36]

The long-range goal of the Muslim movement was to entice Blacks away from the churches and to bring the entire race into the Nation of Islam. But a certain ambivalence in its operative strategy was forced by the massive reality of the organized church. For all its passivity in the face of the needs of the ghetto, the Black church still occupied an almost impregnable position. There is evidence that Elijah Muhammad, cognizant of this fact, has all but given up a frontal assault upon the church and is satisfied, at least temporarily, to work with churchmen in the name of racial unity. Appeals for cooperation across religious lines are replacing the uncompromising hostility of the past. After his break with Muhammad in 1964, Malcolm founded the Muslim Mosque, Inc., and announced that it would welcome the participation of all Negroes "despite their religious or non-religious beliefs." Further, his association with Black preachers like Detroit's Albert B. Cleage and New York's Milton Galamison made him realize that there were ministers whose radicalism matched his own, and he could not afford to alienate them. It is significant that he founded a religious organization, the Muslim Mosque, Inc., before he founded the Organization of Afro-American Unity.[37]

Malcolm recognized the historic importance of religion in the lives of Black people and, if his teaching turned many away from Christianity, they would require a spiritual foundation, a more profound anchorage for faith than was provided by a purely secular movement for Afro-American unity. It is true that he once said "we [Muslims] don't mix our religion with our politics and our economics and our social and civil activities,"[38] but that was an interim strategy—a calculated bid to remove the scandal of religious particularity from a movement which he hoped would solidify the entire Black community—Christians, Muslims and atheists—around the core idea of Black liberation. He was too aware of the false dichotomy between the sacred and secular and the hypocrisy which that separation had produced in white religion. He knew too well the history of Black people and had seen too much of the influence of religion as a motive force in Black radicalism to discard it, either in his own personal life or as a means of inspiring the masses to adopt Islam as the true faith. Keeping Islam available as a live option to Christianity provided him with one of his most potent ideological weapons for weening Blacks away from American values and radicalizing them for solidarity with other non-white peoples.

The assassination of Malcolm X in 1965 brought to an end one of the great prophets of Black liberation—a man whose influence, at his death, extended far beyond the borders of the United States to the Middle East, Africa and Latin America. It is impossible to calculate the extent to which

he would have redirected the course of Black history had
he lived. The Black revolution he envisioned was primarily
secular, but his incisive analysis of the role of Christianity
as an exploitative religion and his understanding of the
spiritual quality of an ultimate commitment—the power of
faith which had shaken the foundations of his own life and
impelled him to give himself to the liberation struggle—gives
him unquestionable standing as a religious leader, if one
understands the meaning of religion in the Black experience.

No facile appropriation of Marxist dogma or of some
purely materialistic philosophy of social change could have
awakened within this hipped cat from the streets of Harlem
the profound sense of mission and prophetic gifts which were
released by his conversion. Even after his discovery of the
apostasy of Elijah Muhammad he cherished the experience of
visiting Mecca and the confirmation of his faith by the great
seers and scholars of Islam, who welcomed him as a Black
brother. "The only true world solution today," he wrote, "is
governments guided by true religion—of the spirit. Here in
race-torn America, I am convinced that the Islam religion
is desperately needed, particularly by the American black
man."[39]

The truth that Malcolm perceived was not only cognitive,
but also revelational. His study of Western civilization opened
his eyes to the whole demonic structure of evil that had
been erected by the perversion of one of the world's great
religions. By his own estimate of the depth of that perversion
he came to the conclusion that the distortions of the Christian
view and the system of values which undergirded it could
not serve the purpose of restoring manhood and self-respect
to the Black man. But it was the compulsion of religious
faith, not unrelated to the Christian Bible itself, which caused
him to prophesy what had been revealed to him as the judgment of a righteous God upon the unconfessed and un-
repented sins of white Western civilization. And in that
grace:

I believe that God is giving the world's so-called "Christian" white society its last opportunity to repent and

atone for the crime of exploiting and enslaving the world's non-white peoples. It is exactly as when God gave Pharaoh a chance to repent. But Pharaoh persisted in his refusal to give justice to those whom he oppressed. And, we know, God finally destroyed Pharaoh.[40]

Since Malcolm's death various movements within and outside the Black community have laid claim to his legacy.[41] The legacy of Malcolm cannot be the exclusive possession of any one group. It belongs to all Black people who are struggling against racism, colonialism, neocolonialism and imperialism in the world today. It belongs to secularists and religionists alike, for during his brief lifetime Malcolm brought Black religion and Black politics together for the spiritual edification and political empowerment of Black people. Although he repudiated Christianity, his prophetic ministry as a Black Muslim contributed to the further development of that idigenous Black religion which was never exclusively Christian in the historic sense. And what he stood for as an exponent of that ghettoized Black religion—namely, justice and liberation—was the continuation of a great tradition of nativistic-messianic religion in the United States, Africa and the Caribbean. Whatever else Black Christianity may be, it is also a part of the tradition he shared, and it is precisely for this reason that many Black churchmen are saying today, "The God who spoke by the prophets and in the fullness of time by his Son, *now in this present time, speaks to us through Brother Malcolm.*"[42]

No one outside the church has spoken more clearly concerning the relationship of the religious faith of Black people to Black awareness, pride and empowerment than Malcolm. His was a polemical message directed against white Christianity, but its real strength was not in its sectarianism, but in the difference a militant religion could make in the life of a young Harlemite who was bound for self-destruction until— as he wrote: "Every instinct of the ghetto jungle streets, every hustling fox and criminal wolf instinct in me . . . was struck dumb."[43] Its strength was in the extraordinary insight it gave him into a truth about Black life that was validated in the experience of every Negro, and the courage it gave him to speak that unvarnished truth unflinchingly. The common people heard him gladly and were purified and ennobled by his words. The Black church, smug in its complacency and hiding behind the façade of what Nathan Wright calls "a honkyfied version of the faith," was forced to acknowledge that its vision of an integrated, nonviolent America as the *telos* of powerless love, had alienated large numbers of Black people. That acknowledgment was not to come, as often with prophets, until after Malcolm's death, and it must be conceded that it has not yet come to the majority of Black Christians in America. But the religiopolitical legacy of Malcolm X awakened the spirit of dissidence in the Black church, and white Christianity will never again find easy acceptance among Black people.

Despite the dechristianization process, the separation of Black radicalism from its Christian roots was never wholly achieved. Even the Muslims were influenced by patterns of Black church life, by former Christian ministers who crossed over with vestiges of their old faith still clinging to their preaching, and particularly by the fact that the Muslims acknowledged the historical Jesus. In a negative way their anti-Christian polemics backed them into a grudging esteem of authentic Christianity.[44] In somewhat the same way Black nationalists groups took cognizance of the civil rights movement and were affected by it even as they repudiated its goals. Rejecting the idea that the Black man could "overcome" as long as he desired to be integrated into a sick society, they regarded every apparent victory within the system as mere tokenism which simply blinded more Blacks to the real truth. Also, the fact that the movement was led by a Black preacher invited their contempt. But again the popularity of Martin Luther King and the widespread response of Black folk to the day-to-day struggle to restrain the lawlessness and violence of whites made it impossible to mount a frontal attack against King and maintain, at the same time, a good relationship with thousands of Blacks. Moreover, the Muslims did not deny the necessity of justice and equality. They differed with King and Wilkins over strategy and long-range goals. Elijah Muhammad said:

> We have not been opposed to the NAACP's cause for the National Advancement of the so-called Negroes. Only we feel that the NAACP should have at its head a Black Man, and not a white man . . . and should not at this late date seek integration of the Negroes and Whites . . . Seeking love and equal recognition among this people is the most foolish and ignorant thing that a Negro leader could do in this late date and it would eventually prove the total destruction of us, as a people.[45]

Nor did the Muslims and other nationalists yield to the attempt of the white press to incite an internecine struggle in the Negro leadership ranks. They were sometimes attacked publicly by Negro leaders, but more often they avoided public laundering and reserved their most inflammatory rhetoric for whites. Criticism of King, Wilkins and Young continued in the relatively closed circle of the radical movements and only occasionally seeped into the public arena. When it did, the exchange was sharp and brief. For the most part, the relationship between the Muslim and Christian leaders, such as King and Abernathy, could be described as a restrained cordiality. Although King rejected what he called "hate groups," he secretly admired the way the Muslims "took care of business."[46] On their part, both Malcolm and Muhammad welcomed dialogue with the civil rights leaders, and occasionally Muhammad invited them to meet with him at his headquarters in Chicago. Wyatt T. Walker tells how once Malcolm and Martin happened to meet in an airport, and the Muslim leader told King that what he was doing was actually helping the civil rights movement.[47] Muslim ministers still accept invitations to speak at church-sponsored meetings, and although the areas of disagreement are recognized, there is usually fundamental concurrence on the necessity of maintaining unity in the face of the white conspiracy to "divide and conquer."

It is, therefore, important to recognize that the relationship between the dechristianization tendencies within the nationalistic movements and the rechristianizing efforts of King was one of both competition and interdependence. It is possible that one could not have existed without the other. Although Malcolm was a converted Muslim three years before the Montgomery bus boycott, he did not reach the zenith of his ministry until the late 1950s and early 1960s, when the climate of Black resistance to institutionalized racism had been heated to the boiling point by King's direct-action program. Northern Blacks were elated over the movement's successes in the South, but frustrated by the difficulty of translating those victories into anything meaningful for the big-city ghettos. Malcolm found a ready audience in this milieu because Blacks were looking for a strategy of involvement more appropriate to their needs in the North than the marches, rallies and picketing which were desegregating lunch counters in the South.

Conversely, the international attention and the power of the national coalition King was able to secure by the time of the March on Washington, received considerable impetus from Blacks (and whites) outside the South who had been radicalized by the Black Muslims and other nationalist groups. King had, of course, already earned his reputation, but during the period 1963–64 resistance to his leadership was rising among those who were listening intently to Malcolm and were beginning to push Martin toward a more radical posture if he were to keep younger Blacks in the movement. Their aggressive tactics and tougher ideological line also forced the power structure in Washington to take King's church-oriented movement more seriously as a desirable alternative. Thus, pushed from behind by the radical sentiment building up outside of SCLC and pulled forward by his own diagnosis of fundamental issues, King took the offensive against the Vietnam War and moved toward a more political stance in the sanitation workers' strikes and the Poor Peoples' Campaign.

One cannot fully understand the contemporary Black revolution without grasping the complementary functions of independence and interdependence between Malcolm and Martin which bound them together in a dialectic of social action in the sixties that was, at one and the same time, cultural and political, Christian and non-Christian, separatist and integrationist. They learned from one another and received impelling power from one another. Little had been written about how they reached to one another in private, or whether or not they were really conscious of reciprocal roles in the drama being played out in the Black community. But it does seem incontrovertible that their contributions cannot be evaluated separately. These two men, both of whom were struck down by assassins' bullets at the peak of their careers, approach the vocation of Black liberation from two profoundly political-religious perspectives which had been growing silently, side by side, in the fecund soil of the Black folk tradition. They shared the nourishment of that tradition together and received tremendous moral and spiritual power by calling forth from each other, perhaps unconsciously, the single, full-orbed interpretation of Black reality which caught and held in tension the antimonies of the centuries-old yearning for Black manhood and liberation.

What could have been a more radical understanding of Black America than Malcolm's when he called for Black people to give up the "slave religion" of Christianity and discover integrity and brotherhood in the Nation of Islam? Not only that, but to turn their backs, once and for all, physically and ideologically, on all that America offered or promised. Not only that, but joyfully to take up the gun, if that became necessary, to protect themselves and make their freedom secure. And what could have been more radical than Martin's daring belief that in twentieth-century America—after two world wars, a devastating economic depression, and a series of ill-advised imperialistic adventures in Latin America and Southeast Asia—it was possible to make white people Christians, to make love the operative agent of reconciliation between Black and white, rich and poor? What could have been more radical than, after all the dismal trials and failures, to suppose that the Christian Church could become Christian, become the Church of the Sermon on the Mount and the Good Friday crucifixion?

It is no wonder that Harold Cruse could write that "The historically true, native American radicalism is black radicalism."[48] But what Cruse did not perceive was that this unique Black radicalism has religious roots that lie deep and unseverable in the soul of Black folk. His otherwise perceptive analysis of "the crisis" scarcely recognizes the existence of religion in the Black community. Its stark reality must not be overlooked in any examination of what has been occurring in the Black world. The radical faiths of Malcolm and Martin coalesce in the opaque depths of a Black spirituality that is neither Protestant nor Catholic, Christian nor Islamic in its essence, but both comprehends and transcends these ways of believing in God by experiencing his real presence, by becoming one with him in suffering, in struggle and in the celebration of the liberation of man.

CHAPTER VIII

Black Power, Black People and Theological Renewal

> Black Theology is a theology of black libera-
> tion. It seeks to plumb the black condition in
> the light of God's revelation in Jesus Christ, so
> that the black community can see that the
> gospel is commensurate with the achievement
> of black humanity . . . The message of liber-
> ation is the revelation of God as revealed in
> the incarnation of Jesus Christ. Freedom IS the
> gospel. Jesus is the Liberator!
>
> National Committee of Black Churchmen

THE CIVIL RIGHTS movement began to show signs of serious
disability when Martin Luther King, Jr., and the SCLC staff
ran afoul of northern white power in the form of the Chicago
Board of Realtors and the Daley machine during the long,
hot summer of 1966. It rallied momentarily in 1967 when, with
symptoms of desperation, it turned its attention to Washington, D.C., and the buildup for the Poor Peoples' March. But
finally, amid great consternation and confusion, it died with
the tragic assassination of Dr. King on April 4, 1968. During
those three fitful years, 1966 to 1968, the Black community in
the United States went through a hardening process from
which it is not likely to recover for many years.

When the shouts of anger, the sounds of violence and the

weeping died away, when the smoke cleared from the streets of Washington and Martin King was laid to rest on the campus of his beloved Morehouse College, a great and terrible silence settled down upon Black communities all over the nation. It was as if a dark shadow, as when there is an eclipse of the sun, was sweeping silently and swiftly across the broad lap of the land—from the wealthy upper-class neighborhoods of suburban Atlanta, across the tarpaper sharecropper cabins of the Mississippi Delta, to the lonely, dilapidated rooming houses of the Albina area of Portland, Oregon. Black people turned off their radios and televisions and settled back to think in the gathering darkness. What was the meaning of the events just past? What was the meaning of the last ten or twelve years of the civil rights struggle which had claimed so much of the flower of Black youth and now, in this swift and terrible way, had snatched away this brilliant young Baptist preacher who called himself a "drum major for justice"?

That rethinking of the meaning of the Black experience in America has not yet ended. But it is now possible to assume, on the threshold of the 1970s, that the buoyant optimism of the King era passed that April night into the custody of history, and a new tough-minded skepticism, self-interest and sense of survival has slowly taken over Black America. At first there was fierce anger, then frustration, and finally deep despair. But the long years of adamantine resistance and suffering had taught lessons that could not be so easily forgotten. Those lessons—scarcely remembered during the almost light-hearted days of the civil rights movement—began to be dredged up from the depths of the collective consciousness of the masses and the old feeling of closing ranks, of insularity and of inner-directedness, in the face of the overwhelming coercion and repression of the white community, generated a new confidence and hope which rested upon foundations deeper and firmer than anything America had promised or withheld.

It would not again be possible to make Black people forget who they were, from whence they had come, and what were the necessities of true manhood and womanhood in the land that was soaked in the blood of their martyrs and whose people had betrayed Black trust, perhaps for the last time. In community meetings, schools and churches all over the nation, Black people were singing once again, the magnificent words of James Weldon Johnson's anthem:

> Lest our feet stray from the paths
>   of the place where we met Thee,
> Lest our hearts, drunk with the wine
>   of the world, we forget Thee.
> Shadowed beneath Thy hand,
> May we forever stand,
> True to our God, true to our native land.

The development generally described as the Black Power movement was heightened and consolidated by the assassination of King. It was, in a way, the inevitable and historic response of the Black community to white perfidy—this time to a series of so-called "backlashes" in the white community, beginning in 1964, to the retreat of the Federal Government from both the so-called "War on Poverty" and Johnson's commitment to enforce the Civil Rights Act of 1964 and the Voting Rights Act of 1965, and finally, to the election of Richard M. Nixon to the presidency in the fall of 1968. Although the movement was born on Highway 51, between Memphis, Tennessee, and Jackson, Mississippi, its true home and its most rapid gains were made in the great central cities of the nation's largest metropolitan areas, where there were in excess of 12,000,000 Blacks in 1966 and where they were to increase by an average annual growth of 316,000 per year through 1985.[1] This was unmistakably, as James Boggs has said, "the Black man's land." The most important contribution of the Black Power concept was the recognition of the crucial importance of land and the control of land—and the recognition that for the people who lived on this increasingly Blackenized land, which whites had already declared unfit for white habitation by a plebiscite of white feet running to the nearest suburb, racial integration was an idle dream. Black Power meant that only by Black people solidifying their ranks through a new consciousness of history and culture, building political and economic power, and being willing to legitimize ethnocentrism, group self-interest and even defensive violence, if necessary, could they hope to survive the onslaught of repression following in the wake of disillusioned white liberalism, and take control of their own future.

It was not that all Black people in America became, between 1966 and 1968, advocates of Black nationalism. *All* black people have never been the advocates of anything except the respect, freedom to live and to prosper accorded other segments of American society. But despite the white-controlled public polls which attempted to prove the contrary, Black people of all classes and levels of education shared in common a general disenchantment with the professed goals of American democracy, a new sophistication about power—about what survival in the United States *really* requires—and a new feeling of pride in the strange and wonderful beauty of being Black and "letting it all hang out," because the era of humiliation, self-delusion and dishonesty was over and gone forever.

The old authoritarian leadership of the Black community and the great national movements with their grand designs for making America live up to her ideals, were relegated to somewhere near the bottom of the Black agenda, and highest priority was given to the confrontation of white power in one's own private, daily life and in one's own neighborhood or city. Ocean Hill-Brownsville became the national symbol of Black localism and realism. New and younger leaders and prophets emerged from among the people themselves and somehow knew, without having to be told, that they were accountable to the masses and could speak for them only when given license to do so. From the first Black Power Conference, meeting against the flickering backdrop of random fires in the closing days of the Newark rebellion in the summer of 1967, the white press and television news services expressed astonishment at the decision of Black groups to bar them from press conferences and to prohibit their receiving statements and personal interviews from Black leaders. The ranks were closing around a new style of Black liberation and leadership. There was a feeling of obdurancy and hipness in the air. Black people had torn away the mask of white superiority and had stared into the watery, lackluster eyes behind it to see fear, ignorance and demoralization.

At a time when white morale was at its lowest ebb, with white young people running amuck from their middle-class parents and teachers, when the white community was reeling from the daily exposés of drug abuse and sexual perversion, when a pervasive hopelessness over inflation and Vietnam gripped the nation, the Black community was swinging with new life in a renascence of history and culture, a sense of pride and power, and a new feeling of identity with Africa and the revolutionary peoples of the Third World. It was a strange situation. White liberals bristled with indignation. Conservatives muttered about detention laws and concentration camps. And the Black community, for the first time in many years, ignored the reaction of the majority and went on getting itself together, planning ghetto economic development, community control of schools, Black studies, the culture of "the black world" and talking about "Soul" and liberation.

The final stages of the Meredith Mississippi Freedom March in June, 1966, saw many Black churchmen from the North participating. They were, perhaps, less shaken than their brothers-in-the-cloth from the South when the overalled young SNCC workers defied King and belligerently raised the cry of "Black Power!" at the closing ceremony in Jackson. The northern-city rebellions and the proliferation of militant ghetto community organizations in Chicago, Detroit, New York, and a score of other cities from Baltimore to the San Francisco Bay area, had already heralded the shift of the movement toward a more race-conscious and political posture. Many of the clergy who worked within the structures of the predominantly white churches had been fighting a growing backlash in the religious establishment as the Saul Alinsky-style community organizations came into disfavor and church funds began to be cut off.[2] Men like Dr. Benjamin A. Payton, the executive of the Commission on Religion and Race of the National Council of Churches, and Dr. Edler G. Hawkins, then pastor of the St. Augustine Presbyterian Church in New York City, the undisputed leader of Black Presbyterians in the North, had already received a prevision of the breakup of the white middle class-Black churchman coalition, which since 1963 had supported Dr. King and the Southern Christian Leadership Conference.

Early in July, 1966, Payton called a meeting in his office at the Interchurch Center in New York, which was attended by Dr. Anna Arnold Hedgeman, his associate in the Commission on Religion and Race, Dr. J. Oscar Lee, the National Council executive for racial and cultural affairs, Rev. H. R. Hughes, pastor of the Bethel A.M.E. Church of New York, and the author. The purpose was to discuss the almost hysterical reaction of the white clergy to Black Power, the way in which the slogan was being distorted by white churchmen and bandied about wildly and thoughtlessly by Black spokesmen, and the obvious inability of the Southern Christian Leadership Conference to respond positively to the new situation and mobilize the increasing numbers of radical Black clergy in the North for leadership in the next stage of the struggle. It was decided to form an ad hoc group called the National Committee of Negro Churchmen and to publish a statement on Black Power that would clear the air, clarify the position of northern Black church leadership, and point to some of the theological implications of the concept.

Within a few days a draft statement was prepared by Payton and was revised and adopted by a small group of churchmen who met at the Bethel Church in Harlem. The group pledged to raise $10,000 for a full page in the New York *Times* and planned for a subsequent organizing meeting of the Ad Hoc Committee at Mother Zion A.M.E.Z. Church. Those who formed the nucleus of the new organization included, in addition to those named above, Dr. Nathan Wright, who later was chairman of the first National Conference on Black Power, Methodist Bishop Charles F.

Golden of Nashville, Rev. Horace Sharper of Newark, Rev. M. L. Wilson, whose Convent Avenue Baptist Church became the first headquarters of NCNC, and Rev. J. Metz Rollins, later elected the first full-time executive of the organization.

The Black Power statement, published in the July 31, 1966, edition of the New York *Times* and in several other newspapers during the following weeks, received widespread recognition and support both in the United States and overseas. It was the first carefully reasoned, analytical pronouncement on Black Power to get wide publicity, and the fact that among its signatories were some of the best-known and most powerful Black preachers in America made it fall upon the white leadership of both the church and society with shock and disquietude. Although it was intended to be read by the masses of Negroes, its real target was "the leaders of America" —the white ecclesiastical and secular bureaucracies which molded the opinion of the American public regarding race relations and who had recoiled in horror at what it considered the dangerous trend of the Black community toward lawlessness and reverse racism. The Black churchmen's statement declared forthrightly:

> As black men who were long ago forced out of the white church to create and to wield "black power," we fail to understand the emotional quality of the outcry of some clergy against the use of the term today. It is not enough to answer that "integration" is the solution. For it is precisely the nature of the operation of power under some forms of integration which is being challenged . . . Without . . . capacity to *participate with power*—i.e., to have some organized political and economic strength to really influence people with whom one interacts—integration is not meaningful . . . We regard as sheer hypocrisy or as a blind and dangerous illusion the view that opposes love to power. Love should be a controlling element in power, but what love opposes is precisely the misuse and abuse of power, not power itself. So long as white churchmen continue to moralize and misinterpret Christian love, so long will justice continue to be subverted in this land.[3]

By all counts, despite its call for organizing the Black masses and the "rebuilding of our cities," the NCNC statement was a moderate document, although by the standards of the time it read like a radical manifesto. Vincent Harding rightly observes that:

> Its definition of black goals was thoroughly American. The churchmen repeatedly claimed that black people wanted power, "to participate more effectively at all levels of the life of the nation." At the same time they condemned programs of either "separation" or "domination," and made a point of referring to America as "our beloved country" and our "beloved homeland."[4]

But it is important to recognize that the theological and political definitions of the statement were considerably to the left of a broad spectrum of the Black middle-class. It placed the leaders who signed it in unapologetic discontinuity with the civil rights movement and the liberalistic, reconciliation strategy of King and the SCLC. King had talked a great deal about Christian love, and many white liberals rested easy in their compromises because they believed that they could depend upon what they considered the Negro's love-of-the-enemy tradition not to place white liberal friends in an intolerable position with their peers and masters. The critique of the love ideal as the motivating force of the freedom movement cast a shadow of doubt across the assumption that the conscience of white people could any longer be appealed to by the redemptive suffering of Black people and warned white America that power, not love, was the matter at issue. "Powerlessness," said the NCNC statement, "breeds a race of beggars. We are faced now with a situation where conscienceless power meets powerless conscience, threatening the very foundations of our nation."

There is no evidence that King took more than a glancing notice of the Black Power statement or recognized in it a challenge to the SCLC domination of the Christian forces for racial justice, even though some close friends in the North and even members of the SCLC Board of Directors were among the signatories. Moreover, the historic Black Methodist denominations and the three major Black Baptist Conventions followed King in taking no official notice of the NCNC. Indeed, one or two of the Black denominations came perilously close to repudiating Black Power. The NCNC, however, went on to establish headquarters at the Convent Avenue Church in Harlem and to erect a permanent organization in Dallas in November 1967. Although it was studiously ignored by the hierarchy of the Black churches, it did receive considerable attention from Black nationalist groups in the North. Stokely Carmichael quoted freely from the Black Power statement in various speeches around the country. The Black Power Conference in Newark had a religion workshop which was well attended by nonchurch radicals and was dominated by NCNC members and representatives of Maulana Ron Karenga's US. Floyd McKissick, the national director of CORE, who himself had attempted to articulate a responsible doctrine of Black Power, entered into conversations with NCNC officials exploring areas of collaboration. Finally, the National Council of Churches and a few of the predominantly white denominations, faced with the rebellion of their most respected Black leadership, found it expedient to give at least tentative recognition to the legitimacy of the concept of Black Power and to counsel white churchmen to give serious consideration to the need for power and self-determination in the Black community.[5] A few white churchmen were genuinely sympathetic, and occasionally NCNC spokesmen found more acceptance of the concept in white congregations than in middle-class Black congregations.

In September 1967, the National Council of Churches Division of Christian Life and Work sponsored a conference on the urban crisis in Washington, D.C. The conference brought together Black and white church activists and religion and race executives from several denominations and many parts of the country. In the opening session the Black delegates, many of them members of NCNC, which was still an ad hoc confederation representing both all-Black denominations and those that were predominantly white, insisted that the conference be divided into two caucuses, one Black and one white. It was further proposed that the caucuses should meet separately for most of the conference and come together for a final plenary session. It was the first time such a proposal had been made in the history of the ecumenical movement in the United States. The white churchmen made a weak gesture of remonstrance, but the Blacks were firm and uncharacteristically aggressive. The motion to divide was sustained, and the two groups retired to separate meeting rooms with an incredible feeling in the air that something of grave significance was taking place—not unlike the action of Richard Allen and Absalom Jones in 1786—and that this historic decision of 1967 would be irreversible.

The conference finally ajourned, after a tumultuous closing session, with the adoption of a statement prepared by each of the caucuses, the white group having divided in confusion over the issue of separation and having ejected some of its dissenting members. The statement of the Black churchmen supported Black Power, advocated the creation of Black caucuses, and called for a more radical involvement of church structures in the problems of the cities. The white churchmen once again deplored the faithlessness of the white churches, but in an unprecedented statement affirmed the position of the Blacks unequivocably and called upon whites to return to the white community to deal, as they had not done before, with the virulence of white racism.

The NCC Washington conference was held two months prior to the first convocation of the NCNC, which in Dallas became the National Committee of Negro Churchmen (later to become the National Committee of Black Churchmen, NCBC). It went far beyond the usual pronouncement-making of interdenominational assemblies. The rapid development of Black consciousness in American Protestantism and the desire of Blacks to organize pressure groups in almost every major white denomination, including the Roman Catholic Church, is directly traceable to the Washington meeting, and within a year Black clergy caucuses had been established or revitalized (as in the case of the United Presbyterians and the United

Church of Christ) in nine national denominations, representing the vast majority of organized Christians in the United States.[6] It was the most dramatic demonstration of the influence of the Black Power movement within the sacred precincts of the American religious establishment and inaugurated an era of confrontation and negotiation between Black and white churchmen which was unprecedented in the twentieth century.

It cannot be doubted that the impetus for this turn of events within American Christianity came from outside the organized church. It was the Black folk of Watts, Newark, Detroit, and hundreds of other communities across the nation and the young Black radicals of SNCC and the northern Black nationalist groups—including the Nation of Islam—who convinced Black preachers that the church was expendable if it was unwilling to immerse itself in the vortex of the Black Power movement. The Black Power motif was pregnant with moral and religious meaning, and the Black churchmen could not evade its magnetic force once the people took the cause of liberation into their own hands.

Although King did not immediately participate in this development, he gradually became aware of its significance for both the Black revolution and for American Christianity. During the Poor People's Campaign he strengthened his relationships with Black churchmen at the Interchurch Center in New York City. His tremendous work load of administering the affairs of SCLC, organizing opposition to the war and developing the second March on Washington, prevented him from joining the small group of preachers in the Northeast who were plotting the course of dissident Black churchmen and making new contacts with the Black Power leaders. It is clear, however, that by late 1967 he was well on his way to a basic shift in his own theological and ideological referents and saw the necessity of NCBC's attack on the entrenched power of the white denominational structures. Not only did he call upon NCBC leadership for support in training cadres of Black ministers in key cities under a grant from the Ford Foundation, but he sent SCLC staff to NCBC meetings. Some of his closest associates, like Hosea Williams, T. Y. Rogers and Wyatt T. Walker, became members of the new organization.

The logic of the NCBC policies was inescapable, although as Harding's excellent critique of its public statements demonstrate, the group has yet to prove that it has more to contribute than revolutionary rhetoric and is prepared to "find, educate and mobilize their logical constituencies around the positions taken . . ."[7] The day King was assassinated in Memphis the Board of Directors of NCBC was meeting in Chicago, where it supported the Poor People's March on Washington and issued a highly significant and much neglected statement to the white denominations. The statement, entitled "Urban Mission in a Time of Crisis," raised serious questions about the work of the white denominations in Black communities. It called upon the white mission agencies to "surrender" their hegemony over ghetto social-service institutions and "come to the bargaining table" with Black churchmen for the transfer of power to those who were the legitimate religious leaders of the Black community.[8]

In January 1967, when the enemies of Adam Clayton Powell succeeded in unseating him from his strategic position in the U. S. Congress, NCBC blasted the "arbitrary and cynical use of power" by the white members of the House of Representatives and called for Powell's re-establishment and a uniform standard of ethics which would expose and discipline every member of the Congress who not only shared his foibles, but exceeded him in manipulating the system for political favor and personal aggrandizement. In the same year, NCBC projected plans for a National Renewal and Development Corporation to enable the Black community to develop an economic power base by controlling the selection of sites and personnel for urban renewal and community development under the Model Cities and other government programs. Earlier Benjamin Payton, its first national coordinator, had conceived of a program for metropolitan development by government and private industry, calling for a minimum budget of 8.4 billion dollars per year for a five-year period. Payton's plan predated similar proposals by the National Urban League and the A. Philip Randolph Institute and greatly influenced the later NCBC efforts in this direction. The collapse of Lyndon Johnson's Great Society and the reluctance of the National Council of Churches to support ambitious and Black Power-generating approaches to the urban crisis eventually forced the organization to abandon the proposal for the Renewal and Development Corporation and an Economic Development Bank. The irony did not pass unremarked in the NCBC Board that, its pretensions toward Black Power notwithstanding, it had neither the expertise nor the financial resources necessary to launch a national ghetto-development scheme.

A continuing frustration of the NCBC during the late sixties was the problem of encouraging the organization of powerful Black caucuses within the predominantly white churches while, simultaneously, welding those caucuses together in such a way that their prior loyalty would be given to NCBC. For example, as the Unitarian, Methodist and Lutheran caucuses received funds for program implementation, they began to develop staffs and convene expensive national meetings, diverting much-needed resources that might otherwise have been used to undergird the National Committee. The consequence was the inability of the new interdenominational body to produce rapidly the apparatus of an efficient national movement—regional offices, membership drives, fund raising, educational and action programs, and the integration of Black laity into its clergy-dominated structures. Moreover, despite the fact that several powerful bishops and pastors were members of NCBC, the great Black denominations stood aloof and regarded it with suspicion.

In the first place, NCBC was too closely identified with men who served in the white denominations—particularly the United Presbyterians, Episcopalians and Unitarian-Universalists—whose congregations were largely composed of the top layer of the Black bourgeoisie and whose training and work habits were conspicuously under the influence of white norms. Secondly, the leaders of the Black communions were no more willing to permit this new northern-based group to encroach upon their power and prerogatives than they were prepared to be relegated to a subordinate position by King's southern-based SCLC. Accordingly, many Black ministers assumed a "wait and see" attitude toward NCBC and kept an alert eye open for signals from their bishops and denominational leaders.

American Christianity exists, like the society, in two worlds, one white and the other Black. Because the primary leadership and power of NCBC, in its early years, was in the white rather than the Black world, this fact prevented the coolness of the Black denominations from freezing it to death before it had an opportunity to develop its internal vitality. Although the Black churches of the white denominations are resident in Black neighborhoods and have their institutional roots and branches in the Black community, their ministers have fought their way, over the years, into the white structures of which they are a part. In recent years they have succeeded in garnering a few committee memberships and chairmanships in key national programs. In a few denominations they have even acquired an impressive number, relatively speaking, of top-echelon staff positions. The linkages between NCBC and these strategic outposts made it possible for the organization to continue to exist, if not thrive, without the wholehearted support of the hierarchy and grass-roots following of the Negro Baptists and Methodists.[9] The Black caucuses of the white churches, while proliferating their own structures, were an important political factor in obtaining access for NCBC spokesmen to national decision-making bodies like the National Council of Churches' Crisis in the Nation Program and in releasing denominational funds for the administration of NCBC.

Shortly after the creation of the Interreligious Foundation for Community Organization (IFCO) in 1966, a strong Black caucus emerged in the interracial Board of Directors and controlled most of its deliberations.[10] The leaders and most of the members of the IFCO caucus were active members of NCBC, and the policies of the two organizations were generally coordinated. When the director of IFCO, Rev. Lucius Walker, introduced the idea of a National Black

Economic Development Conference to be held in Detroit in April 1969, he was not operating out of an ideological and institutional vacuum. Already, in 1966, Benjamin Payton, Albert Cleage, Bryant George and other Black ministers who were instrumental in the formation of both IFCO and NCBC had discussed Black economic development as the next stage of the civil rights struggle. By 1968, NCBC had organized itself into five regional areas and was seeking funds for large-scale regional meetings to discuss the feasibility of church-sponsored economic development along the lines suggested by the concept of an Economic Development Bank.

The IFCO-sponsored National Black Economic Development Conference was, therefore, a direct outgrowth of trends which had been discernible for at least two years in Black church circles and among those community organizations which had been funded by IFCO. It was inevitable that the Black churchmen, particularly those from the predominantly white denominations, would be deeply implicated in the most important action to come out of the Conference— the Black Manifesto. It is not possible to understand why NCBC moved as it did to support the Manifesto and IFCO, or the essential meaning of the crisis which was precipitated, without understanding the close relationship between IFCO and the mission agencies of the white churches in which a few Black churchmen played key roles, the interlocking membership between IFCO's Black caucus, the Black caucuses of the white denominations and NCBC, and the primary leadership of Black churchmen from the white denominations and the National Council of Churches on the Board of NCBC. For the most part, these organizations and the crisis of the Black Manifesto in which they were all involved, were outside the institutional life and work of the historic Black denominations. What occurred in Detroit, and later at the Riverside Church in New York City, was the culmination of many years of institutionalized racism in the white structures of American Protestantism and Roman Catholicism, but also the curiously ironic consequence of an intricate pattern of good intentions and bad strategy, miscalculated superiority and incompetence, inaction and over-reaction on the part of the white liberal church establishment. The Black churches of the nation, and Black religion as one *genre* of American religiosity, were drawn into the gravitational field of the social and religious forces which were joined in the Detroit Conference and which will continue in the future to unite and radicalize Black religionists in the United States.

The Black Economic Development Conference (BEDC) met April 25–27 in Detroit. It was attended by more than 600 persons from all segments of the Black community, many of them coming as delegated representatives of ghetto community organizations. The purpose was to "help coordinate Black economic development and community organization efforts and to give members of the Black community a chance to develop an agenda for total community development."[11] The delegates heard James Boggs, the Detroit socialist theoretician; Robert S. Browne, an economist from Fairleigh Dickinson University in New Jersey; Milton Henry, then Vice-President of the Republic of New Africa; Lucius Walker, the executive director of IFCO, James Bond of Atlanta, and many of the leading advocates of Black Power in the nation. In numerous resolutions the Conference rejected "Black capitalism" and "minority entrepreneurship" and emphasized the importance of land ownership, cooperatives and mass-based organizations in urban areas for political and economic control. It also voted for the continuation of the Conference as a clearinghouse for national strategies for Black economic development.

On the night of April 26, James Forman, the International Affairs director of SNCC and one of the leaders of its famous Mississippi Project, presented the Black Manifesto, which he announced as a consensus of the Conference.[12] Forman himself had written the preamble to the Manifesto and had discussed it with several persons, including churchmen, before making it his address to the delegates. There was some question, in view of the rules of order of the Conference, of the parliamentary correctness of the procedure by which the document reached the floor, but on the next day Lucius Walker, the chairman, declared that the Black Manifesto had been approved by a vote of 187 to 63, with many delegates abstaining,[13] and in any case, Forman's presentation expressed both the spirit and the ideological conviction of a majority of the grass-roots leadership in attendance. Neither BEDC nor IFCO attempted to rescind or withdraw from the demands Forman put forth, although some leaders expressed reservations about the preamble.

The Manifesto's preamble was a caustic indictment of Black moderation and white racism. It called for the identification of Black America with Africa and the rejection of American capitalism and imperialism. "We are dedicated," said Forman, "to building a socialist society inside the United States . . . led by Black people . . . concerned about the total humanity of the world." He broadly hinted at the seizure of state power and guerrilla warfare and declared that the power of the Conference was being taken over by "revolutionary right," while complimenting IFCO for "a magnificent job" and promising the Conference leadership a place in the vanguard movement being launched by the Manifesto. According to one observer, Lucius Walker deliberately had no prior agenda for the Conference and wanted it to be "taken over." "The hope was that something like a strategy of action and consensus would emerge from the delegates themselves."[14] Forman was an invited delegate and had a plan of action.

Actually, it was the introduction, or preamble, rather than the Manifesto itself, that caused the greatest consternation and the strongest statements of repudiation from white churchmen. Rabbi Marc Tanenbaum, the president of IFCO and National Director of Interreligious Affairs for the American Jewish Committee (which subsequently withdrew from IFCO over the Manifesto), complained of the "Marxist-Leninist doctrine" and the "use of force."[15] Edwin H. Tuller, General Secretary of the American Baptist Convention, could not agree with "the complete elimination of capitalism" and deplored "the military and guerrilla stance taken by

Mr. Forman."[16] While the Manifesto also used the rhetoric
of violence, it was somewhat qualified by the disclaimer
"that this is the road we want to take . . . but let us be
very clear that we are not opposed to force . . . and violence,"
and by stating in the final paragraph: "Our demands are
negotiable, but they cannot be minimized."

The main text of the Manifesto called for reparations to
Black people of $500,000,000, an exceedingly modest sum,
to be paid through BEDC by the white Protestant and
Catholic churches and the Jewish synagogues of America.
Repeating the theme that was dealt with more fully in the
preamble, the Manifesto declared that the white churches
and synagogues are "part and parcel of the system of capitalism" and Black exploitation. "For the sake of the churches
and synagogues," it continued, "we hope that they have the
wisdom to understand that these demands are modest and
reasonable." In detailing the uses to which the money would
be put, the Manifesto enumerated the following programs,
to which sums from $10 million to $200 million dollars were
to be allotted:

—A southern land bank to secure land for Black farmers;
—Black-controlled publishing and television broadcasting
facilities;
—Research and training centers for community organization needs and the development of various communication skills;
—Funding of organizations assisting welfare recipients to
secure rights and influence the welfare system;
—Establishment of a National Black Labor Strike and Defense Fund for workers fighting racist employers;
—Establishment of an International Black Appeal for
financing cooperative businesses in the United States
and Africa;
—Establishment of a Black university.

In commenting upon these programatic items, Forman said
at St. George's Episcopal Church in New York on June 8,
1969:

Those are basically the uses we are talking about . . .
they are not a total solution, but they are a new departure. It's certainly a new departure to the poverty
program whose funds are sapped up by the politicians
making twenty-five to thirty thousand dollars a year. It's
certainly a new departure to so-called Model Cities, and
it is most definitely a new departure to whatever Nixon
was going to propose about bringing business into the
community, which is really a tax gain, you see, because
he is going to give them the same kind of favored
status that many other businesses have overseas.[17]

It is quite clear, however, that the program of the Manifesto
went far beyond being merely a "new departure" from the
Great Society program and the Nixon proposal for "Black
Capitalism." What the Black Manifesto contained was the
organizational and communications machinery for radicalizing
and institutionalizing Black Power in the United States. It
was a comprehensive strategy for the development of pride,
unity and self-determination as the first step toward the
orderly and intelligent controll of the Black community, its
institutions, resources and skills. It is not so much that the
Manifesto demands were new. Many of them had already
been projected by Black churchmen and others, and some—
like the support of the National Welfare Rights Organization,
the utilization of Black-owned land in the South, and the
development of research and training in community organization, had even been on the drawing boards of the white
mission boards, in consultation with Black strategists. The
difference was that the Manifesto combined these programs,
in the context of Black Power and Third World revolutionism,
and gave them a new urgency as a total program of Black
liberation. Forman then backed up his demands with coercive
tactics which refused to permit the issue to be sidetracked
by bureaucratic procrastination and red tape.

This was precisely the purpose of the confrontation which
took place on Sunday, May 4, 1969, a few days after the
Detroit Conference, when Forman walked down the aisle of

Riverside Church in New York City and hurled a series of demands at its minister and people. Similar confrontations and church-building "liberations" took place in the ensuing months in various parts of the nation and overseas, where Black expatriates took up the reparations issue with American churches in foreign cities and with the World Council of Churches.[18] It was, however, the dramatic appearance of Forman at Riverside Church which galvanized the attention of the nation and brought a storm of outraged protest from white clergy and laity. Unquestionably, the bold disruption of the Riverside service alienated many liberal white churchmen from the aggressive position advocated by NCBC, and not a few Black church leaders outside of NCBC deplored Forman's action as "extreme and sacrilegious." The middle-class New York *Amsterdam News* echoed the shocked re-action of the Black establishment with the comment that "busting up church services is not our idea of how to gain any demands, no matter how righteous they may be."

The fact remains, nevertheless, that the tactics of Forman and BEDC representatives in other cities, achieved what years of genteel prodding by Black church executives and others had not been able to do—the short-circuiting of the normal decision-making processes of the denominations and the sounding of a clear note of urgency which sent their officials and those of the NCC scurrying into emergency sessions. It is of more than passing interest in this regard to note that when Dr. Charles Spivey, the top Black executive of the NCC, Leon Modeste, the Black executive of the Episcopal Church's Special Program, and J. Metz Rollins, Executive Secretary of NCBC, presented impassioned statements on the Crisis in the Nation Program before the May 1–2, 1969, NCC General Board meeting, their addresses were received with polite applause. But the docket was amended to hear Forman repeat the Manifesto demands. A committee was immediately formed to take the matter under advisement, and the General Board recorded "its deep appreciation to Mr. James Forman for his presentation of an explanation concerning the Black Manifesto . . ." The General Board then instructed its Executive Committee to bring "the most appropriate course of action that the Council should take on this important matter" to a special meeting on June 23.

Despite numerous expressions of mortal pain and sorrow from the denominations and the NCC, no major church body in the United States actually acknowledged the legitimacy of the demand for reparations, publicly recognized the Black Economic Development Conference as a negotiating agent, or fulfilled the specific demands made in the various appearances and communications of Forman and the BEDC Steering Committee. The prophetic confrontation, which was a modern-day re-enactment of Amos before the temple at Bethel, only momentarily perturbed America's three great, predominantly white religions. Both Black and white Amaziahs arose to defend the religious and civil establishment. With profuse apologies and hard eyes, they called mayors, police, private detectives, law firms and ad hoc "defense leagues" to restrain this wild Black man who talked about "reparations," and rapidly adjusted the delicate mechanism of their bureaucracies to absorb the impact of the Manifesto and go on to the usual business of being the Church. Arnold Schuchter correctly observes:

> It was asking a great deal of churchmen and laity to rejoice in the opportunity for moral convolutions. God's choice of a black anti-church, a seemingly atheistic, revolutionary and socialistic mouthpiece, certainly did not make the task easier. Forman brought the judgment of Jeremiah down on the heads of Christians and Jews, who were supposed to respond by welcoming repentance and embracing a radically new mission likely to turn America's churches upside down. To no one's surprise, the churches thanked God for the challenge and then went about business as usual. Institutional momentum may have been deflected briefly, but observers should not indulge any fantasies about the short- or long-term impact of the Black Manifesto.[19]

The role of IFCO, BEDC and NCBC in this ecclesiastical brouhaha is a matter of considerable dispute. IFCO and

NCBC immediately supported the Manifesto, and certainly IFCO did so at great risk to its preferential position between the white church structures and the minority communities. NCBC could handle the matter with more aplomb, and its Board of Directors, meeting in Atlanta on May 7, issued a statement which had the intention of putting it on record in support of the Manifesto without an unqualified endorsement of its program. The issue at the Atlanta meeting was whether or not Forman had selected the most strategic programs for meeting the needs of Black people, the specific processes by which his proposals could be implemented, and the viability of BEDC as an instrument for negotiating with the intricate bureaucracies of the churches. Nevertheless, the group clearly affirmed Forman as "a modern day prophet" and called upon foundations, corporations and other elements of the private sector to join the churches in providing "millions of dollars for the economic and social development in the black community." As the days passed it became increasingly clear that NCBC's major problem was with the denominational caucuses. To a greater or lesser degree, all of them supported the Manifesto and BEDC, but the question was whether they could maintain their credibility with their constituents and their authority with the officialdom of their respective denominations if they did not force BEDC to filter its demands through their own negotiating machinery. On its side, NCBC—still in a tenuous relationship with the powerful Methodist, Episcopal and Unitarian caucuses—urged them to "unify their efforts of advocacy and implementation of the Manifesto through coordination provided by the NCBC" and instructed Rollins to "immediately begin this coordinating activity."[20]

By the end of May, Forman was closely coordinating his activity with Rollins and the NCBC. The Black Economic Development Conference had become independent from IFCO and elected Rev. Calvin Marshall, an A.M.E.Z. pastor and member of the NCBC Board, as its chairman. When it became obvious to everyone that the line of demarcation between BEDC and NCBC had practically dissolved, the white churches began to yield to the demands of the caucuses which had previously been given only token recognition. This strategy served both to draw the caucuses that were fighting for their own lives away from Forman and made it possible for the churches to make small, indirect grants to BEDC *through* the caucuses without incurring the wrath of whites who were angrily demanding total disengagement. Throughout this period Forman, completely overwhelmed by the bewildering convolutions of church politics, vacillated between a grudging endorsement of this strategy and bitter denunciations of it. In his report to BEDC on June 5, he related how he had accepted the advice of a group of Black Methodists that their caucus would be the channel for Methodist reparations, but . . .

> Lo and behold, the next meeting when we came to the meeting where we were supposed to present our demands and argue them, we found out that a few well-chosen house niggers inside the Methodist Church who are on the paid staff of the masters inside that shop had agreed to accept a lousy $300,000 with a promise of a million more if the money was given to the Black task force.[21]

But five days later he issued a memorandum to his Steering Committee and field staff which urged:

> We must work with the staff and laymen of the denominations. We should touch bases with as many of them as possible. They are willing, for the most part, to help, and they can neutralize some of the flak from the local Toms. In addition, they know the church structure and can save us time in research and intelligence.[22]

This last point was the nub of the matter. Ironically, one of the principal reasons why Forman was rarely able to negotiate directly with the denominations and met with little success when he did, was his lack of knowledge and experience in dealing with white church structures. Although he was briefed, the caucus leaders became increasingly convinced that his impatient tactics had failed and that, left to his own devices, he would make it impossible for either BEDC or themselves to obtain a victory. In this they may have erred, and Schuchter's analysis that the Episcopal caucus and NCBC "prostituted themselves by taking money from the various Protestant denominations and the National Council of Churches" may be correct. But the situation was more complicated than he suspects. In point of fact, Forman and Marshall concurred with this procedure as a last resort, and this concurrence made it possible for at least some funds to reach the BEDC treasury.[23] The caucuses knew better than Forman the mysterious and labyrinthine channels of church funding, under pressure or otherwise. They also comprehended the necessity of meeting some of the needs of their ghetto churches, and to have evaded those needs would have robbed them of credibility and the possibility of pressing the demands of the Manifesto on another day. The weakness in the caucuses' position was not in their playing the role of conduit for reparations and siphoning off something to repair their own crumbling defenses, but in their unwillingness or inability to permit themselves to be coordinated by NCBC, thereby combining their political strength in a uniform process of negotiation.

An unrepentant conservatism and a dismal failure of creative imagination are revealed by the churches in the crisis brought on by the Manifesto. But what is also most patently revealed is the naïveté and fallibility of powerlessness in any competition for scarce resources and the lingering and negative effects of denominationalism within the National Committee of Black Churchmen. The caucuses helped to bring NCBC into existence, and they were, undoubtedly, the advance guard from which a successful attack on racism within the churches had to begin. And yet the Manifesto controversy, which was taken up by NCBC and became almost exclusively its domain, convincingly demonstrates that unless the caucuses surrender their autonomy and decline to develop their own infrastructures further, Black ecumenism will fail to exploit the historical continuity and integrity of the Black religious experience in the United States. While the Negro churches of the white denominations do not represent that Black religious mainstream, they are only slightly marginal to it and have made important contributions. Under the umbrella of a Black Power-oriented movement like NCBC, the Black churchmen of these predominantly white communions could become the single most significant factor in the renewal and extension of Black religion in America and the Third World. Their experience and power position within the citadel of American Protestantism and Roman Catholicism give them a peculiar aptitude for strategic churchmanship within those structures and the national and international ecumenical bodies. But whether they will be able to develop a new and more effective mission at home and overseas depends, in large measure, upon rapprochement with the historic Black churches and the extent to which the latter will embrace a new theological perspective that breaks with the opiate spirituality and generalized religion of "the American Way of Life."

The Manifesto controversy illuminated, more than the King-led church freedom movement, the contours of America's civil religion and spurred the development of the Black theology which had laid dormant within the amalgam of Black religion and Black radicalism for more than a half century. Even before 1966, a few Black churchmen within and on the fringes of the Southern Christian Leadership Conference had begun to explore prospects for the revitalization of the Black church and the renewal of its distinctive theological perception of the relationship between redemption and liberation. The publication of Joseph R. Washington's *Black Religion* in 1964, almost by way of negative reaction rather than positive response, accelerated this development. But it was the groundswell of political activity, ideological reflection and cultural education among the masses of the ghetto, induced by the Black Power movement, which provided the incentive for a genuine theological renewal within the Black church.

The Black Manifesto served as the final booster stage for a

development which was adumbrated in the 1966 Statement on Black Power of the National Committee of Negro Churchmen. When the organization met in its first convocation in Dallas in 1967, there was unanimous agreement that further theological work needed to be done, and a Theological Commission was created and instructed to report to the St. Louis convocation in November 1968.

The discussion in Dallas generated excitement and enthusiasm for a "prospective" theology, building upon militant Black preachers of the past, which would break new ground in the dialogue between religionists and secular radicals in the Black Power movement—a dialogue which had become stultified by the domination of the nonviolence, redemptive suffering ethics of Martin Luther King, Jr. Moreover, the charge by Joseph R. Washington that the Black church was bereft of an authentic theology was regarded by many as an obsequious imitation of E. Franklin Frazier's sociological reductionism regarding the Black church.[24] The work group on theology rejected both of these analyses and recommended that the new Commission conduct a survey among Black seminary professors and "scholarly pastors" to determine what might be the ingredients of a basic theological position paper which would clarify the growing interest in "Black Theology" and provide churchmen with a conceptual framework for "a new dialogue and confrontation with both conservative 'whitenized' black Christians and liberal, but paralyzed white Christians, whose accommodation to the religious and secular status quo has all but robbed American Christianity of its vitality and credibility—especially among the poor, the black and the young."[25]

The publication of Washington's *The Politics of God* in 1967 pointed toward a revision of certain previous assumptions and, despite its essentially integrationist flavor, provided a new context for reflection on the theological basis for involvement with the Black masses in community organization and political action. Washington's theology was a defensive polemic against the "ghettoization" of the Negro, and the reconstruction of his folk-religion thesis moved toward a conception of the Negro's "suffering servant" role as a divine vocation to release white Christianity from its Puritan ethnocentrism.[26] He did, nevertheless, indicate the possibilities of a radical theology within the Black church that would incorporate the passion and experience of the Black masses for a new expression of the Kingdom of God within the structures and institutions of a white-dominated society. He writes:

> In order to meet the needs of the Negro, which are the demands of the Kingdom of God, Negro ministers, laymen and denominational institutions require a conscious rejection of white theological and ecclesiastical doubletalk and a conscious acceptance of their black promise. . . . The inclusion of the Negro in the society is the demand of the Kingdom for the health of whites and blacks, but is dependent for extensity upon black cohesion in the present for the fullness of black dispersion throughout the society with equality in the future and as a whole.[27]

Between 1966 and 1970 a spate of articles by Black writers in the national religious press heralded the beginning of a new era of Black theological reflection and began to sound the themes and motifs which have been developed in depth by a few scholars scattered in a half-dozen Black and predominantly white seminaries. The venerable interdenominational journal *Christian Century* published articles by C. Eric Lincoln and Vincent Harding on Black Power from a theological perspective. Harding's "Black Power and the American Christ" came to the defense of Carmichael and McKissick and declared that for Black Christians, "Christ is the Lord of this too."[28] A Mennonite churchman who was chairman of the History Department at Spelman College in Atlanta, Harding brought an impressionistic but keenly insightful view of what Nathan Wright called "the dehonkification of black Christianity." His famous essay, "The Religion of Black Power," which appeared in 1968, caused a flurry of excitement in both Black and white theological circles and brought to the fore the mixture of old and new Black folk traditions in the religious ferment swirling around the Black Power movement. Harding, whose penchant has been to raise questions rather than suggest answers, boldly affirmed in "The Religion of Black Power" that "Allah and other gods of Africa enter into competition with Yaweh, Jesus and Buddha" in the ideological and theological winds rising in the Black community. "It is," he wrote, "joyously difficult, but part of the affirmation of Black Power is 'We are a spiritual people.' "[29]

Harding's equation of Black religion with the eclectic religiosity of Black Power was the contribution of an academician whose major interests were outside of organized Black religion in the United States. As such, it lacked the practical realism and authority of a Black churchman who could view the function of Black theology from within the church and would be obliged to test its validity in the sanctuary and on the streets. Such a man was Albert B. Cleage, Jr., a minister of the United Church of Christ and pastor of the Shrine of the Black Madonna in Detroit, a Black nationalist congregation which experienced a new birth during the rise of the Black Power fervor in the mid-sixties. Cleage's *The Black Messiah* was a collection of sermons preached during the tumultuous years in the Detroit ghetto, where one of the most devastating riots in the nation occurred during the summer of 1967.

No Black theologian has been more controversial than Cleage. His thesis, drawn from the radical Black preachers of the nineteenth century and the religious cults of the urban ghetto, was that Jesus is the Black Messiah, the descendant of the Nation of Israel, which became Black during its sojourn in Babylon and Egypt, and that he was part of a small underground movement, a Zealot, whose revolutionary message of separation and liberation from Rome was corrupted by the Apostle Paul and the theologians of white, Western civilization. Cleage told his Detroit congregation, once heavily infiltrated by movement people:

So then, I would say to you, you are Christian, and the things you believe are the teachings of a Black Messiah named Jesus, and the things you do are the will of a black God called Jehovah; and almost everything you have heard about Christianity is essentially a lie.[30]

Like other Black theologians, Cleage attacked the traditional Christian concept of love and redemptive suffering. He also declared that only the Old Testament was canonical for the Black Nation. He pressed the idea of Blacks as God's Chosen People called to purify the authentic religion of Israel, which the white man had despoiled, and to undertake revolutionary political action "to build one Black community, one Black Nation, all stemming from the hub which is the Shrine of the Black Madonna."[31] Deeply involved in the Black Power movement in Detroit and much sought for as a spokesman and organizer for Black nationalist causes, he worked to assimilate the radical, anticlerical element of the movement into a reconstructed Black church which had divested itself of the norms of white Christianity. A recurring proposition in his work is the brotherhood of Black people who prefer one another to the white enemy and who rebuilt the ghetto by self-help and mutual aid—a familiar theme in the history of the Black community. "Jesus was black," he writes, "and he did *not* preach universal love . . . God is working with us every day, helping us find a way to freedom. Jesus tried to teach the Nation Israel how to come together as black people, to be brothers one with another and to stand against their white oppressors."[32] Harding is similarly emphatic about the pastoral care of Blacks for one another. Commenting on the alienation of Black youth from the church and the need of the Black church to address itself to them, he writes:

The issue of religion is constantly before many of the young persons who are drawn back into the ghettos by the urgent logic of Black Power. As they return— from college or from prison—to struggle against what can be reasonably described as "principalities and powers" which seem anonymously but fiercely to control the life of their people, they find themselves often insufficient as autonomous sources of inner strength . . . a few black Christian churches have responded fully to the call of Black Power. In Detroit, the pastor of one such congregation, the Reverend Albert B. Cleage, Jr., of the Central United Church of Christ, preaches of a black revolutionary Jesus who came to set the nonwhite peoples free. A Black Madonna is the focal point of worship, and the church has probably attracted more persons committed to Black Power than any single institution still connected to the Christian churches.[33]

It is, perhaps, a matter of speculation whether James Forman, who spent considerable time in Detroit, was influenced by Cleage. But it is certainly true that he and other young Blacks, who were drawn into the orbit of IFCO and BEDC, were among those who returned to the northern ghetto with the highest humanitarian motives and sought, in the loneliness and anguish of their struggle, a greater sense of mission and a more profound resource of spirit than the crass secularism of the white Left.

The Manifesto incident and the involvement of Black churchmen in Forman's confrontation of the white religious establishment underscored the alienation of young Blacks from the doctrinaire politics of Marxism. It also indicated the alienation of Black religious thought from white theology and the quasi-fundamentalism of much of the historic Black church. In the midst of the struggle a little-known scholar with a doctorate in systematic theology from Northwestern University joined the faculty of Union Theological Seminary in New York City. James H. Cone's first book, *Black Theology and Black Power*, was published during the Manifesto controversy. Even before its publication date advance notices made it a sensation among Black religionists. Cone, the youngest of the new theologians, was the first to suggest the broad outlines of a Black theology based upon an essentially classical interpretation of the Christian faith. Calling upon Protestant theologians, from Karl Barth to Jurgen Moltmann, Cone showed how a radical, but historically accurate, inter-

pretation of the Biblical story and a thorough reading of
Paul Tillich, Albert Camus and Franz Fanon leads to the
indisputable conclusion that Black Power is the affirmation
of Black being and humanity against the nonbeing and dehumanization of white racism. Not only is it a correlative
of Black theology, but it is essential to a Christian understanding of freedom. He writes:

> It would seem that Black Power and Christianity have
> this in common: the liberation of man! If the work of
> Christ is that of liberating men from alien loyalties, and
> if racism is, as George Kelsey[34] says, an alien faith,
> then there must be some correlation between Black
> Power and Christianity . . . Black Power is the power
> to say No; it is the power of Blacks to refuse to
> cooperate in their own dehumanization. If Blacks can
> trust the message of Christ, if they can take him at his
> word, this power to say No to white power and domi-
> nation is derived from him.[35]

Cone attended the Theological Commission of NCBC meeting at the Interdenominational Theological Center in Atlanta
on June 13, 1969. The first public statement of the Commission on the nature and meaning of Black theology unmistakably shows his influence, and its opening paragraph re-
flects one of the principal motifs of his work:

> Black people affirm their being. This affirmation is made
> in the whole experience of being black in the hostile
> American society. Black theology is not a gift of the
> Christian gospel dispensed to slaves; rather it is an
> *appropriation* which black slaves made of the gospel
> given by their white oppressors. Black theology has been
> nurtured, sustained and passed on in the black churches
> in their various ways of expression. Black theology has
> dealt with all the ultimate and violent issues of life
> and death for a people despised and degraded.[36]

It is again the influence of Cone, supported by Preston N.
Williams, Henry Mitchell and Deotis Roberts—all seminary

professors—which comes through in the key section of the statement, which has become almost standardized as the main line of the NCBC. This concept of Black theology provided a guideline for the NCBC debates with white churchmen during the Manifesto crisis:

> Black Theology is a theology of black liberation. It seeks to plumb the black condition in the light of God's revelation in Jesus Christ, so that the black community can see that the gospel is commensurate with the achievement of black humanity . . . The message of liberation is the revelation of God as revealed in the incarnation of Jesus Christ. Freedom IS the gospel. Jesus is the Liberator![37]

The NCBC understanding of Black theology issued out of the existential situation the organization faced in its attempt to make the white church acknowledge what Black churchmen believed to be God's judgment upon the American church and society as stated in the Black Manifesto. "Black Theology," said the statement, "must confront the issues which are a part of the reality of Black oppression." A basic reality was the refusal of the American people, after years of tokenism in state and federal programs, to make massive funds available for the social and economic reconstruction of the Black community. The theological statement, therefore, eschewed the abstractions of the debate among white theologians about the possibility of a self-consciously *Black* theology which could, at the same time, be a *Christian* theology. The issue at Atlanta was not whether Black theology could be authenticated to white colleagues and churchmen as having universal applicability, apart from immediate and self-serving contingencies, for oppressed people everywhere and in every circumstance, but whether or not it could serve the needs of Black people who were caught up in a struggle for manhood and self-determination with the structures of White Power. At the heart of the Theological Statement was the issue of reparations and the Black Manifesto. Thus it reads:

Reparation is a part of the gospel message. Zaccheus knew well the necessity for repayment as an essential ingredient in repentance. "If I have taken anything from any man by false accusation, I restore him fourfold" (Luk 19:8). The church which calls itself the servant church must, like its Lord, be willing to strip itself of possessions in order to build and restore that which has been destroyed by the compromising bureaucrats and conscienceless rich. While reparation cannot remove the guilt created by the despicable deed of slavery, it is, nonetheless, a positive response to the need for power in the black community . . . As black theologians address themselves to the issues of the black revolution, it is incumbent upon them to say that the black community will not be turned from its course . . . This is the message of black theology. In the words of Eldridge Cleaver: "We shall have our manhood. We shall have it or the earth will be leveled by our efforts to gain it."

Since the Black theology statement of NCBC, an unpublicized, quiet controversy has raged in theological circles over the justification of a "Black Theology." The warrant for Black theology is Black oppression. The religion of Israel depended solely upon Israel's need for deliverance from Egyptian bondage. Thus, Yahweh was not the object of philosophical speculation, but the subject of a subjugated and yearning people. He refused to give Moses ontological and epistemological answers to the question, "What shall I say to the people when they ask me, 'Who is this God who has sent you to summon us?'" The answer: "I AM WHO I AM. I AM has sent you," terminates the discussion. Any further inquiry is not only irrelevant but blasphemous. The fundamental explication of Jewish theophany and the warrant for both Judaism and for Black theology are the words of Exodus 3:16–17:

I have observed you and what has been done to you in Egypt; and I promise that I will bring you up and out of the affliction of Egypt, to the land of the

Canaanites, the Hittites, the Amorites, the Perizzites, the Hivites, and the Jebusites, a land flowing with milk and honey.

James Cone, as the leading exponent of Black theology, has taken the brunt of the criticism that Blackness is an illegitimate basis for a Christian theology. The argument has been that there is nothing unique in the historical experience of Black people that justifies the particularity of the claim that the whole of Biblical revelation points to what is being called Black theology.[38] In his first book Cone states that "Black Theology is Christian theology precisely *because* it has the black predicament as its point of departure."[39] White Christians, therefore, must become Black in order to be Christians. But in his effort to lay the groundwork for a systematic theology of the Black experience which meets the requirement of universality, Cone adds:

> Being black in America has very little to do with skin color. To be black means that your heart, your soul, your mind, and your body are where the dispossessed are . . . Therefore, being reconciled to God does not mean that one's skin is physically black. It essentially depends on the color of your heart, soul and mind.[40]

In *A Black Theology of Liberation,* Cone further develops this position by a reference to Paul Tillich's description of the symbolic nature of all theological speech. He writes:

> The focus on blackness does not mean that *only* blacks suffer as victims in a racist society, but that blackness is an ontological symbol and a visible reality which best describes what oppression means in America . . . Blackness, then, stands for all victims of oppression who realize that their humanity is inseparable from man's liberation from whiteness.[41]

Cone's struggle with the legitimation of a Black theology, as such, is commendable and he satisfies the norm of universality, which he sometimes seems to believe is necessary for an acceptable systematic. The question is whether the Black religious experience requires such validation by the norms of white systematic theology, and whether the strain toward universality does not, *ipso facto,* rob Black religion of its freedom as *one* approach to the knowledge of God and, thereby, of its existential singularity. As J. V. L. Casserley reminds us:

> The advent of Christianity forced a new problem upon the attention of the ancient world—the problem of the singular . . . There is a profound distinction between the term "particular" and the term "singular." The "particular" is the individual as seen by the man who is looking for the universal, and who will feel baffled intellectually until he finds it; the "singular," on the other hand, is the individual seen from the point of view of the man who is out to capture and enjoy the full flavor of its individuality.[42]

Is Black theology simply the Blackenization of the whole spectrum of traditional Christian theology, with particular emphasis upon the liberation of the oppressed, or does it find in the experience of the oppression of Black people, as *black,* a singular religiosity, identified not only with Christianity, but with other religions as well? To say that being Black in America has little to do with skin color is, at best, only half true. It is possible to argue that in a world dominated by white power that has been inextricable from white Christianity, being Black, or identifiably "Negroid," is a unique experience and has produced a unique religion, closely related to, but not exclusively bound by, the Christian tradition. Simply being oppressed or psychologically and politically in sympathy with the dispossessed does not deliver one into the experience of Blackness any more than putting on a blindfold delivers one into the experience of being blind.

There is no attempt here to denigrate the sensitivity to divine revelation of other oppressed peoples or even to invalidate the provisional authenticity of white Christianity as a true religion—one of several valid approaches to the One

Eternal God. It is simply to affirm that Black theology authenticates itself in the unique religious experience of Black people in the particular circumstance of white, Western civilization since the beginning of slavery in the New World. That Cone himself also recognizes this difference is seen in his statement that:

> Black Theology seeks to create a theological norm which is in harmony with the black condition and the biblical revelation . . . Theology cannot be indifferent to the importance of blackness by making some kind of existential leap beyond blackness to an undefined universalism.[43]

He can even speak of "Jesus as the Black Christ who provides the necessary soul for black liberation."[44] In so doing he opens up the possibility of a Black theology which is neither Protestant nor Catholic, but the way Black people *think, feel* and *act* with the intensity of ultimate concern about their liberation from oppression and racism. Such a theology is rooted in the resistance of the historic Black church, but it extends beyond organized religion. It embraces also the attempt of Black secular and non-Christian groups to express verbally and to act out the meanings and values of the Black experience in America and Africa.

Black theology expresses both affirmation and negation. It affirms the real possibility of freedom and manhood for Black people, and it negates every power that seeks to demean and rob Black people for the determination of their own destiny. Black theology's contribution to the universal knowledge of God does not lie in its being only the reverse side of traditional Christian theology—white theology in Black vesture. In this, Leon E. Wright is correct to say that a judgment and protest against white Christianity is not enough. Rather, in its illumination of the religious meaning of Black liberation, Black theology breaks with the determinative norms of white theology and unveils the deepest meaning of human freedom for all men.

The informal, unsystematic and, to a large degree, inarticulated "'theology" of the Black folk has spoken, and still speaks, to their distinctive, singular needs. That theology, confirmed and nurtured not only in the church, but in every institution of the Black community, was oriented toward an indestructible belief in freedom. Although political emancipation was the concrete expression of that freedom, it did not exhaust its meaning. The freedom toward which the Afro-American religious experience and early Black theology tended was freedom as existential deliverance, as liberation from every power or force that restrains the full, spontaneous release of body, mind and spirit from every bondage which does not contribute to the proper development of the whole person in community. Not simply political freedom, but the freedom of the human being as a child of God, to be himself; to realize the deepest and highest potentialities of his psychosomatic nature. In short, the freedom to be a man or a woman, rather than a brain, a muscle, or a subhuman appendage to an IBM computer.

The first source of Black theology is in the existing Black community, where the tradition of Black folk religion is still extant and continues to stand over against the institutional church—merging with it at times in the ministry of such men as Henry M. Turner, Adam Clayon Powell, Jr., and Martin Luther King, Jr. This Black folk religion has never ceased providing the resources for radical movements in the Black community while the organized church receded into white evangelical pietism. Movements of Black nationalism, from the Moorish Science Temple to the Shrine of the Black Madonna, have their roots in a tradition which maintained a tenuous but persistent connection with Voodooism and the spirituality of the religions of Africa. It continues to be represented in the sects and cults of the Black ghetto and has periodically been enlisted as the base of contemporary movements led by such men as Imamu Tmeer Baraka, Maulana Ron Karenga, and Brother Imari of the Republic of New Africa. It is reflected in the National Negro Evangelical Association. It breaks out in Black music, Black drama, and the writing of the new Black "alienation" poets. The Black middle class has generally sought to evade these influences, but even they are too deeply rooted in the masses, of whom Langston Hughes wrote:

> But then there are the low-down folks, the so-called common element, and they are the majority—may the Lord be praised! The people who have their nip of gin on Saturday nights and are not too important to themselves or the community, or too well fed, or too learned to watch the lazy world go round. They live on 7th Street in Washington, or State Street in Chicago and they do not particularly care whether they are like white folks or anybody else. Their joy runs, bang! into ecstasy. Their religion soars to a shout. Work maybe a little today, rest a little tomorrow. Play awhile. Sing awhile. O, let's dance! These common people are not afraid of spirituals, as for a long time their more intellectual brethren were, and jazz is their child. They furnish a wealth of colorful, distinctive material for any artist because they still hold their own individuality in the face of American standardization.[45]

This spirit is still the soul of Black religion and Black culture. Black theology must begin to understand and interpret it before it turns to white theologians for the substance of its reflection. The ebb and flow of Black folk religion is a constituent factor in every important crisis and development in the Black community. When the community is relatively integrated with the white society it recedes from Black institutions to form a hard core of unassimilable Black nationalism in an obscure corner of the social system—biding its time. When the community is hard-pressed, when hopes fade and the glimmer of light at the end of the tunnel is blocked out by resurgent white racism, then the essential folk element in Black religion exhibits itself again and begins anew to infiltrate the institutions which had neglected it. That is the meaning of the religion of Black Power today and the renewal of a radical Black theology within the contemporary Black church.

The second source of Black theology is in the writings and addresses of the Black preachers and public men of the past. As white theology has its Augustine, its John Calvin, Martin Luther, Ulrich Zwingli, and John Wesley, Black theology has its Nat Turner, its Richard Allen, Martin Delany, Edward Blyden, and W. E. Burghardt Du Bois. Not all Black thinkers were ministers, but all of them were greatly influenced by Black religion. One cannot understand the genius of Black spirituality or the work of charismatic leaders like Martin King, Malcolm X or James Forman, without understanding how their interpretations of the Black experience were conditioned by great Black men of the past. Forman and Malcolm X belong as much to this theological tradition as Powell or King. In an important and neglected article written in 1964 Carleton Lee indicated the significance of prophecy in the Black community as spiritual vision, as a way of "forth-telling" the transcendent meaning of history revealed to the inspired imagination.[46] To the extent that secular prophets draw upon the history of suffering and struggle in the Black community and point to its destiny as the fulfillment of the faith and hope of a stolen and oppressed people, they deal with insights, themes and motifs of the Black religious consciousness and interpret Black reality in ways that are either religious or are readily incorporated into a basically religious view of life.

As we have seen in the earlier chapters of this book the writings of the nineteenth-century Black philosophers and preachers lift up some of the seminal ideas of a Black Theology—liberation, self-help, elevation, chosenness, emigration and unity. These are some of the major themes, charged with religious significance, with which men like Payne, Crummell, Turner and Grimke were obsessed. The broad vistas of Black reality which these concepts encompass need to be prospected for the rich veins of theological insight they contain. Cone has made a beginning of this development of a theology rooted and grounded in the Black experience, but even in *A Black Theology of Liberation* he retains the traditional categories, and in so doing finds it necessary to use the arguments of white theologians to buttress his position. This is certainly not prohibited, but neither is it the only option available to Black theologians whose ancestors have not produced a systematic theology.

Black theology's interests lie in another direction. What is needed to think theologically about the corpus of Black opinion—both written and oral—a "new consciousness," a new way of perceiving and ordering religious, cultural and political data from the Black community. This, of course, requires a new set of interpretative tools, a new hermeneutic. Henry H. Mitchell recognizes the need for the Black theologian to break the interpretative strictures of white theology when he observes:

Just as the new hermeneutic of Ebeling and others has sought to recapture the vital message of Luther and the Reformation Fathers for the benefit of their sons, so must the Black hermeneutic seek to look into the message of the Black past and see what the Black Fathers could be saying to Black people today.[47]

Mitchell has not, however, developed that hermeneutic in his two propositions of communicating in the argot of the uneducated Black Baptist preacher, and "Putting the gospel on a tell-it-like-it-is, nitty-gritty basis."[48] The problem is infinitely more difficult than that. It has to do with unpacking the mythology, folklore and norms of the Black community as reflected in its verbal tradition and literature, in order to discover the ways in which Black people have acted out and linguistically communicated their provisional and ultimate concerns under an exploitative system. What Franz Fanon has done for the native people of Algeria and the Antilles, must yet be done for the oppressed Blacks of the United States.[49]

Although Fanon would not agree with its utility, such a Black hermeneutic will deal with the morphology of Black language, the meaning of Black music, poetry, the dance, and, as Mitchell himself has suggested, not only the content, but the accent and cadences of Black preaching. In other words, if the God of justice and liberation has identified himself with the struggle of Black humanity and has manifested himself, in special ways, in the Black subcommunity of the United States, then theologians need to know much more about the life style of that community and look at it through the eyes of its formal and informal leaders of the past and present. Only so will they be able to unlock the secrets of understanding and communicating the gospel of freedom in a new and meaningful way.

Black people, as Du Bois continually reminded us, are "a spiritual people." The theology of the Black community is developed not in theological seminaries, but on the streets, in the taverns and pool halls, as well as in the churches. The evolution of the first African Societies into the African Methodist church or a group of Black youths from a fighting gang to a Black nationalist club, reforming ex-convicts and fighting dope pushers, will suggest more about the operative religion and ethics of the Black community than a study of the literature of the neighborhood Sunday schools. It is out of this welter of knowledge of the thought, feeling and action of the Black fathers and the contemporary Black ghetto that a hermeneutic can be constructed which will make it possible for Black theologians to read back to the community an interpretation of its indigenous religion that will clarify its basic commitments and integrate Black values and institutions around the core of liberation.

The third source of Black theology are the traditional religions of Africa, the way those religions encountered and assimilated, or were assimilated by, Christianity, and the process by which African theologians are seeking to make the Christian faith indigenous and relevant to Africa today. Black people are not only a spiritual people—they are also an African people. The dispute about African survivals in Negro culture and religion will go on, but it is clear that Black people did not begin on the auction blocks of Charlestown and New Orleans, nor did their religious consciousness commence with the peaching of Christianity to the slaves. It is still possible to recover some of the major beliefs of the traditional religions of Nigeria, Dahomey, Ghana, and other parts of Africa from which our ancestors came. Their development and alteration may be traced to the islands of the Caribbean and, to a lesser extent, to the mainland. It may be true that the contributions of African religion have all but evaporated from Black Christianity in the United States, but we do not know enough about the psychic structure of Black people, about what the Jungian psychologists call "the collective unconscious," of Black Americans to be able to say with absolute assurance that nothing of African spirituality lies deeply impregnated in "the souls of black folk." In any event, Black people who have struggled for their humanity against the suffocating domination of a racist, Anglo-Saxon culture, need to examine in much greater detail the religious contributions of their ancient homeland, which arise out of a vastly different cultural matrix than Europe and America. Professor Charles Long of the University of Chicago has written:

> Our colleague Mircea Eliade said long ago that the West was in danger of provincialism through a lack of attention to the orientations and solutions of non-Western man. It would be difficult, if not impossible, to make the case for the non-Western identity of the black community in America, though several make this claim. The element of truth in this claim is that though we are Westerners, we are not Western in the same way as our compatriots, and thus we afford within America an entree to the *otherness* of America and the otherness of mankind.[50]

Those contributions, among others, are: a deep sense of the pervasive reality of the spirit world, the blotting out of the line between the sacred and the profane, the practical use of religion in all of life; reverence for ancestors and their real or symbolic presence with us, the corporateness of social life, the source of evil in the consequences of an act rather than in the act itself, and the imaginative and creative use of rhythm—singing and dancing—in the celebration of life and the worship of God. All of these aspects of African religions were found in some form, however attenuated, in the Black religion of the eighteenth and nineteenth centuries and were absorbed into Black Christianity in the Caribbean,

South America and the United States. The feeling, spontaneity and freedom in Black religion and life had much to do with their resistance to complete whitenization, but this is also related to the intrinsic discontinuity between African and European religiosity. Black theology must be concerned about the recovery of those values, particularly the recovery of the achievement of freedom, the freedom to be *Muntu*— a man or a woman—in the most profound meaning of that profound Bantu word.

The theological program of African scholars for the Africanization of Christianity in modern Africa has much to say to Black theology's "ghettoization" of the Christian faith in the United States. In either case, the purpose is not to impose the sterile thought-forms and traditions of Western Christianity upon the Black community, but by a new approach to general revelation to discover a new and creative *Theologia Africana* which can unveil the reality of the Eternal Christ in the life and destiny of his Black people. Related to this quest are the urgent political issues of liberation in southern Africa and the United States, social justice and development, the relationship of Christianity to the separatist and independent churches on both sides of the Atlantic, and the contribution of Africa and Black America to the great social revolution of the Third World. Only by a sympathetic and intensive dialogue between the new younger theologians of Africa and Black theologians in the United States and the Caribbean will it be possible to uncover the harmonies and disharmonies in Black religion and forge the theological and ideological links which can bind modern Africa and Black America together for the unimaginable possibilities of the future.

What of that future? Perhaps the most that can be said is that the reformation and revivification of the faith that has come down to us from Jesus of Nazareth awaits the unhindered contribution of the nonwhite peoples of the world and that Black people of Africa and America will play a crucial role in that development. It will be preceded by the end of divisive sectarianism and the beginning of ecumenism in the institution of Black religion in the United States, by increasing communication and emigration between African and Black American churchmen, and by the development of an incisively relevant theology—on both continents —which will free itself from the false consciousness and impiety of white Christianity and bind Black people together, inside and outside of churches, in the solidarity of a new faith in God and humanity.

It can only be a matter of judgment, based upon the history of the Black race, and faith in the grace of a God who does not reward us according to our iniquities, to affirm that the Black world will not repeat the inhumanities of the white world. And if this judgment and faith are vindicated, mankind will be the beneficiary and the reconciliation for which the whole Church of Christ prays will become a realized eschatological event.

Until that time, too remote to deflect Black people from the revolutionary tasks which lie at hand today, white men must take, with utmost seriousness, the words of the National Committee of Black Churchmen in its "Message to the Churches from Oakland" in 1969—the year of the Black Manifesto:

> We black people are a religious people. From the earliest time we have acknowledged a Supreme Being. With the fullness of our physical bodies and emotions we have unabashedly worshipped Him with shouts of joy and tears of pain and anguish. We neither believe that God is dead, white, nor captive to some rationalistic and dogmatic formulation of the Christian faith which relates Him exclusively to the canons of the Old and New Testaments, and accommodate Him to the reigning spirits of a socio-technical age. Rather, we affirm that God is Liberator in the man Jesus Christ, that His message is Freedom, and that today He calls all men to be what they are in themselves, and among their own people, in the context of a pluralistic world society of dignity and self-determination for all. We believe that in a special way God's favor rests today upon the poor and oppressed peoples of the world and that He calls them to be the

ministering angels of His judgment and grace, as His
Kingdom of freedom and peace breaks in from the
future upon a world shackled to ancient sins and
virtues.

The 1969 *Message to the Churches from Oakland* of the
National Committee of Black Churchmen and the *Black Manifesto* of the Black Economic Development Conference are,
one must concede, merely words on paper, not ideas that have
been actualized nor deeds performed. But they are prophecies
of things to come and to be worked for. They belong together,
and in the course of events they sought each other out. These
two documents represent, each in its own way and together,
the basic theme we have explored throughout this book,
namely, that Black religion and Black radicalism are historic
and complementary aspects of an essential characteristic of
the Black experience in America—a pervasive "pragmatic
spirituality" which, in a world dominated by the peculiar
racism and oppression of Anglo-Saxon or Euro-American
civilization, has always expressed itself in terms of a religiopolitical struggle for humanization and liberation. Black
nationalism and panAfricanism, hard-pressed and poverty-
stricken, may surrender to the rising forces of political repression non-white people and white radicals are now experiencing
in the United States, and the main-line Black churches, piously
complacent, may yet succumb to the temptation of solemn assemblies and bourgeois captivity. If that happens in our time,
it will be a retreat in a long history of retreats, but not a
decisive repudiation of the fundamental meaning of our striv-
ing. That is to say, we will never give up the right to be what
we are. We are a spiritual people. We are an African people.
And we are determined, by the power of God or of Satan, to
be free.

FOOTNOTES TO CHAPTER I

1. James Ramsay, *An Essay on the Treatment and Conversion of American Slaves* (London, 1784), p. 173.
2. Newbell N. Puckett, *Folk Beliefs of the Southern Negro* (Chapel Hill, Univ. of North Carolina Press, 1926), p. 545.
3. W. E. B. Du Bois, *The Negro Church* (Atlanta, Atlanta Univ. Press, 1903), p. 5.
4. Benjamin Brawley, *A Social History of the American Negro* (New York, Macmillan Co., 1921), p. 7.
5. *Ibid.*, pp. 4–5.
6. Melville Herskovits, *The Myth of the Negro Past* (Boston, Beacon Press, 1958), p. 106.
7. *Ibid.*
8. Carter G. Woodson, *The History of the Negro Church* (Washington, Associated Publishers, 1945), p. 7; Lorenzo J. Greene, *The Negro in Colonial New England* (New York, Columbia Univ. Press, 1942), p. 282.
9. W. E. B. Du Bois, *The Souls of Black Folk* (Chicago, A. C. McClurg & Co., 1929), p. 141.
10. E. Franklin Frazier, *The Negro Church in America* (Liverpool, Univ. of Liverpool, 1963), p. 11.
11. See Clifton H. Johnson, Ed., *God Struck Me Dead* (Philadelphia, Pilgrim Press, 1969); Benjamin E. Mays, *The Negro's God* (Boston, Chapman and Grimes, Inc., 1938); Miles M. Fisher, *Negro Slave Songs in the United States* (New York, Russell & Russell, 1968); Newbell N. Puckett, *Folk Beliefs of the Southern Negro* (Chapel Hill, Univ. of North Carolina, 1926); LeRoi Jones, *Blues People* (New York, William Morrow Co., 1963).
12. Charles C. Jones, *The Religious Instruction of Negroes in the United States* (Savannah, T. Purse Co., 1842), pp. 125ff.
13. *Ibid.*
14. Henderson H. Donald, *The Negro Freedom* (New York, H. Schuman Co., 1952), pp. 110–11, quoting C. Stearns, *The Black Man of the South and the Rebels* (New York, American News Co., 1872).
15. Donald, *op. cit.*
16. William Jay to Bishop Ives, Dec. 1846, in *Miscellaneous Writings on Slavery* (Boston, John P. Jewett & Co., 1853), p. 471.
17. Jones, *op. cit.*, p. 126.
18. Joseph B. Earnest, *The Religious Development of the Negro in Virginia* (Charlottesville, The Mitchie Co., 1914), p. 134.
19. Puckett, *op. cit.*, p. 526.
20. John S. Mbiti, *African Religions and Philosophy* (New York, Frederick A. Praeger, Inc., 1969), p. 207.
21. Donald G. Mathews, *Slavery and Methodism* (Princeton, Princeton Univ. Press, 1965), p. 76.
22. Jones, *op. cit.*, p. 126.
23. *Ibid.*, p. 127.
24. See Herskovits, *op. cit.*, Janheinz Jahn, *Muntu* (New York, Grove Press, 1961); Lorenzo D. Turner, "African Survivals in the New World with Special Emphasis on the Arts" in *Africa Seen by American Negroes*

(Paris, 1958); LeRoi Jones, *Black Music* (New York, William Morrow Co., 1967). Some more recent work on African survivals in Black religion is being done by Dr. Vincent Harding at the Institute of the Black World and by Professor George Thomas of the Interdenominational Theological Center (I.T.C.) in Atlanta, Georgia.

25. See Mbiti, *op. cit.*; E. Bolaja Idowu, *Olodumare, God in Yoruba Belief* (London, Longmans, 1962); C. G. Baeta, Ed., *Christianity in Tropical Africa* (London, S.C.M. Press, 1962); Kwesi A. Dickson and Paul Ellingworth, *Biblical Revelation and African Beliefs* (London, Lutterworth Press, 1969); and J. V. Taylor, *The Primal Vision* (London, S.C.M. Press, 1963).

26. Mbiti, *op. cit.*, pp. 15–16; 29–57.

27. *Ibid.*, p. 52.

28. *Ibid.*, p. 170.

29. See Puckett, *op. cit.*

30. Herskovits, *op. cit.*, p. 107.

31. Joseph J. Williams, *Voodoos and Obeahs* (New York, Dial Press, 1933); Janheinz Jahn, *Muntu* (New York, Grove Press, 1961), especially Chapter 2; and Alfred Metraux, *Voodoo in Haiti* (New York, Oxford Univ. Press, 1959).

32. See article in the *New Catholic Encyclopedia*, Vol. 14, p. 752, and Alfred Metraux, *op. cit.*, pp. 30ff.

33. Geoffrey Parrinder, *West African Religion* (London, Rev. Ed., Epworth Press, 1961), pp. 35ff. However, Herskovits in his study *Trinidad Village* (New York, 1947) reports a native as saying, "All obiamen keep snakes," p. 225. Also, J. J. Williams refers to an official document published in London in 1789, which says that Obeah (witchcraft or sorcery) derives from the Egyptian *Ob* (serpent), which applies to "one particular sect, the remnant probably of a very celebrated religious order in remote ages . . ." Williams, *op. cit.*, p. 109.

34. Metraux, *op. cit.*, p. 28.

35. *Ibid.*, p. 34. Metraux follows the early descriptions of Moreau de Saint-Méry, but doubts the centrality of snake worship, which he says, in any case, died out in the nineteenth century.

36. *Ibid.*, p. 364.

37. Mbiti, *op. cit.*, pp. 209–10.

38. Metraux, *op. cit.*, p. 48. Lerone Bennett says that Toussaint's nephew tells of the deposed general's renunciation of Christianity when he walked to the altar of a village church and hurled the crucifix to the floor with the words, "You! You are the God of the white man, not the God of the Negroes! You have betrayed men, and deserted me! You have no pity for my race!" *Before the Mayflower* (Baltimore, Penguin Books, 1966), p. 108.

39. Vittorio Lanternari, *The Religions of the Oppressed* (New York, Alfred A. Knopf, Inc., 1963), p. 140.

40. Metraux, *op. cit.*, p. 41.

41. Mathews, *op. cit.*, p. 77.

42. Anson West, *A History of Methodism in Alabama* (Nashville, Publishing House, Methodist Episcopal Church, South, Barbee & Smith, agents, 1893).

43. W. E. B. Du Bois, *The Negro Church* (Atlanta, Atlanta Univ. Press, 1903), p. 11.

44. *Ibid.*

45. For a discussion of freedom in primitive religions, see Mircea Eliade, *Myths, Dreams and Mysteries* (New York, Harper & Row, 1967), pp. 103–6.

46. Joseph R. Washington, Jr., *Black Religion* (Boston, Beacon Press, 1964), p. 33. Although Washington raised a storm of controversy over his low estimate of the theological and ecclesiastical credentials of the independent Black churches, he was the first scholar, in recent years, to examine the unique nature and function of Black religion in the United States as differentiated from Protestantism, Roman Catholicism and Judaism. His work led to fruitful debate in the National Committee of Black Churchmen in 1966–67, and in the theological seminaries subsequently. His earlier misrepresentation of the Black church was corrected in his second book, *The Politics of God* (Boston, Beacon Press, 1967).

FOOTNOTES TO CHAPTER II

1. Herbert Aptheker, *American Negro Slave Revolts* (New York, International Publishers, 1943), p. 162. Aptheker reports some 250 "revolts and conspiracies" during the history of American slavery. He does not include in this number many which took place in the Caribbean, Central America and South America.

2. James Redpath, *The Roving Editor, or Talks with Slaves in the Southern States* (New York, A. B. Burdick, 1859), pp. VI–VII.

3. Quoted by Joe Grady Taylor, *Negro Slavery in Louisiana* (Baton Rouge, Burns and MacEachern, 1963), p. 222.

4. Aptheker, *op. cit.*, p. 177.

5. *Ibid.*, p. 190.

6. Quoted by James Hugo Johnston, "The Participation of White Men in Virginia Negro Insurrections," *Journal of Negro History*, Vol. 16, 1931, p. 159.

7. Aptheker, *op. cit.*, pp. 106–7.

8. Sterling Stuckey, in an article which throws new light on the protest role of the Negro spiritual and folk song, writes: "There seems to be small doubt that Christianity contributed in large measure to a spirit of patience which militated against open rebellion among the bondsmen. Yet to overemphasize this point leads one to obscure a no less important reality: Christianity, after being reinterpreted and recast by slave bards, also contributed to that spirit of endurance which powered generations of bondsmen, bringing them to that decisive moment when for the first time a real choice was available to scores of thousands of them." "Through the Prism of Folklore," in *Black and White in American Culture*, Jules Chametzky and Sidney Kaplan, eds. (Amherst, University of Massachusetts Press, 1969), p. 183.

9. Carter G. Woodson, *The History of the Negro Church* (Washington, Associated Publishers, 1945), pp. 32–33.

10. Herbert Aptheker, A *Documentary History of the Negro People in the United States* (New York, Citadel Press, 1951), p. 9.

11. *Ibid.*, p. 11.

12. For recent research on the attitude and activity of Black churchmen, especially those in New York, regarding slave revolts in contrast to the nonviolent-resistance philosophy of Garrison and the Quakers, see Carleton Mabee, *Black Freedom* (Toronto, Macmillan Co., 1970), pp. 51–56; 276ff., 293ff.

13. Aptheker, *op. cit.*, pp. 91–92.

14. *Ibid.*, p. 92.

15. *Ibid.*, pp. 92–98. It is not known whether or not Nat Turner, who certainly read widely, ever came into possession of the Ethiopian Manifesto. He did, however, have certain strange marks at birth which he and his parents took to be signs of a divine commission to do some great work for his people. The Bashilele peoples of the Congo, under anti-European prophetic movements dating back to 1904, looked for a Black Messiah to fight against the whites. Also Andre Matswa, the successor to Simon Kimbangu—the great religious leader of the Congo whose church has been received into the World Council of Churches—was regarded as the Messiah during his lifetime, and after his death, in 1942, was called Jesus Matswa—the Black Christ. Vittorio Lanternari, *The Religions of the Oppressed* (New York, Alfred A. Knopf, Inc., 1963), pp. 24–27.

16. Aptheker, *"One Continual Cry," David Walker's Appeal* (New York, Humanities Press, 1965). pp. 45ff.

17. Henry Highland Garnet, *Walker's Appeal, With a Brief Sketch of His Life* (New York, J. H. Tobitt, 1848), p. V.

18. Charles M. Wiltse, *David Walker's Appeal* (New York, Hill and Wang, 1965), p. VIII.

19. *Ibid.*

20. Garnet, *op. cit.*, p. VII.

21. *Ibid.* Wiltse says that Walker was found dead near the doorway of his shop, which suggests that death was sudden and without warning. There are grounds for suspicion that he met a violent death either in Boston or Richmond. Aptheker cites a letter which appeared in January, 1831, over the signature of "A Colored Bostonian," which alleges that after painstaking investigation the writer learned that southern planters had spread the word in Boston that $3000 would be given for the life of David Walker. *"One Continual Cry,"* p. 53.

22. Garnet, *op. cit.*, p. VIII.

23. Aptheker, *"One Continual Cry,"* p. 138.

24. *Ibid.*, p. 80.

25. *Ibid.*, p. 104.

26. *Ibid.*, pp. 128–29.

27. *Ibid.*, p. 89.

28. *Ibid.*, p. 137.

29. *Ibid.*, p. 133.

30. *Ibid.*, p. 137.

31. Walker was able to get some copies into southern ports by slipping them into the pockets of Negro sailors who reclaimed their clothing at his shop on Brattle Street.

32. Wiltse, *op. cit.*, p. X.

33. *Ibid.* See also Samuel J. May, *Some Recollections of Our Anti-slavery Conflict* (Boston, Fields, Osgood & Co., 1869), pp. 133–34.
34. Quoted by Carleton Mabee, *Black Freedom* (Toronto, Macmillan Co., 1970), p. 277.
35. See Benjamin Quarles, *Black Abolitionists* (New York, Oxford Univ. Press, 1969), pp. 47–50, 53.
36. Aptheker, *American Negro Slave Revolts*, pp. 105–6.
37. *Ibid.*, p. 139.
38. W. E. B. Du Bois, *The Souls of Black Folks* (New York, Avon Books, 1965, p. 146.
39. *Ibid.*, pp. 147–48. Italics mine.
40. Joseph C. Carroll, *Slave Insurrections in The United States, 1800–1865* (Boston, Chapman & Grimes, 1938), p. 14. Aptheker, *American Negro Slave Revolts*, p. 166.
41. Joseph B. Earnest, *The Religious Development of the Negro in Virginia* (Charlottesville, The Machine Co., 1914), p. 27.
42. Joshua Coffin, *An Account of Some of the Principal Slave Insurrections* (Westport, Conn., Negro Universities Press, 1970), p. 9.
43. Carroll, *op. cit.*, p. 18.
44. *Ibid.*, p. 14. See also Woodson, *The Education of the Negro Prior to 1861* (Washington, D.C., 1919), p. 27, and Benjamin Brawley, *A Social History of the American Negro* (New York, Macmillan Co., 1921), pp. 36–40.
45. Carroll, *op. cit.*, p. 14.
46. Faith Vibert, "*The Society for the Propagation of the Gospel*", *Journal of Negro History*, Vol. 18, p. 176.
47. In order to allay the fear that conversion would require manumission, the Bishop of London laid down a fundamental principle in 1727 which was to become the basis of law in the colonies: "The freedom which Christianity gives," he wrote to the American missionaries, "is a freedom from the bondage of sin and Satan and from the dominion of men's lusts and passions and inordinate desires; but as to their *outward* condition, whatever that was before, whether bond or free, their being baptized and becoming Christian, makes no matter of change in it." Charles C. Jones, *The Religious Instruction of Negroes in the United States* (Savannah, T. Purse Co., 1842), pp. 20–22.
48. Aptheker, *op. cit.*, p. 179.
49. Gooch to the Bishop of London May 28, 1731, in the *Virginia Magazine of History and Biography*, Vol. 32, pp. 322–23.
50. Carroll, *op. cit.*, p. 22.
51. Cyril Lionel Robert James, *A History of Negro Revolt* (New York, Haskell House, 1969), p. 22.
52. Aptheker, *op. cit.*, pp. 188–89.
53. *Ibid.*, p. 190.
54. Carroll, *op. cit.*, pp. 27–30. See also Brawley, *op. cit.*, pp. 43–47. Aptheker cites a letter from a Massachusetts correspondent to one Cadwallader Colden in which the hysteria which seized the populace is compared to the Salem witchcraft panic. In this connection see also Charles A. Beard and Mary R. Beard, *The Rise of American Civilization —The Agricultural Era* (New York, The Macmillan Co., 1927), p. 81.

55. Benjamin E. Mays, *The Negro's God* (Boston, Mt. Vernon Press, 1938), pp. 26ff.

56. R. A. and Alice Bauer, "Day to Day Resistance to Slavery," *Journal of Negro History*, Vol. 26, pp. 388ff.

FOOTNOTES TO CHAPTER III

1. Joseph C. Carroll, *Slave Insurrections in the United States, 1800–1865*, p. 49.

2. Brawley mentions that during this unusual storm the original force dwindled to three hundred men, and many of these were paralyzed by fear and superstition. *A Social History of the American Negro* (New York, Macmillan Co., 1921), p. 87.

3. Carroll, *op. cit.*, p. 50. Aptheker, *American Negro Slave Revolts* (New York, International Publishers, 1943), p. 225.

4. Aptheker, *op. cit.*, p. 222.

5. Carroll, *op. cit.*, p. 56.

6. Aptheker, *op. cit.*, pp. 226–61, p. 261n.

7. Carroll, *op. cit.*, p. 63.

8. *Ibid.*, p. 70.

9. Aptheker, *op. cit.*, p. 246.

10. Carroll, *op. cit.*, p. 74.

11. *Ibid.*, p. 85.

12. Orville J. Victor, *The History of American Conspiracies* (New York, J. D. Torrey Co., 1863), p. 377. One of the first revolts in Africa occurred in Sierra Leone in 1898. It was led by the Mende, who objected to corporeal punishment and the poll tax. The insurgents killed every missionary they could find and also certain Europeanized Blacks. See C. L. R. James, *A History of Negro Revolt* (New York, Haskell House, 1969), p. 42.

13. Victor, *op. cit.*, p. 376. Carroll, *op. cit.*, p. 86.

14. Note the use of the number seven also in Vesey's battle plan. There were seven attack forces or groups prepared, with Vesey himself in command of the seventh, which was to march on the main guardhouse. See John Loften, *Insurrection in South Carolina* (Yellow Springs, Ohio, Antioch Press, 1964), p. 141.

15. Carroll, *op. cit.*, pp. 87–88.

16. John Loften, *Insurrection in South Carolina* (Yellow Springs, Ohio, Antioch Press, 1964), p. 136.

17. Loften, *op. cit.*, p. 91.

18. *Ibid.*, p. 92. See also Du Bois, *The Negro Church* (Atlanta, Atlanta Univ. Press, 1903), pp. 11–12.

19. Carroll, *op. cit.*, p. 87. Also Jones, *The Religious Instruction of Negores in the United States*, p. 214.

20. George Sheppardson and Thomas Price, *The Independent African* (Edinburgh, Edinburgh Univ. Press, 1958), p. 107.

21. Loften, *op. cit.*, p. 92.

22. Carroll, *op. cit.*, p. 96.

23. Victor, *op. cit.*, p. 378.

24. Henry Bibb, *Slave Insurrection in 1831, in Southampton County, Va.*, (New York, Wesleyan Book Room, 1850), p. 3.

25. Carroll, *op. cit.*, pp. 100–1.

26. Brawley, *op. cit.*, p. 139. Peter Poyas deserves much more attention than has been given to him. He was a devout layman of the Black A.M.E. Church and had 600 names on his assault group's list, yet not one of them was arrested or betrayed his companions. Victor, *op. cit.*, p. 385.

27. Carroll finds no discontent among the slaves until 1826. Aptheker, however, cites evidence to show that there were risings in Virginia, South Carolina and North Carolina before that date; *op. cit.*, pp. 276–77.

28. Aptheker, *op. cit.*, p. 275.

29. William Styron, *The Confessions of Nat Turner* (New York, Random House, 1966).

30. John Henrik Clark, ed., *William Styron's Nat Turner* (Boston, Beacon Press, 1968), pp. VIII–IX.

31. Charles V. Hamilton, "Our Nat Turner and William Styron's Creation," in Clark, *op. cit.*, p. 74.

32. F. Roy Johnson, *The Nat Turner Insurrection* (Murfreesboro, N.C., Johnson Publishing Co., 1966), p. 16. Johnson, more than Aptheker and others, appreciates the African background of Nat Turner's early religion. He also recognizes the influence of West Indian spirituality in Black religion and reports that Voodoo was present in the area of Virginia where Turner preached: pp. 15, 56.

33. William Sidney Drewry, *The Southampton Insurrection* (Washington, D.C., The Neale Co., 1900), pp. 31–33.

34. Mike Thelwell, "Back With the Wind: Mr. Styron and the Reverend Turner," in Clark, *op. cit.*, p. 86.

35. This particular parable is also found in Matthew 24:45–51.

36. Johnson, *op. cit.*, p. 76.

37. Drewry, *op. cit.*, p. 114.

38. *Ibid.*, p. 115.

39. *Ibid.*, p. 33n. It is an interesting conjecture which only Mr. Styron could validate, whether upon finding the word "intercourse" in Drewry his rather florid imagination leaped to the idea of substituting Willis for Brantley in the baptism scene and linking Turner with homosexuality. See the novel, pp. 203–7, and pp. 238–39.

40. Carroll, *op. cit.*, p. 133.

41. *Ibid.*

42. Nelson Williams was thought to be a sorcerer, like Gullah Jack, the companion of Denmark Vesey.

43. George W. Williams, *A History of the Negro Race in America, 1619–1883*, Vol. I (New York, G. P. Putnam Sons, 1883), pp. 88–90.

44. Aptheker, *op. cit.*, p. 298.

45. *Ibid.*, p. 300.

46. Carroll, *op. cit.*, p. 137.

47. *Ibid.*, pp. 139–40.

48. Drewry, *op. cit.*, pp. 101–2.

49. Cited by Aptheker, *op. cit.*, p. 305.

50. Du Bois, *The Negro Church*, pp. 25–26.

51. Drewry, *op. cit.*, p. 116.
52. Carter G. Woodson, ed., *The Works of Francis J. Grimke*, Vol. I (Washington, D.C., Associated Publishers, 1942), p. 354.

FOOTNOTES TO CHAPTER IV

1. Philip A. Bruce, *The Plantation Negro as a Freeman* (New York, G. P. Putnam Sons, 1889), pp. 73–74.
2. Carter G. Woodson, *History of the Negro Church* (Washington, D.C., Associated Publishers, 1921), p. 49.
3. *Ibid.*, p. 53.
4. Henry Evans, a Methodist, held secret meetings after he was persecuted by the town council of Fayetteville, N.C. Black Harry Hosier was a colorful Methodist preacher who attracted the attention of Bishop Asbury. It was said that Asbury learned to preach by listening to him. Benjamin Rush called Black Harry the greatest orator in America. See Woodson, *op. cit.*, pp. 56–57, and George W. Williams, *History of the Negro Race in America* (New York, G. P. Putnam Sons, 1883), Vol. II, pp. 466–67.
5. Benjamin Brawley, *Social History of the Negro in the United States* (New York, Macmillan Co., 1921), p. 51.
6. Woodson, *op. cit.*, pp. 73–85.
7. *Ibid.*, pp. 87–89.
8. Marcia M. Mathews, *Richard Allen* (Baltimore, Helicon Press, 1963), p. 47.
9. Richard Allen, *The Life Experiences and Gospel Labors* (Philadelphia, F. Ford and M. A. Ripley, 1880), p. 13.
10. Mathews, *op. cit.*, p. 55.
11. Allen, *op. cit.*, pp. 14–21. See Charles H. Wesley, *Richard Allen, Apostle of Freedom* (Washington, D.C., Associated Publishers, 1935), p. 81.
12. Wesley, *op. cit.*
13. Daniel A. Payne, *History of the African Methodist Episcopal Church* (Nashville, Book Concern of the A.M.E. Church, 1891), p. 14. For more recent research on the beginning of African Methodism, see also Grant S. Shockley and Leonard L. Haynes, "The A.M.E. and the A.M.E. Zion Churches," in E. S. Bucke, ed., *The History of American Methodism* (New York, Abingdon Press, 1964), Vol. II, pp. 527–63, and George A. Singleton, *The Romance of African Methodism* (New York, Exposition Press, 1952), pp. 19–24.
14. Richard R. Wright, Jr., *The Centennial Encyclopedia of the African Methodist Episcopal Church, 1816–1916* (Philadelphia, A.M.E. Church, 1916), p. 11.
15. David H. Bradley, Sr., *A History of the African Methodist Episcopal Zion Church* (Nashville, Parthenon Press, 1956), Part I, pp. 45–46. The question of how long a group of Blacks may actually have been meeting under Williams' auspices is a matter of scholarly debate. The controversy over which group of the various branches of Black Methodism was the first to move toward the organization of a separate congregation is still unresolved, although the Allenites of Philadelphia are gen-

erally considered to have been the first. It is nevertheless true that at
least five denominations have claimed that honor. See J. W. Hood, *One
Hundred Years of the African Methodist Episcopal Zion Church* (New
York A.M.E. Zion Book Concern, 1895), p. 6.

16. Quoted by Bradley, *op. cit.*, p. 47.

17. *Ibid.*, p. 48.

18. Shockley and Haynes, *op. cit.*, p. 563.

19. While Hood calls Varnick "the first regularly elected bishop of the
connection," Bradley states that the Zionites did not change the name of
Superintendent to Bishop until 1864. Bradley, *op. cit.*, p. 156.

20. James A. Handy, *Scraps of A.M.E. History* (Philadelphia, A.M.E.
Church, 1901?), p. 78.

21. Payne, *op. cit.*, pp. 45, 50, 84.

22. *Ibid.*, p. 339.

23. Handy, *op. cit.*, p. 141.

24. Payne, *op. cit.*, pp. 344–45.

25. Bradley, *op. cit.*, p. 108.

26. The Jamestown *Sun*, September 3, 1950.

27. Bradley cites from *The Life of Thomas James, By Himself*, but
gives no other information about this autobiography: *op. cit.*, p. 115. This
remark about the Zionite preachers is interesting in view of the New
York origin of the denomination as compared with the more conservative
climate in Philadelphia, where the A.M.E.s originated. Mabee comments
on the difference between the Negroes of the two cities and the militancy of the New Yorkers. Carleton Mabee, *Black Freedom* (London,
Ontario, Macmillan Co., 1970), p. 58. See also Leon F. Litwack, *North
of Slavery* (Chicago, Univ. of Chicago Press, 1961), pp. 239–46.

28. Bradley, *op. cit.*, pp. 113–15.

29. Hood, *op. cit.*, pp. 541–42.

30. W. D. Weatherford, *American Churches and the Negro* (Boston,
Christopher Pub. House, 1957), p. 195.

31. Andrew E. Murray, *Presbyterians and the Negro* (Philadelphia,
Presbyterian Historical Society, 1966), pp. 32–33.

32. At least the southern wing which met in Montgomery, Alabama, in
1861, was treated with the utmost deference by the northern bishops,
and the designations of the southern dioceses remained on the Convention rolls throughout the war. Weatherford, *op. cit.*, pp. 43–44.

33. George Bragg, *History of the Afro-American Group of the Episcopal Church* (Baltimore, Church Advocate Press, 1922), pp. 61–64.

34. See Murray, *op. cit.*, pp. 29, 32, 239.

35. Leon F. Litwack, *North of Slavery* (Chicago, Univ. of Chicago
Press, 1961), p. 196.

36. It is difficult to understand how Frederick Douglass, who rejected
the idea of a Black church, could have persuaded himself—given what
he saw of the Presbyterians and Episcopalians—that the white churches
of the North were ready to accept Black people on a basis of equality.
The situation which obtained in the Methodist Church when Richard
Allen and Absalom Jones withdrew, continued to exist in many white
churches into the twentieth century. Even after segregated seating was
abolished in the North, Blacks continued to be discriminated against in
many subtle ways, such as being passed over for pastoral visitation, elec-

tive offices and being excluded from the more fashionable and intimate social functions of the city congregations.

37. Howard H. Bell, *A Survey of the Negro Convention Movement,* an unpublished Ph.D. dissertation, Northwestern Univ., 1953, pp. 7–8. For the role of Black preachers in the early convention movement, see also George W. Williams, *op. cit.,* Vol. II, pp. 61–63 and John W. Cromwell, "The Early Negro Convention Movement," Occasional Papers, No. 9, The American Academy, 1904.

38. Mabee, *op. cit.,* p. 58.

39. *Ibid.,* pp. 57–58.

40. Quoted in Melvin Drimmer, ed., *Black History—A Reappraisal* (Garden City, N.Y., Doubleday & Co. Anchor Books, 1969), p. 213.

41. Education and their relatively low status in the white denominations are factors in the militance of these men in the Black Church movement today.

42. Mabee, *op. cit.,* p. 59.

43. Carter G. Woodson, ed., *Negro Orators and Their Orations* (Washington, D.C., Associated Publishers, 1925), p. 155.

44. *Ibid.,* p. 157.

45. Quoted by Mabee, *op. cit.,* p. 60.

46. John H. Bracey, Jr., August Meier and Elliott Rudwick, *Black Nationalism in America* (Indianapolis, Bobbs-Merrill Co., 1970), p. 67. Leon Litwack claims that the pamphlets were published at the expense of John Brown, *op. cit.,* p. 243. See also Arthur Zilversmit, "The Abolitionists," in James C. Curtis and Lewis L. Gould, *The Black Experience in America* (Austin, Univ. of Texas Press, 1970), pp. 61–63. Zilversmit's comment on Garnet's effect upon Black abolitionism strikes a note of sober warning for today. He writes: "For other abolitionists the frustrations of their situation, the frustrations engendered by not having an audience that would respond to reasoned argument, led to the conclusion that a society so immoral, so impervious to reasoned argument, was not worth saving and had to be destroyed. They were led finally to a commitment to violence as a substitute for reason.

47. Douglass, in a speech in Rochester in 1848, had said, "I am aware of the anti-Christian prejudices which have excluded many colored persons from white churches, and the consequent necessity for erecting their own places of worship. . . . But such a necessity does not now exist to the extent of former years. There are societies where color is not regarded as a test of membership, and such places I deem more appropriate for colored persons than exclusive or isolated organizations." Quoted by Benjamin Brawley, *op. cit.,* pp. 239–40. Douglass, however, could not disassociate himself from such organizations in the discharge of his duties as a professional abolitionist.

48. Woodson, *The Negro Church,* p. 123.

49. Benjamin Quarles, *Black Abolitionists* (New York, Oxford Univ. Press, 1969), p. 82.

50. Wesley, *op. cit.*

51. *The Genius of Universal Emancipation,* March, 1831, Vol. I, p. 185. See also Daniel M. Baxter, *Bishop Richard Allen and His Spirit* (Philadelphia, A.M.E. Church, 1923), *passim.*

FOOTNOTES TO CHAPTER V

1. Benjamin Brawley, *Social History of the American Negro* (New York, Macmillan Co., 1921), pp. 174–76.
2. John H. Bracey, Jr., August Meier, and Elliott Rudwick, *Black Nationalism in America* (Indianapolis, Bobbs-Merrill Co., 1970), p. XXXI.
3. Brawley, *op. cit.*, p. 124.
4. Black churches in the West Indies played their own part in sending money and missionaries to Africa. The missionary societies in Jamaica, for example, trained men for work in Africa as early as the 1840s, and individual Jamaicans, such as Thomas Keith and James Keats, went to Africa on their own initiative to bring Christianity to Nigeria. Rex Nettleford writes: "A Mr. Jameson, a missionary who worked at Goshen between 1836 and 1846, wrote in 1839 that 'the people's hearts are turning to Africa' and it was not surprising that as early as 1841 the Jamaica Presbytery decided to train 'black and coloured' Jamaicans for the African missions." "The Africa Connection—the Significance for Jamaica," in *Our Heritage*, by John Hearne and Rex Nettleford, A Public Affairs in Jamaica Pamphlet (Univ. of West Indies, 1963), p. 44.
5. Edwin S. Redkey, *Black Exodus* (New Haven, Yale Univ. Press, 1969), p. 17.
6. Leon F. Litwack, *North of Slavery* (Chicago, Univ. of Chicago Press, 1961), pp. 24–25.
7. See Forten's letter to Paul Cuffee in Bracey, *et al*, p. 46.
8. George W. Williams, *History of the Negro Race in America* (New York, G. P. Putnam Sons, 1883), Vol. II, pp. 69–70.
9. Artishia W. Jordan, *The AME Church in Africa* (New York, A.M.E. Press, 1960), p. 45.
10. James W. Rankin, "The Missionary Propaganda of the AME Church," *The AME Review*, Jan., 1916, p. 175.
11. Quoted by Daniel A. Payne, *History of the African Methodist Episcopal Church* (Nashville, A.M.E. Church, 1891), p. 91.
12. From Daniel Coker to Jeremiah Watts, April 3, 1820. *Journal of Daniel Coker* (Baltimore, Press of Edward J. Coate, 1820), quoted in Bracey, *et. al.*, p. 47.
13. Booker T. Washington, "The Mission Work of the AME Church," *The AME Church Review*, Jan. 1916, p. 186.
14. L. L. Berry, *A Century of Missions of the A.M.E. Church, 1840–1940* (New York, Missionary Department of the A.M.E. Church, 1942), p. 44.
15. Monica Schuler, "Akan Slave Rebellions in the British Caribbean," in *Savacou*, Vol. 1, No. 1, June 1970, p. 24. Shepperson and Price write: "The slave disturbances of 1831 in Jamaica were spoken of as 'the Baptist war,' and after the abolition of slavery two years later, the Baptist name was linked to the whole train of troubles which resulted in the Jamaica Rebellion of 1865 under Governor Eyre." George Shepperson and Thomas Price, *The Independent African* (Edinburgh, Univ. of Edinburgh Press, 1958), p. 423.

16. Grant S. Shockley and Leonard L. Haynes, "The A.M.E. and the A.M.E. Zion Churches," in *The History of American Methodism*, E. S. Bucke, ed. (New York, Abingdon Press, 1964), Vol. II, pp. 554–55.

17. Redkey, *op. cit.*, pp. 73–126.

18. August Meier, *Negro Thought in America, 1880–1915* (Ann Arbor, Univ. of Michigan Press, 1963), p. 63.

19. Payne, *op. cit.*, pp. 293–94.

20. *Ibid.*, p. 220.

21. Martin R. Delany, *Official Report of the Niger Valley Exploring Party* (New York, Thomas Hamilton Co., 1861), pp. 50–51. Delany was also critical of white missionaries. For example, he often accused them of destroying African culture, such as changing the names of converts, which, Delany believed, led to a loss of identity. He vigorously upheld Black identity, and either he or Edward W. Blyden was the first to use the slogan "Africa for the Africans."

22. Benjamin Brawley, *Negro Builders and Heroes* (Chapel Hill, University of North Carolina Press, 1937), p. 93.

23. Delany, *The Condition, Elevation, Emigration and Destiny of the Colored People of the United States, Politically Considered* (Philadelphia, 1852), p. 38.

24. *Ibid.*, p. 40.

25. *Minutes of the African Civilization Society*, Nov. 7, 1861.

26. Delany, *op. cit.*, p. 183.

27. *Ibid.*, pp. 61–62.

28. See Delany's address, "Civilization, the Primal Need of the Race," 1897.

29. Meier, *op. cit.*, p. 43.

30. Howard Brotz, ed., *Negro Social and Political Thought, 1850–1900, Representative Texts* (New York, Basic Books, 1966), pp. 174–75.

31. *Ibid.*, p. 176.

32. George Shepperson, "Notes on Negro American Influences on the Emergence of African Nationalism," *Journal of African History*, I, 2 (1960), p. 299.

33. Edward W. Blyden, *Christianity, Islam and the Negro Race* (Edinburgh, Aldin Pub., 1967), p. 45.

34. Shepperson, *op. cit.*, p. 310. See also James S. Coleman, *Nigeria—Background to Nationalism* (Berkeley, Univ. of California Press, 1963), p. 176ff.

35. Edward W. Blyden, *Liberia's Offering* (New York, John A. Gray, Printer, 1862), pp. 71–72.

36. *Ibid.*, p. 8.

37. Brotz, *op. cit.*, pp. 121–22.

38. Melvin Drimmer, ed., *Black History—A Reappraisal* (Garden City, Doubleday & Co., 1969), p. 243.

39. See James M. McPherson, "The Negro: Innately Inferior or Equal?" in Drimmer, *op. cit.*, p. 241.

40. See also Psalms 16:21, 22; 78:51; 105:23, 26–27.

41. James W. Hood, *One Hundred Years of the African Methodist Episcopal Zion Church* (New York, A.M.E. Zion Book Concern, 1895), p. 55.

42. Redkey, *op. cit.*, p. 30ff.

43. Bracey, et. al. *op. cit.*, pp. 172–73. Turner's radicalism was without peer in the early twentieth century. He spoke of the United States as "this bloody, lynching nation," and President Theodore Roosevelt, according to a letter written to the bishop by Booker T. Washington in 1906, once suggested to the latter that Turner might be tried for treason for referring to the American flag as "a bloody rag."

44. Henry M. Turner, "The Races Must Separate," in Willis B. Parks, ed., *The Possibilities of the Negro–In Symposium* (Atlanta, Franklin Co., 1904), pp. 91–92.

45. Henry M. Turner in *The Christian Recorder*, February 22, 1883.

46. Henry M. Turner in *The Voice of Missions*, February 1, 1898. This position was strongly criticized by white theologians, but for a contemporary discussion of the Christian symbolism of color against which Turner inveighed, see Roger Bastide, "Color, Racism and Christianity," in John Hope Franklin, ed., *Color and Race* (Boston, Houghton Mifflin Co., 1968), pp. 34–49.

47. Berry, *op. cit.*, pp. 72–73. Josephus R. Coan's unpublished doctoral dissertation "The Expansion of Missions of the A.M.E. Church in South Africa, 1896–1908" (Hartford Seminary, 1961) is the authoritative work on Turner and South Africa. See also J. M. Batten, "Henry M. Turner: Negro Bishop Extraordinary," *Church History*, September 1938. The most recent research on Turner and Black Nationalist is in Edwin S. Redkey's *Black Exodus: Black Nationalist* and *Back to Africa Movements, 1890–1910* (New Haven, Yale Univ. Press, 1969).

48. Turner ordained 31 elders and 29 deacons—a total of 60 ministers during his six-week visit. This, naturally, became a matter of anxiety among the white missionaries. A.M.E. agents were designated by them as Ethiopians and considered unwelcome and dangerous interlopers in South Africa. The South African Native Affairs Commission shared this view. See Coan, pp. 169–72, 174.

49. Jordan, *op. cit.*, pp. 59–60. For a discussion of Ethiopianism in this relationship, see also Vittorio Lanternari, *The Religions of the Oppressed* (New York, Alfred A. Knopf, Inc., 1963), pp. 40–41; Bengt G. M. Sundkler, *Bantu Prophets in South Africa* (London, Oxford Univ. Press, 1961), pp. 53–59; Thomas Hodgkin, *Nationalism in Colonial Africa* (London, Frederick Muller Co., 1960), pp. 99ff.

50. Quoted in Edward Roux, *Time Longer Than Rope: A History of the Black Man's Struggle for Freedom in South Africa* (Madison, Univ. of Wisconsin Press, 1964), p. 81.

51. *General Conference Minutes* for 1892, p. 83. Coan, *op. cit.*, p. 50.

52. Roux, *op. cit.*, p. 85.

53. Shepperson and Price, *op. cit.*, p. 98.

54. *Ibid.*

55. *Ibid.*, p. 91.

56. Roux, *op. cit.*, pp. 135–39.

57. *Ibid.*, p. 140.

58. Shepperson and Price, *op. cit.*, pp. 427–28.

59. Coleman, *op. cit.*, p. 177.

60. For a recent analysis of factors affecting African independence movements, see David B. Barrett, *Schism and Renewal in Africa* (Nairobi, Oxford Univ. Press, 1968), pp. 142–50. Also G. C. Oosthuizen,

Post-Christianity in Africa (Grand Rapids, Eerdmans Co., 1968), pp. 30–61.
61. Stanley Shaloff, "Presbyterians and Belgian Congo Exploitation," *Journal of Presbyterian History*, June 1969, pp. 173–94.
62. Shepperson and Price, *op. cit.*, pp. 427–28.
63. E. U. Essien-Udom, *Black Nationalism: A Search for Identity in America* (New York, Dell Publishing Co., 1962), pp. 30–75. Dr. Benjamin E. Mays should also be mentioned in this connection because of his work on the Black church and his recognition that its emphasis on justice, though muted at times, was never totally absent. See Benjamin E. Mays, *The Negro's God* (Boston, Chapman & Grimes, Inc., 1938).
64. Horace Cayton, "E. Franklin Frazier: A Tribute and a Review," *Review of Religious Research*, Vol. 5, No. 3 (1964), p. 141. See E. Franklin Frazier, *The Negro Church in America* (New York, Schocken Books, 1963).
65. Essien-Udom, *op. cit.*, pp. 37–38.
66. Payne, *op. cit.*, pp. 150–51.

FOOTNOTES TO CHAPTER VI

1. However, Du Bois recognized the crucial importance of the Black church. See his *The Soul of Black Folk* and *The Gift of Black Folk* (New York, Washington Square Press, 1970), pp. 178–90. His private religion obtrudes through his secular writings under a nimbus of African spirituality and mystique. He was once Knight Commander of the Liberian Order of African Redemption. On his 25th birthday he vowed to become the Moses of Black people and improvised a ritual of regeneration, using wine, candles, oil and oranges. In the throes of the rite he prayed, sang and made "a sacrifice to the *Zeitgeist* of Work, God and Mercy." Cited by L. Bennett, Jr., *Pioneers in Protest* (Chicago, Johnson Publishing Co., 1968), pp. 241–42.
2. See August Meier, *Negro Thought in America, 1880–1915* (Ann Arbor, Univ. of Michigan Press, 1963), pp. 218–19.
3. Edwin S. Redkey, *Black Exodus* (New York, Yale Univ. Press, 1969), p. 277.
4. *Voice of Missions*, March–May 1897.
5. Redkey, *op. cit.*, pp. 229–30.
6. New Orleans *Times-Democrat*, July 29, 1900.
7. See Redkey's detailed account of Turner's final emigration efforts, *op. cit.*, pp. 258–76.
8. *Crisis*, July 1915.
9. Benjamin Brawley, *Social History of the American Negro* (New York, Macmillan Co., 1921), p. 295.
10. C. Vann Woodward, *Strange Career of Jim Crow*, 2nd Rev. (New York, Oxford Univ. Press, 1966), pp. 97–102.
11. *Voice of the People*, March 1903.
12. The A.M.E. Annual Conference of 1912, however, after hearing Washington speak, approved a report from H. T. Kealing's committee

calling on Blacks to resist like men the mob violence to which they were being subjected. See Meier, *op. cit.*, p. 220.

13. August Meier and Elliott M. Rudwick, *From Plantation to Ghetto* (New York, Hill & Wang, 1966), p. 194.

14. Nancy J. Weiss, "The Negro and the New Freedom," in Allen Weinstein and Frank O. Gatell, eds., *The Segregation Era, 1863–1954* (New York, Oxford Univ. Press, 1970), p. 142.

15. See De Berry's 1901 study of St. John's Church, Springfield, Mass., in Du Bois, *The Negro Church*, pp. 149–51. Also Report No. 37 on an Atlanta A.M.E. church: "As the church grew a cleft appeared between the richer and poorer members and the result was that some thirty or more members of the poor class withdrew.' *Ibid.*, p. 77. This was not untypical. An examination of Du Bois's and other studies will bear out the contention that social stratification within congregations and class churches were developing at the turn of the century and before. See also Gunnar Myrdal, *An American Dilemma*, Vol. I (New York, Harper & Bros., 1944), p. 196n. and E. Franklin Frazier, *Black Bourgeoisie* (New York, Collier Books, 1962), pp. 98–110, 173.

16. Gary Marx, *Protest and Prejudice; A Study of Belief in the Black Community* (New York, Harper & Row, 1967).

17. *Crisis*, Jan., 1914.

18. Meier and Rudwick, *op. cit.*, p. 190.

19. The dramatic increase of the Negro church population of the North and West is illustrated by the fact that in twelve states of the South in 1890 there were 2,348,549 Black church members and only 225,428 in the rest of the nation. By 1926 the Black church population of the South had not quite doubled, with a total of 4,288,621, while the numbers in the North and West had more than quadrupled to 914,866. These figures are from comparisons of U. S. Eleventh Census and statistics in *Negroes in the United States, 1920–1932*, Bureau of the Census, 1931, p. 536.

20. Frazier, *op. cit.*, *Black Bourgeoisie*, p. 99.

21. Joseph R. Washington, Jr., *Black Religion* (Boston, Beacon Press, 1964), pp. 30–162.

22. *Ibid.*, p. 35.

23. Edmund D. Cronon, *Black Moses* (Madison, Univ. of Wisconsin Press, 1962), p. 7.

24. Amy Jacques-Garvey, ed., *The Philosophy and Opinions of Marcus Garvey*, Vol. II (New York, The Arno Press and *The New York Times*, 1969), p. 126.

25. *Ibid.*, p. 128.

26. Amy Jacques-Garvey, *Garvey and Garveyism* (Kingston, United Printers, Ltd., 1963), p. 91.

27. Amy Jacques-Garvey, *Philosophy and Opinions*, II, pp. 37–38.

28. *Ibid.*, p. 98. Garvey was, of course, not without guile.

29. *Ibid.*, p. 95.

30. Amy Jacques-Garvey, *Garvey and Garveyism*, pp. 133–34.

31. His frequent criticism of preachers was that they were tools of the politicians and the real-estate interests. The latter talked them into putting the energies of "religious suckers" into buying new buildings which wasted money. For more on this particular problem among Black city

churches see Carter G. Woodson, *History of the Negro Church*, pp. 230ff. and St. Clair Drake and Horace R. Cayton, *Black Metropolis* (New York, Harcourt, Brace and Co., 1945), pp. 414–29.

32. Amy Jacques-Garvey, *Philosophy and Opinions*, II, p. 288.
33. *Ibid., Garvey and Garveyism*, p. 133.
34. *Ibid.*, p. 61.
35. Amy Jacques-Garvey, *Philosophy and Opinions*, II, p. 16.
36. A. C. Terry-Thompson, *The History of the African Orthodox Church* (New York, African Orthodox Church, 1956), pp. 49–50.
37. Cronon, *op. cit.*, p. 42. Jamaicans were not securely attached to their denominations, and in the eclectic, revivalistic atmosphere of the island many Catholics and Church of England members participated in other sects.
38. Terry-Thompson, *op. cit.*, p. 55.
39. Cronon, *op. cit.*, p. 178.
40. Quoted by Cronon, *op. cit.*, p. 182.
41. Edward Roux, *Time Longer Than Rope: A History of the Black Man's Struggle for Freedom in South Africa* (Madison, Univ. of Wisconsin Press, 1964), p. 112N., 236: Vittorio Latineri, *The Religions of the Oppressed*, (New York, Alfred A. Knopf, Inc., 1963), p. 39.
42. M. G. Smith, Roy Augier and Rex Nettleford, *The Rastafari Movement in Kingston, Jamaica* (Kingston, Jamaica Univ. College of the West Indies, 1960), pp. 4–12.
43. *Ibid.*, p. 7.
44. Nils Bloch-Hoell, *The Pentecostal Movement; Its Origin, Development, and Distinctive Character* (Oslo, Universitetforlaget, 1964); *God's People, West Indian Pentecostal Sects in England* (London, Oxford Univ. Press, 1965); Walter J. Hollenweger, "Black Pentecostal Concept," in *Concept*, World Council of Churches Studies in Evangelism, June 1970.
45. Hollenweger, *op. cit.*, p. 11. See also Stanley H. Frodsham, *With Signs Following, The Story of the Pentecostal Revival in the Twentieth Century* (Springfield, Missouri, Gospel Publishing House, 1946), p. 31.
46. Hollenweger, *op. cit.*, p. 9.
47. *Ibid.*, p. 45.
48. David Barrett, *Schism and Renewal in Africa* (Nairobi, Oxford Univ. Press, 1968), p. 34.
49. See Raymond J. Jones, *A Comparative Study of Religious Cult Behavior Among Negroes with Special Reference to Emotional Group Conditioning Factors* (Washington, D.C., Howard Univ. Graduate School, 1939), pp. 7–34.
50. Arthur H. Fauset, *Black Gods of the Metropolis* (Philadelphia, Univ. of Pennsylvania Press, 1944), p. 55.
51. *Ibid.*, p. 55. See also Washington, *op. cit.*, pp. 122–25.
52. Richard R. Mathison, *Faiths, Cults and Sects of America* (Indianapolis, Bobbs-Merrill Co., 1960), p. 246.
53. George Padmore, *History of the Pan-African Congress* (London, Hammersmith Bookshop, Ltd., 1947), pp. v, 13.
54. C. Eric Lincoln, *The Black Muslims in America* (Boston, Beacon Press, 1961), p. 51.

55. *Ibid.*
56. Woodson, *op. cit.*, p. 254.
57. Mays and Nicholson estimated that the average Black church had a membership of 586 in 1930.

A 1930 investigation by the Greater New York Federation of Churches was probably closer to the real situation in the city. It found three out of four Black churches with an average membership of 122. These smaller churches were largely supported by women, and their primary activities were Sunday worship, Sunday school and choir. They had small effect upon the political and economic life of the community.

58. Seth M. Scheiner, "The Negro Church and the Northern City, 1890–1930," in William G. Shade and Roy C. Herrenkohl, eds., *Seven on Black* (Philadelphia, J. B. Lippincott Co., 1969), p. 99.
59. Drake and Cayton, *op. cit.*, p. 381.
60. *Ibid.*, p. 419.
61. Scheiner, *op. cit.*, p. 105.
62. Archibald Robinson, *That Old Time Religion* (Boston, Houghton Mifflin Co., 1950), pp. 195ff.
63. Drake and Cayton, *op. cit.*, p. 429.
64. Liston Pope, *The Kingdom Beyond Caste* (New York, Friendship Press, 1957), p. 115.
65. Ruby F. Johnston, *The Religion of Negro Protestants* (New York, Philosophical Library, 1956), p. 212.

FOOTNOTES TO CHAPTER VII

1. Wilson Record, *Race and Radicalism* (Ithaca, Cornell Univ. Press, 1964), pp. 8–31.
2. *Philosophy and Opinions*, I, pp. 18–19.
3. James Baldwin, *Go Tell It on the Mountain* (New York, Dell Publishing Co., 1952), p. 163.
4. Herbert Hill, ed., *Soon One Morning, New Writing by American Negroes* (New York, Alfred A. Knopf, Inc., 1963), p. 560.
5. Record, *op. cit.*, p. 60.
6. Reported by members of the National Committee of Negro Churchmen at a meeting in November 1966. Despite the close association of the Blackstone Rangers with the First Presbyterian Church of Chicago, some of the church's leaders believe that they are hostages to the Rangers' contempt for all churches, and if the facilities were closed to them they would "burn it down to the ground."
7. Forman sought the advice of some clergy friends who had worked with him in the Conference of Federated Organizations in Mississippi in 1964, and decided to seek the collaboration of Black clergy rather than alienate them by assault on all Black churchmen.
8. C. Eric Lincoln, *The Black Muslims in America*, p. 79.
9. *Mr. Muhammad Speaks*, May 2, 1959.
10. Gertrude Samuels, "Two Ways: Black Muslims and N.A.A.C.P." August Meier and Elliott Rudwick, eds., *Black Protest in the Sixties* (Chicago, Quadrangle Books, 1970), August 1970, p. 40.

11. Lerone Bennett, *What Manner of Man; A Biography of Martin Luther King, Jr.* (Chicago, Johnson Pub. Co., 1964). See also Rudwick, *op. cit.,* and "The Conservative Militant," C. Eric Lincoln, ed., *Martin Luther King, Jr., A Profile* (New York, Hill & Wang, 1970), p. 147.

12. Joseph R. Washington, Jr., *Black Religion* (Boston, Beacon Press, 1964), p. 3.

13. James Baldwin, "The Highroad to Destiny," in C. Eric Lincoln, ed., *Martin Luther King, Jr., A Profile,* p. 96.

14. Martin Luther King, Jr., *Stride Toward Freedom* (New York, Harper & Bros., 1958), p. 46.

15. *Ibid.,* p. 54.

16. *Ibid.,* p. 96.

17. *Ibid.,* p. 101. See also *Strength To Love* (New York, Harper & Row, 1963), pp. 137–39.

18. Lerone Bennett, *op. cit.,* p. 72.

19. Claude Detton, "Sheriff Harasses Negroes at Voting Rally in Georgia," *The New York Times,* July 27, 1962.

20. W. Haywood Burns, *The Voices of Negro Protest in America* (London, Oxford Univ. Press, 1963), p. 43.

21. The Congress of Racial Equality (CORE) came into existence during a sit-in protest in a downtown Chicago restaurant in 1942. It was interracial from the beginning with strong participation from white pacifists and members of A. J. Muste's Fellowship of Reconciliation. CORE was founded by James Farmer, a former Methodist minister, who became its first national director. Farmer focused his activity in the North, but as early as 1947 CORE sponsored Freedom Rides through the South to test compliance with Interstate Commerce Commission regulations and the Supreme Court decisions regarding segregated transport facilities.

22. Quoted in Burns, *op. cit.,* p. 46.

23. Martin Luther King, Jr., *Where Do We Go From Here: Chaos or Community?* (New York, Harper & Row, 1967), p. 124.

24. *Ibid.,* p. 96. See also *Stride Toward Freedom,* pp. 205–11; *Strength To Love,* p. 47, and his "Letter from the Birmingham Jail," April 16, 1963.

25. See Robert W. Spike, *The Freedom Revolution and the Churches* (New York, Association Press, 1965).

26. Harold Cruse discusses the clash of the old Communist left and the Socialist Workers party in the leadership of the Freedom Now party in *The Crisis of the Negro Intellectual* (New York, William Morrow Co., 1967), pp. 414–19. Despite the internal conflict which doomed the Freedom Now Party, it was probably from these circles that the concept of Black Power first arose during 1963–64.

27. Chuck Stone, "The National Conference on Black Power," in Floyd B. Barbaus, ed., *The Black Power Revolt* (Boston, Porter Sargent, 1968), p. 189.

28. King, *op. cit.,* pp. 30–31.

29. Joseph H. Jackson, pastor of the Olivet Baptist Church in Chicago, has led the convention since 1953. His position among rights-conscious Black ministers has been enigmatic. He was instrumental in a Baptist

land-investment program to develop farms on 100,000 acres in Liberia and in the purchase of 400 acres in Fayette County, Tennessee. He has supported Negro civil rights, but has also been highly critical of the movement and reactionary in his rejection of Black militancy. King's discontent with his leadership and the "fusty status quo" among Black Baptists led to his involvement in a revolt which led to the organization of the Progressive Baptist Convention. William Robert Miller, *Martin Luther King, Jr.* (New York, Weybright & Tally, 1968), p. 295.

30. José Yglesais, "*Dr. King's March on Washington,*" Part II, *The New York Times Magazine,* March 31, 1967.

31. Eldridge Cleaver, *Post-Prison Writings and Speeches* (New York, Ramparts Books, 1969), p. 50.

32. Malcolm X, *The Autobiography of Malcolm X* (New York, Grove Press, 1964), p. 75.

33. *Ibid.,* p. 180.

34. *Ibid.,* p. 200. See also pp. 220, 241–42, 247, 368ff.

35. Lincoln, *op. cit.,* pp. 155–56.

36. New York *Amsterdam News,* April 26, 1958, quoted by Lincoln, pp. 157–58.

37. George Breitman, *The Last Year of Malcolm X* (New York, Schocken Books, 1967), p. 73.

38. *Ibid.,* p. 74.

39. Malcolm X, *op. cit.,* p. 369.

40. *Ibid.,* p. 370.

41. The Muslim Masque, Inc., the Organization of Afro-American Unity, The Black Economic Development Conference. The National Black Power Conference, the Republic of New Africa, the Black Panthers, certain factions of the Socialist Workers Party—and others.

42. See "The Black Church in Search of a New Theology," by the author, in Kendig B. Cully and F. Nile Harper, *Will The Church Lose The City?* (New York, World Publishing Co., 1969), pp. 137–39.

43. Malcolm X, *op. cit.,* p. 163. His experience of conversion is strikingly reminiscent of Paul's on the Damascus road. He speaks of the truth which came to him as "a blinding light," p. 164.

44. See George Breitman, ed., *Malcolm X Speaks* (New York, Grove Press, 1965), p. 24.

45. "Mr. Muhammad Speaks," Los Angeles *Herald-Dispatch,* November 21, 1959.

46. King, *op. cit.,* p. 125.

47. Breitman, *op. cit.,* p. 125.

48. Cruse, *op. cit.,* p. 328.

FOOTNOTES TO CHAPTER VIII

1. *Report of the National Advisory Commission on Civil Disorders* (New York, Bantam Books, 1968), p. 390.

2. Saul Alinsky, the radical leader of the Industrial Areas Foundation, organized The Woodlawn Organization (TWO) in Chicago and other militant mass-based organizations in northern Black ghettos in the early

1960s. His techniques were copied by the Students for a Democratic Society (SDS) and, to some extent, by SNCC and CORE workers in the North. Alinsky and his staff lost favor with many movement people following the 1964 purge of white students from the southern projects, but his work was continually the subject of controversy within the churches which gave many of the organizations their initial funding.

3. The New York *Times*, July 31, 1966, p. E5.

4. Vincent Harding, "No Turning Back," *Renewal*, October–November 1970, p. 8.

5. For example, the 179th General Assembly of the United Presbyterian Church in 1967 encouraged its members "to view the phenomenon of Black power within the context of the white power we exercise, seeing in it both the legacy of frustrated aspiration and the promise of a newly assertive self-identity." The Assembly also commended the NCNC Statement on Black Power to the churches and recommended the study of its "action implementations" for predominantly white congregations.

6. The denominations which now have national Black caucuses are the United Methodists, the three Lutheran bodies, the United Church of Christ, the American Baptist Convention, the Disciples of Christ, the Episcopal Church, the Presbyterian Church in the United States (Southern), the United Presbyterian Church in the U.S.A., and the Unitarian-Universalist Church. Black Roman Catholic priests and nuns have also organized. The A.M.E.Z. Church has a radical clergy group called the Sons of Varick. Other Black denominations which do not have Black caucuses, as such, have clergy—usually younger men—who are strongly committed to the National Committee of Black Churchmen and form an informal caucus of NCBC members within their respective denominations. See Leon W. Watts, "The National Committee of Black Churchmen," *Christianity and Crisis*, November 2 and 16, 1970, pp. 237–43.

7. Harding, *op. cit.*, p. 13.

8. The statement, drafted by Rev. John H. Adams, held it to be "a tragic mistake" to attempt to bypass the Black church in an effort to relate directly to the ghetto. It was adopted April 4, 1968, the day King died, and mailed to more than 800 denominational executives, many of whom replied that they resented the language of confrontation and polarization, calling upon them to "negotiate" and "surrender" power. *NCNC Newsletter*, June 1968, p. 1.

9. It must nevertheless be said that the majority of NCBC's more than a thousand members today are ministers of all-Black denominations. They are generally younger, seminary-educated men. Many are disenchanted with the conservatism of their churches.

10. IFCO was created by ten national white churches as a coalition for the development and funding of indigenous community organizations in Black and brown communities. In 1969 its Board consisted of 23 Black and brown, and 17 white representatives of national religious and community agencies. IFCO's first directors—Lucius Walker, Jr., a Baptist minister, and Louis Gothard, a Unitarian layman—were among those who conceived of the National Committee of Black Churchmen.

11. IFCO News Release, May 5, 1969.

12. James Forman was born in Chicago in 1928. He was baptized and

confirmed in the A.M.E. Church. He served four years in the military and earned a B.A. in political science and public administration at Roosevelt College in Chicago. Later he did graduate work in government and African studies at Boston University. Between 1963 and 1965, Forman took over the SNCC project in Hattiesburg, Mississippi, from Bob Moses, and during that period met and worked with many Black and white ministers from the North who participated in the project, first under the auspices of the National Council of Churches Commission on Religion and Race, and later under a similar program of the United Presbyterian Church.

13. Arnold Schuchter, *Reparations: The Black Manifesto and Its Challenge to White America* (Philadelphia, J. B. Lippincott Co., 1970), p. 4. See also Robert S. Lecky and H. Elliott Wright, eds., *The Black Manifesto* (New York, Sheed and Ward, 1969), pp. 66–67, 102–3.

14. Stephen C. Rose, "Putting It to the Churches," in Lecky and Wright, p. 102.

15. *Tempo*, June 1, 1969, p. 7.

16. *Ibid.*

17. "Rationale for Restitution," pamphlet of St. George's Church, Stuyvesant Square, New York City.

18. A Declaration of Revolution presented on May 23, 1969, to the World Council of Churches meeting at Notting Hill, England, demanded £500,000 for establishing a defense fund for political prisoners in South Africa (including the Panther 21), various sums for African liberation movements, funds to establish an international publishing house, and the public disclosure of assets and investments of the Council. A direct outgrowth was the creation of the WCC Program to Combat Racism, which allocated $200,000 to liberation movements and racial-justice causes in 1970.

19. Schuchter, *op. cit.,* p. 62.

20. *Minutes* of the NCBC Board of Directors meeting, May 7, 1969.

21. *Action Training Clearing-House Notes,* Metropolitan Urban Service Training Facility, June 1969, pp. 4–5.

22. *Ibid.,* p. 53.

23. The major portion of the BEDC money finally came through undesignated grants to IFCO by the churches and through NCBC, which accepted Episcopal funds for this purpose by agreement between NCBC, BEDC, and the Episcopal Black caucus.

24. E. Franklin Frazier, *The Negro Church in America* (New York, Schocken, 1962), pp. 44–46, 85–86, and Joseph R. Washington, Jr., *Black Religion: The Negro & Christianity in the United States* (Boston, Beacon Press, 1964), pp. 140–43.

25. *NCNC Theological Commission Project: A Summary Report,* November 1968, p. 4.

26. Joseph R. Washington, Jr., *The Politics of God* (Boston, Beacon Press, 1967), pp. 170–71.

27. *Ibid.,* p. 185. For the further development of his thought toward the Black Power position, with an obvious Fanon influence, see his *Black and White Power Subreption* (Boston, Beacon Press, 1969), pp. 124–27.

28. Vincent Harding, "Black Power and the American Christ," *Christian Century*, January 4, 1967, p. 10.

29. Harding, "The Religion of Black Power," Donald R. Cutler, ed., *The Religious Situation: 1968* (Boston, Beacon Press, 1968), p. 31.

30. Albert B. Cleage, Jr., *The Black Messiah* (New York, Sheed and Ward, 1968), p. 37.

31. *Ibid.*, p. 277.

32. *Ibid.*, p. 111.

33. Cutler, *op. cit.*, pp. 29–30.

34. George D. Kelsey was one of the first Black Christian ethicists to teach at a major white seminary. A professor at Drew in New Jersey, his principal work, *Racism and the Christian Understanding of Man* (New York, Charles Scribner's Sons, 1965), antedates the Black theology movement.

35. James H. Cone, *Black Theology and Black Power* (New York, Seabury Press, 1969), pp. 39–40.

36. "Black Theology—A Statement of the National Committee of Black Churchmen," *Christian Century*, October 15, 1969, p. 1310. See in the same issue commentary on the statement by Preston N. Williams, chairman of the NCBC Theological Commission.

37. *Ibid.*

38. Leon E. Wright writes: "It would be hazardous to insist . . . that one has made a case for a uniquely oriented world-view—'Black Theology'—whose posture consists essentially in judgment and protest of 'White Christianity' and/or 'racist' society. Though such judgment can be shown to be supremely righteous and just and the protest seen to stem from deep prophetic depths, there is involved in all this no distinctive alternative to the traditional approaches to 'God-talk' and man's self-understanding." Howard University *Journal of Religious Thought*, Summer 1969, p. 54.

39. Cone, *op. cit.*, p. 118. Italics added.

40. *Ibid.*, p. 151.

41. James H. Cone, *A Black Theology of Liberation* (Philadelphia, J. B. Lippincott Co., 1970), pp. 27–28.

42. J. V. Langmead Casserley, *The Christian in Philosophy* (New York, Charles Scribner's Sons, 1951), p. 31. Perhaps more to the point is Fanon, who writes: "The natives' challenge to the colonial world is not a rational confrontation of points of view. It is not a treatise on the universal, but the untidy affirmation of an original idea propounded as an absolute." Frantz Fanon, *The Wretched of the Earth* (New York, Grove Press, 1963), p. 41.

43. Cone, *op. cit.*, p. 76. Cf. pp. 120–23; 156–57.

44. *Ibid.*, p. 80.

45. Langston Hughes in *Black Protest Thought in the Twentieth Century* (New York, Bobbs-Merrill Co., 1970), ed. by Francis Broderick, et al., p. 92.

46. Carleton L. Lee, "Religious Roots of the Negro Protest" in *Assuring Freedom to the Free*, Arnold Rose, ed. (Detroit, Wayne State Univ. Press, 1964).

47. Henry H. Mitchell, *Black Preaching* (Philadelphia, J. B. Lippincott Co., 1970), p. 27.

48. *Ibid.*, pp. 29–30.

49. Frantz Fanon, *Black Skin, White Masks* (New York, Grove Press, 1967).

50. Charles H. Long, "The Black Reality: Toward a Theology of Freedom," *Criterion,* Univ. of Chicago Divinity School, September 1969.

Index